The Measure of the Years

The Right Honourable
Sir Robert Gordon Menzies
K.T., C.H., F.R.S., Q.C.

PRIME MINISTER OF AUSTRALIA, 1939–41 and 1949–66

THE
MEASURE
OF
THE YEARS

CASSELL · LONDON

CASSELL & COMPANY LTD
35 Red Lion Square, London WC1
Melbourne, Sydney, Toronto
Johannesburg, Auckland

First published 1970

I.S.B.N. 0 304 93646 4

Made and printed in Great Britain by
William Clowes and Sons Ltd, London and Beccles
F.770

FOR MY GRANDCHILDREN

Contents

1

Politics and Politicians

1

A Retrospective Survey of the Science and Art of Politics

We are, in the nature of man, redoubtable partisans. We take sides; sometimes by positive conviction, sometimes by pretty blind prejudice, sometimes just for the fun of it. For most, politics is a spare-time occupation or passion, and vehemence is frequently in inverse ratio to objective knowledge.

The title of this chapter is, I think, appropriate for two reasons.

One is that there is a modern tendency to divide science and art into watertight compartments; which is a grievous error. They are, properly considered, inseparable.

Politics provides the supreme example of how interdependent they are.

I will first take politics as a science, and will begin by defining my terms. In this context, what is science? And what is political science?

Science is a word which, like so many others, has changed its meaning in common usage. Etymologically, it means, of course, knowledge—or *scientia*. In earlier centuries, it was used and understood in this sense. But in modern times it has come to be used in a narrower sense, as having primary reference to the physical or 'natural' sciences. At school or at a university, a student is said to be studying 'science' or 'the humanities' as quite distinct areas of learning.

We are living in a period where the two things are sharply distinguished. So great and dramatic has been the twentieth-century development in pure science and applied science, or technology, that prominent thinkers have become concerned at the cleavage they see existing between such departments of learning and the 'humanities', which, not more than a century ago, were the chief preoccupation of the old universities. We are from time to time told that there are two worlds in the universe of knowledge and that their mutual exclusiveness presents a real menace to modern civilization.

There is, in my opinion, an element of truth in this.

But for my present purpose, I want to say something about that marginal problem, the science of politics.

What is political science? To discover the answer I have examined the curriculum of students in the Department of Political Science in my own university, the University of Melbourne. The matters studied include the institutions of modern government; the political structure, legislative and administrative; the study of comparative politics, with particular reference to the U.S.A., Great Britain, and the Soviet Union; a further course in comparative politics based on China and India; another on international relations and foreign policies; studies in sociology and public administration.

For the honours degree, students engage in studies in history, economics, psychology and philosophy and other allied matters.

It will be seen from this brief summary—which is not, I am sure, peculiar to Australia—that the science of politics spreads its net wide, and acknowledges no artificial or preconceived boundaries.

Now, does this mean that political science is more important than political art; that a political artist must first be a political scientist; or that, in an age in which we glorify science and technology, the art of politics should be regarded merely as the skill of the charlatan?

My first answer is that a political leader should have a sufficient background of political science, not expressed in purely academic terms, but informing his mind for practical purposes.

Thus (and this is particularly true of a federal country like mine) he must have an understanding of the constitutional structure of his own country; he must know broadly (only the courts decide with occasional precision) which problems fall within the federal domain and which are reserved for the States. He is here in the realm of political science.

He must know a good deal about the economic and financial

4

impact of such policies as he may pursue. To do this he must have some knowledge of the broad principles of economics; the extent and character of national resources, their development and use. If, as in Australia, he has a significant responsibility for the handling of international affairs (which will, of course, involve much *art*) he should understand his country's treaty structure and have a general appreciation of international law; though, as this is always in the making, exactness is not attainable.

In particular, he should occasionally read the Charter of the United Nations, without deluding himself into the belief that all of the delegates to the General Assembly in New York have done so.

So here I must postulate a reasonable background of political science. But as we look back over the panorama of history and select (as even the least of us have the privilege of doing) the political giants, we find ourselves identifying them as above all great artists.

For the artist is the man who knows how to use his materials; who has a sensitiveness to his environment and an understanding of humanity, and a great skill in execution.

Let me take, by way of example, two men, one in England and one in the United States, prominent at the time of the First World War—David Lloyd George and President Woodrow Wilson. The fiery and eloquent Welshman did not have the scientific approach. It would have been much too cold for him. He was a magnetic handler of men. In his absence, one could reject his beliefs, even with dogmatism. In his presence, one was tempted to become not only a disciple but an apostle. I think that the judgment of history (that elusive and unpredictable man or men!) will be that he did things for the winning of the war for Great Britain and therefore for Allied victory which the vastly superior intellectual qualities of Asquith could not achieve.

Woodrow Wilson, on the other hand, was an intellectual, a scholar and a thinker. But he lacked the art of the great politician. He thought, perhaps too academically, on the world scale; but he failed to take the ordinary people of the United States with him.

5

In the result, the League of Nations and its covenant were crippled almost at birth; and the subsequent history of the world was changed.

In the Second World War my two examples are Franklin Delano Roosevelt and Winston Churchill.

I would regard each of these as a notable political artist. But they were in some ways quite different.

Roosevelt came to the highest office at a time of economic crisis. He was elected and re-elected because his people trusted his judgment and willingness to act on great domestic issues. He had, of course, some brilliant advisers; but it was his persuasive power which secured a public acceptance of his policies. He had powerful opposition, and no doubt made many enemies, including many of the greatest newspapers. But (and here he was, politically, a pioneer) he used the new instrument of radio with consummate and easy skill. In a real sense, he went to the people, who heard him direct, without false interpretation or distortion, and who believed and trusted him.

He was, in effect, a master politician, judging public opinion accurately, never getting too far ahead of it, never impatient. His strategy and tactics from the outbreak of the war in Europe until the entry of the United States into it were, I thought, superb. The progress from complete neutrality, to benevolent neutrality, to 'all aid short of war', to armed alliance, marked a remarkable period in modern history.

Winston Churchill was an artist of quite a different order. I think that it would be wrong to claim that he was a great political scientist. No political leader known to me ever knew less of the complexities of economics and finance. His grasp of domestic peacetime problems was so imperfect that he had great difficulty, in pre-war years, in holding his parliamentary seat. He would almost certainly not have created or driven through a new or revolutionary New Deal.

But two of the great essentials for an English statesman, a close knowledge of history and a clear understanding of Parliament, he had in full measure. Above all, he knew about war and warriors, and wrote about them in an English prose which has not been surpassed in our time. In the long period of political eclipse which he went through, he wrote three tall volumes on his ancestor John, Duke of Marlborough, the great and triumphant English soldier of the earlier eighteenth century.

It can too easily be forgotten that a vital element in the great battle for Britain was the courageous and serene and humorous quality of the people, men and women. This spirit, always latent, was evoked and inspired by Churchill as never before. He became, as I think I may have said elsewhere, a pillar of cloud by day and of fire by night.

The projection, the almost physical force, of his personality in Cabinet can be fully understood only by those who had the honour to sit with him. But to the beleaguered people he was the symbol of confident defiance and the voice of freedom. A portentous book on political science might give him but brief mention; who can tell? But any sensible book on the art of politics and its impact upon history would contain many a good chapter on Churchill, just as it would, for the reasons I offered a few lines earlier, find rich material in the statesmanship of Franklin Roosevelt.

Having said this, let me return to my thesis. The interdependence of science and art can be illustrated in many fields of activity, but particularly in politics.

I offer a few bold propositions.

The greatest academic political scientist in the country could, in practical politics, involve both himself and his electors in complete disaster, unless he had learned and understood the art of politics, which involves the persuasion and management of men.

The greatest master of the art of the politics of persuasion through clarity or eloquence could bring himself and his country to disaster if he knew too little of the real basis of what he was advocating, had no accurate grasp of the national problems, and, in effect, was saying, however splendidly, things that other people had put into his mouth; things that he did not really understand or believe.

Any man who sets out to lead a political party or a politically minded people must first learn to know the facts and the principles. He must be a student, seeking *scientia*, before he makes his decision. And he may become an apostle only when conviction has come to him.

The art of politics is to convey ideas to others, if possible, to persuade a majority to agree, to create or encourage a public opinion so soundly based that it endures, and is not blown aside by chance winds; *to persuade people to take long-range views.*

Of these elements the last is the most difficult of achievement. For every instrument of publicity encourages and gives significance to the short view. A statesman may, with the knowledge that he has acquired of economics and finance (i.e. the scientific background), believe that a certain policy will, over a period of years, be advantageous to his country. He may know (as many political leaders have known) that in the short run the policy will be unpopular. This is where he will need not only decision but courage and endurance. He will be presented with public-opinion polls of a depressing kind; if his policy has been well thought out, he will do well to ignore them. He will, if he has plenty of time to spare, permit himself to read what some critical commentator has to say. If so, he must read the commentator with a sceptical eye, remembering that problems which have been studied in government with complete access to confidential material, and on which decisions have ultimately been taken, are not so simple that a commentator can dogmatically resolve them, three or even five times a week, as if divinely inspired.

The answer to all this easy criticism is to create in the public mind and heart fire and spirit, as Winston Churchill did during the war. For our people are not fools. They may be temporarily sidetracked by false prophets and false issues, but in the long run they will come back to the truth. That basic fact is, after all, the glory of democracy in an intelligent and educated community.

But this means, as you will not have failed to notice, that the prime art of politics is that of a persuasion which cuts deep into the popular mind and heart, which convinces and satisfies the human spirit.

This means that, political science having been applied and a thoughtful and competent judgment arrived at, the art of speech or of written language becomes supreme. For good or even great ideas can be quite infertile unless they are clearly conveyed to others.

The art of speech is much admired and widely practised. Yet the standard of achievement seems singularly disappointing.

Political leaders, who need to have a great capacity for communication, are in Australia called upon to make far too many speeches—in my case perhaps a hundred a year—on occasions important and unimportant. This tends to debase their own currency by introducing a routine element into what they say.

Because of this, and as part of the exercise of high office, the institution of the speech-writer has arisen, particularly in America. I never employed a speech-writer myself, partly because I had an obstinate objection to having other people's words put into my mouth, and partly because, except for formal lectures and statements on foreign affairs made by me to Parliament, my practice has been to speak from brief notes, allowing the language to come spontaneously as the actual speech developed.

Winston Churchill, to take an infinitely greater example, read practically all of his speeches, which he had first dictated and then corrected; but he had the art of reading a speech to perfection, so garnished with dramatic pauses and chuckling asides that nobody not actually present would have known that he was reading. But he was his own speech-writer, as the language of his speeches will prove to posterity.

Now, there are two defects about a speech written by somebody else.

First, unless the speaker has both eyes on posterity (which may turn out to be singularly indifferent!) his great object must be to move and persuade a contemporary audience. To do this most successfully, the speaker must project his own personality in words which at least appear to come fresh from his mind and lips.

He must be himself. People are roused and stimulated not by the reading of an essay, but by the passion and persuasion of a human being. If President Lincoln had not, on the way to Gettysburg, discarded the prepared speech and resorted to his own language, what he had to say would never have rung around the world or achieved immortality.

Second, we must spare a morsel of pity for the future historian. He will sit down to write of a long-dead statesman whom he neither knew nor heard. He turns to the statesman's recorded speeches, hoping to perceive the man through his words. But if the words are those of the anonymous John Smith and not the statesman, the historian's light on the statesman becomes a little dim. True, the ideas, the policies, may be there, but those sudden phrases and flashing turns of speech, those uncontrived expressions of emotion, which tell us so much about a speaker, will be lacking.

There are some other aspects of political speaking which I, for one, believe to be unfortunate. No doubt modern electronic engineering, which has given us the public-address system, has repaired some of the acoustical defects of large halls or spaces. But unfortunately, and probably inevitably, the interposition of the electronic booster between speaker and audience has in my observation had two regrettable consequences. One is that speakers are forgetting how to produce and use their voices. The other is that audiences find it increasingly difficult to listen to the natural human voice, which still remains the most flexible of all instruments. The listener's ears become less sensitive to fine shades of sound, and more demanding of uproar.

The practice of the great art of politics is discouraged by some other modern developments.

Newspaper reporting is in decline. We live in a period where it is a rare thing—and even then in a rare newspaper—to read a good report of a significant speech. More and more the political contents of a newspaper are to be found in the portentous columns of the commentators, or in the frivolous columns of the gossip-writer.

Inevitably, and again I concede that there are honourable exceptions, political journalism devotes itself more and more to criticism of persons, and less and less to the examination and criticism of ideas.

The reason is not far to seek. To criticize persons is easy, and can no doubt be great fun. It can, indeed, be quite useful if the reasons for it are spelled out. But to criticize an idea, one must first understand it, and such an understanding involves study and serious thought.

Churchill knew, being a Churchill, that he was making speeches that would be read by posterity. He was right. But most of us have no such knowledge. So Churchill wrote his speeches, partly because he knew that he was a man of destiny and that the world, in its supreme anguish, was reading him and listening to him, and getting fire from him; and partly because he conceived them as literary exercises.

Many books will be written about Winston Churchill, most of them dogmatic and superficial. I have tried to write something about him myself. But the great problem for his ultimate biographer will be to discover at what point the great actor, the showman, ended, and the great and dedicated leader took over. Men of genius are not to be analysed by common-place rules. The rest of us who have been or are leaders, more common-place in our quality, will do well to remember two things. One is *never to forget posterity when devising a policy*. The other is *never to think of posterity when making a speech*.

In Australia, in my time, a political leader will be chiefly responsible for the formulation of an election policy, but will by no means be its *sole author*. His colleagues will make their own suggestions, and he will make his. A consensus is arrived at.

From these materials the leader (in my case) writes a policy speech which promotes these joint ideas as persuasively as possible. He accepts a greater responsibility for the policies propounded than does any individual minister.

There is an increasing modern disposition, particularly in the age of the gossip column, for reports of alleged Cabinet discussions

11

(which are in their nature quite confidential) to appear in the Press or in books. If any such report says that A and not B was responsible for some political proposal, nothing can be done about it by B without a disclosure of Cabinet discussions. B, if he be an honourable man, must therefore suffer in silence. He will do this the more readily if he remembers that the Cabinet is a joint body which finally issues a *single decision*. If that decision turns out to be right, and a public benefit results, he will have his share of the credit as a member of the Cabinet.

Any Cabinet in which ministers publicly competed for the credit would be on the road to disaster, for solidarity would have been destroyed.

A man like myself will occasionally be given credit for innovations which were initiated by others, but he will, more than anybody else, accept the major blame for errors made. This is the price of high office, and must be paid cheerfully.

Finally, how far should a government be praised or blamed for national advancement or regression?

To answer this question requires a little analysis of the factors which affect the national economy and social progress.

These factors are not by any means exclusively legislative or even political. No Act of Parliament can make a nation prosperous. No regulations can get rid of human error or, of their own force, create prosperity. For, in a democracy, it is the energetic citizen who produces wealth, and the idler, the non-contributor, who impairs the efficiency of the process.

Governments do not create wealth, though frequently they will distribute it for the public benefit. Governments, contrary to a well-known political superstition, have no money of their own. In the field of public finance, they spend what men and women have earned and have paid to them in either taxes or loans, visible or invisible.

The greatest function of a democratic government is to create a *climate* in which enterprise will flourish and productivity will increase.

2

The Gentle Art of Opposition

When I first went into Opposition in the Federal Parliament in 1941, under the circumstances described in *Afternoon Light*, I had resigned the leadership of my party and sat well back in the Opposition corner. I was not a member of the Opposition executive. I found myself well known, readily listened to, but free. After the incessant labour and continuous responsibility of the Prime Ministership, I was, in spite of my unhappy memories, conscious of great relief. I could decide for myself whether to intervene in a debate or not. I had ample time for reading and preparation. W. M. Hughes had become the nominal leader of my party, but in two years we had only one party meeting. It follows that we sat as a group of individuals, without cohesion or formal communication.

Arthur Fadden, the Leader of the Opposition and leader of the Country Party, was and is a genial and popular soul, thoroughly extrovert, with an unsurpassed fund of anecdote and metaphor. He was a good politician and a good political companion, but as a political general he never seemed to me (and I write of him with great personal affection) to develop a coherent grand strategy or penetrative tactics. He no doubt thought, with Lord Randolph Churchill, that 'the duty of an Opposition is to oppose'.

I do not share that simple belief, though I have seen it being acted upon in several parliaments. But I will return to this matter later on. Meanwhile I proceed to the events preceding the 1943 elections. I conducted an active campaign, and accepted many invitations to speak in the various States, several of my meetings being both crowded and ferocious and, for a man of my nature, most enjoyable. But, as is not uncommon in politics, the size of the audiences, even friendly ones, proved very little. For John Curtin's Government had a landslide victory.

The Opposition's chances were not improved by a well-publicized difference between Fadden and myself. As leader, he had, quite properly, prepared his policy speech in consultation with the Opposition executive, of which, as I have said, I was not a member. One of his proposals was to impose a tax, part of the proceeds of which would be set aside as a post-war credit to the taxpayer. Of this I knew nothing until it was too late. I was having a large meeting in my own electorate, to expound what my ideas were on the issues before the country. At question time I was asked what I thought of the creation of post-war credits. I replied that I would not favour them, because I believed that, having regard to inevitable wartime finance and controls, there would, after the war, be such an accumulation of purchasing-power in the hands of the people that the real problem would be one of inflation, not depression. A mass of post-war credits would, I said, be inflationary in its effects.

This remark was reported to Fadden as he was returning from his meeting in Queensland. Forgetting that I had no part in the preparation of his policy speech, Fadden impetuously denounced my speech as an act of treachery. These were fighting words, even though they were hasty and ill founded, but they got the head-lines, and the Government's inevitable propaganda of a 'divided Opposition' made great headway. So far as Fadden and I were concerned, the matter was cleared up later, and we resumed a friendship which has endured ever since.

After the election, my party, at its first meeting, unanimously requested me to resume the leadership, and I did so, on two con-ditions. Though I have written about this in my earlier book, I will, for the convenience of the reader, repeat them here. The first condition was that, the party being the majority party in the Opposition, I should be Leader of the Opposition. The second was that I should have *carte blanche* to create, out of many fragments, a single party with an appropriate name and a forward-looking platform. That led to the creation of the Liberal Party of Aus-tralia.

Then followed six years as Leader of the Opposition; six years of rich experience, the fruits of which I shall now endeavour to describe; six years in which I may claim to have learned some-

14

thing about the art, the difficult art, of opposition. It is no doubt inevitable that current political commentaries, when they do descend from the heights of government and administration and inspect the lowly plains of opposition, chiefly concern themselves with the examination of persons and personalities and seldom examine either political strategy or tactics.

My first proposition is that the duty of an Opposition, if it has no ambition to be permanently on the left-hand side of the Speaker, is not just to oppose for opposition's sake, but to oppose selectively. No Government is always wrong on everything, whatever the critics may say. The Opposition must choose the ground on which it is to attack. To attack indiscriminately is to risk public opinion, which has a reserve of fairness not always understood.

I can illustrate my view by recounting an experience I had about a year or so after I became Leader of the Opposition. Some of my New South Wales colleagues told me that there was a strong opinion in Sydney that I was not 'in the Press' sufficiently; that I ought to attack the Government, if not daily, at least very frequently. I can remember my reply as if it were yesterday: 'I'm sorry, but I entirely disagree. If I did what your friends think I should do, we would no doubt be regarded by them as a very active Opposition, but we would retain that position of honour for many years. But I want to put the Government out; if not in 1946, at least in 1949. I strongly believe that I should not be attacking them on everything. It would seem quite picturesque for a few weeks, but before long the electors would begin to say, "Oh, here's Menzies again! He wants us to believe that the Government is *always* wrong." And they would soon weary of my attitude. My method requires that, when I make an attack, I should do so on some matter in which most people are very interested. Further, it should be a matter on which I have a powerful case, adequately documented and winnable. If I do this, the Government will feel the full impact of the assault; and so will the electors. I hold this view so strongly that I can't change it; but you may feel that another leader would serve your purposes

15

better.' Well, these were my friends and loyal colleagues, so they smiled and gave me their blessing.

The truth is that a Government is made up of ministers with a far closer knowledge of the problems of their departments and a far greater access to papers and expert advice than an Opposition can have. An attack upon them must therefore be made not on the spur of the moment, but with careful preparation after a careful choice of the subject-matter. With great respect, I distrust what a distinguished member of the House of Commons once christened 'instant politics'; where the parliamentary battle is all too frequently a 'chance medley' and fits into no strategic pattern.

My second proposition is that an Opposition must always remember that it is the alternative Government; that it is unwise, when in Opposition, to promise what you cannot perform; that a quick debating point scored in Parliament against some Government measure will be a barren victory unless you are confident that, in office, you would not be compelled to do, substantially, what the Government is doing. It is always an embarrassment to be confronted by your own words; a procedure well known to parliamentarians as 'making the ghost walk'.

So that opposition is not enough. When you find yourself in Opposition and have recovered from the natural shock which accompanies the process, the first task is a positive one: to reconstruct; to find out what went wrong; to work out a programme of action; to initiate a new phase in political history. In other words, like an advocate and cross-examiner in court, you must never lose sight of the end result to which all your activities must be directed. I found that opposition provided not only a great and enthralling opportunity to create a new and cohesive national party, but also an obligation to rethink policies, to look forward, to devise a body of ideas at once sound and progressive; a political philosophy founded upon the encouragement of private enterprise as the driving and creative element in the economics of society, and at the same time the imposing upon that enterprise of social and industrial obligations appropriate to a modern and civilized community. All of this, essentially work for the study, had to be done while the normal duties of active and campaigning politics were performed. It was not easy, and never will be. But it had to be done if a period in Opposition was to be not merely a period of frustration and dejection, but a splendid opportunity for a revival of the spirit and a replenishment of the mind.

The great error of the Labour Opposition in Australia, under Evatt and then Calwell, was that it tended to live in the past, on old hatreds and shibboleths, pursuing a current policy which demanded bigger and better pensions and other social benefits, fighting old and losing battles about issues long since dead. No symptom emerged of a real study of basic policy. Like the Bourbons, they learned nothing and forgot nothing.

It was always one of my political grievances that when I was in office, working a seventy-hour week on the day-to-day affairs of government, I had no time to do much real thinking and study on important issues except at the week-end, when I could assemble my papers, lock the door, and work my way through some complex matter.

But Opposition, with few administrative duties, gives more time for study and thought. It must be regarded as a great constructive period in the life of a party; properly considered, not a period in the wilderness, but a period of preparation for the high responsibilities which you hope will come.

My third proposition is not so much an assertion as a question. I have noticed with interest that both in London and in Canberra the practice has arisen for an Opposition to have a 'Shadow Cabinet'. This has no appeal for me. True, I can see that there is some advantage in having some member of the Opposition who acquires special knowledge of some individual ministry or department. But there are two disadvantages. The first is that when the Opposition comes home at a General Election, the Leader, the new Prime Minister, will suffer a painful embarrassment if Shadow Minister for X is left in the shadows, and another member preferred. The greater the victory and therefore the greater the numbers to choose from—quite a few having had earlier ministerial experience—the more likely the embarrassment.

An Opposition Leader who wins needs a free hand when he accepts a commission as Prime Minister. He should not be handicapped by too many implied personal promises made when in Opposition.

The second disadvantage is, in my opinion, even more significant. One of the advantages of Opposition is the chance it gives to many members to become all-rounders, well informed on a wide range of topics, competent as flexible debaters, and able to make useful contributions to the formulation of general policy.

There is, of course, another aspect of this matter. If a young Opposition member likes being a member of Parliament, but dislikes the work involved, he may succumb to the temptation to say to himself, 'Leave it to John,' John being the Shadow Minister. This would be a pity, wouldn't it, because it would mean that a possible talent had been wasted.

A good Opposition is one in which quite a few members, while being completely loyal to their leader, can feel that they may have a Field-Marshal's baton in the knapsack. And no man who ever aspired to the baton ever confined himself to a fraction of the great enterprise. In short, a powerful Opposition should contain quite a few potential Prime Ministers!

I concede at once that general rules are hard to formulate when political systems and practices vary. Thus, in the Commonwealth Parliament of Australia, when the Liberal and Country parties win an election, the leader of the Liberal Party becomes Prime Minister. The Prime Minister appoints the ministers. In my time, he suffered no embarrassments arising from having had a Shadow Cabinet in Opposition. True, I had an Opposition executive, but its members were not specifically attached to particular departments, and, in effect, expected to confine their attention to those departments.

But the Labour Party in Australia, unlike its counterpart in Britain, elects its Shadow Cabinet when in Opposition and elects its ministers when victory comes its way. It follows that a member of the Labour Shadow Cabinet who fails to secure election to a real ministry when victory comes has no grievance against the

Prime Minister and must distribute his sorrows over the entire party. Such sorrows soon fade. Both parties in Britain concede to the Prime Minister the right of choosing ministers, and when in opposition concede to the Leader the right to choose (and dismiss) members of the Shadow Cabinet.

My earlier queries therefore, for what they are worth—and I believe that they are important—apply in Britain to both parties, and in Australia to the non-Labour parties.

Though it is not strictly germane to my thesis in this chapter, I should add that there has been in recent years a demand by several Liberal members of the Australian Commonwealth Parliament that ministers should be directly chosen by the party members. Though this practice would obviously make life much easier for the Prime Minister, I always resisted its adoption, for reasons which may be worth recording.

The first was that, in the words of Clement Attlee, 'A Prime Minister who is unfit to choose his ministerial colleagues is unfit to be Prime Minister.'

The second was that you are much more likely to achieve Cabinet cohesion when each minister owes his appointment to his Leader than when the minister owes it to his selection by other people. I believe that Cabinet solidarity is of the first importance. More Governments have been destroyed by internal division than by frontal attack by the enemy. When I was in office and had my weekly party meeting, ministers presented a common front when some Cabinet decision was under criticism, though, of course, a powerful criticism would sometimes result in a Cabinet reconsideration. But in a meeting of a party which elects ministers, some minister whose views have been defeated in Cabinet would be a little more than human if he did not improve the shining hour at a party meeting where he could hope to overthrow a majority Cabinet view. Real Cabinet solidarity cannot long survive in such circumstances.

What does this all amount to? According to your point of view, you may have been reading the somewhat egotistical meanderings of an old politician. It may, on the contrary, have been wisdom for, acting on my principles of opposition, I did manage to win a few seats in 1946 and a slashing majority in 1949.

And, so well founded was the majority in 1949, that thereafter, in 1951, 1954, 1955, 1958, 1961 and 1965, I led my party to victory. I had learned my lessons when in Opposition.

My concluding observation is this. There is a natural tendency, when you are in Opposition, to want to play your opponents at their own game, and beat them. The trouble about this is that it leaves the initiative to your opponent.

To my mind, the chief objective of an Opposition should be to make the voters feel that the Opposition, in both personnel and ideas, is as *different* as possible. All Governments in time begin to decay; people begin to feel that a change would do no harm. But they need to see the nature of the change; to find themselves confronted by a choice, a clear choice between differences. A Government may become unpopular, and begin to lose some of the enthusiasm of its supporters. This does not mean that it is necessarily destined for defeat. If the Opposition has not created positive policies and secured positive support, the public attitude may become 'A plague on both your houses'. And, if this cynicism becomes too deep-seated, there may be strange and unpredictable electoral consequences. In Opposition, it is never very sensible to underestimate your opponent's talents or methods of debate, or to seek always to defeat him in his own field. Better by far to develop and deploy your own talents in your own way; to exhibit the differences between you; to develop your own personality, not his; to help to present to the people a choice, both of men and of ideas, to which you hope they will respond.

In short, I must respectfully reject the Randolph Churchill aphorism about Opposition. It is my own view that the duty of an Opposition which wants to move over on to the Treasury Benches is to be constructive, judicious, and *different*.

3

The Lighter Side of Parliamentary Life

Disputes, personal abuse, breaches of order, and the occasional expulsion are food for the Press. They are usually of no significance, but they get the headlines. The frequent flashes of humour, the hilarious incidents which occur in the corridors and in members' rooms, which serve to sweeten political life, go unrecorded and are therefore largely unknown to the public.

So I will set down some incidents of which I knew during my own time.

No public assembly in Australia is ever without examples of two types each of which could not exist without the other. I will call them those who are destined to be leg-pullers and those who are born victims, those whose legs are pulled.

The great leg-pullers in my time were two Country Party members, Tom Collins from New South Wales and Bernard Corser from Queensland. They were aided and abetted by 'Artie' Fadden until Fadden became absorbed by the duties of the leadership of the Country Party.

I think that I should draw a veil over the names of their chronic victims who were themselves popular members. One of them I shall call G from New South Wales, and another B from South Australia. One illustration about G will suffice.

One night G had been given a drink or two, enough to impair his memory next morning. So it followed that next day the two leg-pullers marked their victim. With a simulated appearance of sympathy, they told G that on the previous night, being in a state of some confusion, he had wandered out of the House and down to the Post Office along the street, and had there, in a frolic, heaved half a brick through one of the windows. They added, for good measure, that the Postmaster demanded an apology, to be personally tendered under the second tree from the Post Office at 9 p.m.

Poor G swallowed the story. In spite of the fact that it was a wet night, he went to the appointed tree at the appointed time, waited in vain for an hour, and went back to the House wet and miserable, only to be received with hoots of laughter by Collins and Corser.

Corser's most famous exploit against B was performed when both were members of a Parliamentary Association delegation in London. Knowing that B was substantially devoid of humour, Corser laid his plans with devilish thoroughness. He had the telephone in B's room switched through to another room in which there was a typewriter. He then burst in on B, and said, 'You are requested by the authorities to broadcast a message to the Australian people; it will be transmitted by the beam wireless; and you are asked to do it at once.'

B swallowed this improbable story without question, and Corser returned to the other room. He picked up the telephone, and in a simulated voice said to the hapless B, 'Wireless here, Mr B, are you ready?' At the same time, 'to lend an air of verisimilitude to an otherwise bald and unconvincing narrative', he began to make tapping noises on the typewriter. 'Yes,' said B, and burst into an eloquent speech. Occasionally, Corser would interrupt him, saying, 'One moment, Mr B, there is an interruption in the circuit.' More tapping sounds. 'Go on, Mr B.' And the speech resumed.

Next day B said to Corser, 'Funny thing that there is no report from Australia as to how the reception went.' Corser's laconic reply was, 'Yes, I can't understand it.'

Tom Collins, who had been a successful country auctioneer, and who became one of my ministers in June 1941, was a fine robust-looking man with the most remarkable photographic memory I have ever encountered. He would read one day, in a country newspaper, a lengthy 'bush ballad' sent in by a contributor. If Tom liked it, he could (and did) recite it that evening without an error. He was, in this sense and in voice, something of an actor. During my first Prime Ministership, I found myself, after the 1941 election, without a majority except the dubious votes of two Independents. I was working like a horse, and was not infrequently worried and unhappy. Emerging from my office at Parliament House and going into my ante-room at about 11 p.m. for a drink, I would say to my messenger, 'Ask Mr Collins to step around, with Mr Corser, if possible.' On their arrival, I would say, 'Tom, tell me a story or recite me a ballad.' The response was instant, and, having been superbly entertained, I went back to my house, at peace with the world.

I have another memory of Tom Collins, one of the agreeable features of which is that the victim came out with a profit. There was a veteran member of Parliament who never ceased to grumble. He felt that he was 'a lone, lorn, creetur' who had never been given his recognition or due. One day Tom Collins decided to take a rise out of him. Tom, who was always well dressed, was this day wearing an aggressively new suit. Across the chamber he went, sat down next to the grumbler in a genial way, and, after a few minutes said to X, as I shall call him, 'How do you like my new suit? Nice bit of worsted, isn't it?' 'Yes,' said the melancholy X, 'you must be pretty well off.' 'Oh, no,' said Tom, 'I voted for the increase of tariff duties on textiles, and one of the companies, as a token of gratitude, sent me a suit-length!' This, of course, was a sheer invention. But it did the trick. X at once said, 'I've always supported protective tariffs, and have never even been thanked.' But Tom had started something. X selected a company, wrote a letter of grievance to them, struck a manager who enjoyed the situation, and *got his suit-length by return*.

There is a whimsical Labour member of the Australian Parliament, still going strong, named Daly—Freddy Daly. One day there was a visitation by Moral Rearmament to Canberra. Two of them were dressed, feathers and all, as Red Indian chiefs, I don't know why.

Some member had them accommodated in the Speaker's gallery, just behind the Government members. Just after they arrived Mr McMahon was speaking at the table. McMahon is bald on top with a tuft of hair on each temple. He, and the Red Indians, were in the direct line of sight of Daly, who in a flash called out, 'Mr Speaker. Look out, they've scalped him!'

But the greatest natural wit of my time was 'Joe' Gander, the Labour member for the Sydney electorate of Reid. Joe had been, in his earlier days, a billiard-marker, and commemorated the occupational hazard of his trade by wearing, in the evening sittings, carpet slippers. He had a statesmanlike shock of white hair, an abiding affection for cricket, a generous disposition, and a lovely sense of timing. He was my political opponent and my great personal friend.

Occasionally an ugly scene would be about to occur, with bad temper flaring. Joe Gander, who hated such things, would intervene, with a remark so hilariously funny that even the contestants roared with laughter, and calm was restored.

He had something of a genius for the unexpected. The House was having a vigorous debate (I don't remember how it cropped up) about the then newly constituted Legislative Council in New South Wales. Labour members were attacking the constitution of the new House as undemocratic. (There had been allegations that some successful candidates owed their election to money rather than talent.)

Horror was registered on the faces of Labour members when suddenly and loudly Joe Gander made an interjection: 'The New South Wales Legislative Council is a good house'—a long pause —'it's the best house that money could buy!'

At the General Election of 1940, Joe was defeated by the notorious J. T. Lang, formerly Premier of New South Wales, the non-Labour party organization in New South Wales having foolishly, on its 'how-to-vote' cards, given its second preferences to Lang and not to Gander. So a man of gentleness and humour went out, and a bitter and ungenerous man came in.

A few days after polling day I was sitting in my office at the Victoria Barracks in Melbourne (the war was on) when in came two leading Labour members to see me. They said they came on behalf of Joe; could I arrange for him to work in some department or other? I said, 'Well, as you know, Joe is a good friend of mine, and I'm very sorry he has lost his seat. But things must be done decently and in order. The final election results are not in yet. Leave it for a week or two.' They laughed and one said, 'Joe told us you would say that; that he knew you were a good friend, but that you were a stickler for correct action. So he said to us, " You tell Bob that in my experience the only time to take up a collection for the widow is at the graveside!"'

Joe got his job.

We had a Country Party member from West Australia, whose name was John Henry Prowse. He fought the battles of his party very tenaciously, but was handicapped by a dreary, ill-tuned, and rather moaning voice and delivery.

He was addressing a meeting of the faithful in a small township in his constituency. It must have been a notable occasion, for he had a full house and, that most priceless of assets to a political speaker, a very noisy interjector, who had 'drink taken', and an unmistakable Irish accent.

John was waxing eloquent about a political opponent: 'He is just like Nero fiddling while Rome burned!' Quick as a flash his little interjector roared out, 'And why did Nero fiddle while Rome burned, Prowse? Answer me that.' Poor old John was a little knocked off his perch. All he could say was, in that curious voice I have endeavoured to describe, 'It's just a bit of a saying, my friend.' This simply would not do. The little man went on to the attack. 'I'll tell you why Nero fiddled while Rome burned, Prowse! It was because he was a bloody Protestant like you, and didn't care whether Rome burned or not!'

As I have said, my majority after the 1940 election was, to say the least of it, not reliable. The passing of measures through the House presented almost daily problems. It was at this time that my friend Walter Lindrum, the greatest billiards-player of all time, as modest as he was talented, was playing exhibition matches in Australia for a fund which he called 'fags for fighters', and by means of which he raised large sums for the benefit of our troops. I invited him to visit Canberra as my guest and carry on his good work.

This he did with success. He was, of course, a miraculous player. I can illustrate this for the benefit of unbelievers. One night when he was my guest at the Lodge, where in those days there was a very fine billiard-table, I invited the then Governor-General, Lord Gowrie, to dinner with a member of his staff. Our wives were not in Canberra at the time, so it was a quite informal night. After dinner, we adjourned to the billiard-room. I asked the Governor-General whether he had ever seen a thousand break scored. He said, 'No.' I thereupon threw the red and the two whites on to the table, and said, 'Walter, you choose spot or plain, start playing as the balls now lie, and show His Excellency how it is done.' I won't be readily believed when I say that he did it! But of course he was incomparable.

Well, during his visit I was busy getting the Estimates passed. In our practice, these are taken in committee of the whole House, department by department. One usually gathers that two or three departments will excite most debate. One morning Walter visited me in my office and, in his charming way, asked me if he could do something for me. Well, it happened that the crucial Estimates, the point of danger for a perilously placed Government, were to come on at about 4 p.m. So I promptly said, 'Walter, I would like you to challenge Mr Hughes to a game of billiards in the billiard-room of Parliament. He enjoys the game but plays it very badly. He will be flattered to be challenged by you. Challenge him to play you at 4 p.m.: I will notify the Whips that the game is on, so that there will be a full attendance of members, and you well know how to prolong the length of the game.'

It all came off. Members enjoyed this quite historic match, and I got my Estimates. For the rest of his life, Walter Lindrum never met me without saying to me, with a twinkle in his eye, 'Don't forget that I put your Estimates through in 1940!' And, indeed, I never have.

When in 1934 I entered the Federal Parliament and became

Attorney-General in the Lyons administration, the Northern Territory returned a member who, by statute, was not 'entitled to vote on any question arising in the House of Representatives'.

At the 1934 election the Northern Territory seat was won by a somewhat eccentric but enthusiastic surveyor from the Territory named Blain. Blain, fully named Macalister Blain, and later inevitably known in Parliament as 'Chil' or 'Chiller', was a swarthy, gaunt man, who had moved around a great deal in the Northern Territory, knew the aborigines well, and always (to our delight) pronounced the word 'aboro*gine*'. He had won the seat from the then voteless incumbent by promising that he would get the member for the Territory a vote inside twelve months, or resign.

And so it was that, shortly after I settled in at Canberra, my door burst open and this quaint character presented himself. 'My name is Blain, from the Northern Territory. I'm in trouble. If I don't get a vote within a year, I've promised to resign!' 'Well, Blain,' I said, 'you'll have to enjoy your year in Parliament, for there's no hope of persuading Cabinet to give you one!' His face fell, but he persisted. 'My cousin Douglas ——' (naming a well-known medical man who was a friend of mine and had been at school with me) 'tells me that I'm in trouble and that you are the only —— who can get me out of it!' The relationship was news to me; I repeated my discouraging advice, but remained conscious of the challenge.

As my colleagues and I saw more of Blain, we came to like him, in spite of and perhaps because of his oddities. The day came when I was pondering over his problem, and had a lawyer's brainwave. We couldn't make him a full voting member, but couldn't we pass an amending Act to give him a vote on a motion to disallow any Ordinance of the Northern Territory? (Ordinances were the executive means of dealing with the Territory but could be disallowed by vote in Parliament.) I put my proposal to Cabinet, who were instantly sympathetic, and approved. An announcement was made. Blain was delighted. Darwin celebrated, and in due course the legislation was passed.

But I was not out of my troubles, nor, as it turned out, was

Blain. Many months later he came to me again. 'The boys up in the Territory, who are great readers of *Hansard*, are saying that they don't believe that I have a vote, because they have never seen my name in a division list.'

So, once more, I tried to come to the rescue. 'It's quite simple, Mac. The Minister for the Interior is tabling a Northern Territory Ordinance. You can move to disallow it. We'll all vote against you because we approve of the Ordinance, but you'll get yourself recorded.' His next question was, 'How do I go about it?' I pointed out the relevant Standing Order, drafted the notice that he was to give, and saw it safely ensconced in the hands of the Clerk, so that it went on to the Parliamentary Orders of the Day. We were getting very near to the end of the session, and the item might not be reached. So off I went to the Prime Minister, Mr Lyons, a most human man, and got his agreement to the bringing-on of Blain's motion.

I then went to Blain and pointed out that he would need a seconder who would vote for him, since it needed two members to secure a division. He said that Norman Makin, of the Opposition, would, for friendship's sake, oblige him.

As the item was about to come on, I went across to Blain and gave him his instructions. 'Now, Mac, I want you to understand what you are to do. When the item is called, you make your speech and move your motion, which Norman will second. The Minister will reply and say that the Government will not accept the motion. There will be no other debate, and the Speaker (who knows what's going on) will put the question and then say, "I think the Noes have it." At this stage you call out, "Division!" Don't forget this, Mac, it is vital.'

Well, everything went right until the moment for Blain's action. He sat in his seat looking like a mesmerized rabbit, in spite of my signals. The Speaker, true to his cue, said, 'Is a division called for?' Blain sat dumb. The Speaker repeated the question, looking at Blain appealingly. No result.

So a division didn't occur, and poor Blain didn't get into a division list! Love's labour was lost.

But he was a brave soul. When the war came, and he was over age, he enlisted, went off to Singapore, and became a prisoner of war. After the war, he lost his seat. Whether he ever secured a place in a division list I do not recall, but I hope so.

In a later chapter I have something to say about George Maxwell as advocate in the courts of law. But he occasionally added to the humour of political life.

He was the member for Fawkner and was addressing an election meeting at the Prahran Town Hall—a rare and invaluable place for a lively meeting. There were men at the back of the hall who constantly and offensively attacked Maxwell, and threatened to break up the meeting.

But George knew how to deal with them. Using his fine Scottish speech to the full, he said:

'Ladies and gentlemen, as you know, I have appeared as counsel in the Criminal Courts, and have frequently had accused persons acquitted of serious charges. When I first stood for Parliament, I had just got a man off in a case in which there was much evidence of guilt. But I managed to get him off.

'A few nights later, I was on the political platform, feeling a little nervous in these new surroundings. But I soon found that I was being vociferously encouraged by a man in the very front row. Everything I said was right and splendid. So I looked down gratefully at my supporter, and saw that he was my client of a few days before!'

He paused, and then went on:

'Tonight, ladies and gentlemen, my clients are all at the back of the hall!'

Maxwell won the meeting, and the seat.

2

Some Highlights of a Long Term of Office 1949–1966

4

Introduction to the Record

Many people have complained to me, in a friendly way, that my earlier book (which did not profess to be a political history) said little or nothing about my experiences during the sixteen post-war years (1949–66) in which I was Prime Minister of Australia. Even now, I would have been content to leave this task to others, but for one curious fact of contemporary politics and journalistic writing. It appears to have become the fashion to hint, or to say openly, that nothing good or memorable happened in my time, which is made to appear to have been a period of inertia and unawareness of the world's problems. This is strange, for those years saw unexampled financial and economic progress in Australia, a growing significance for Australia in international affairs, particularly in the Pacific, the revolutionizing of our relations with the United States, and great happenings at home in such fields as those of development, social welfare and education. These facts cannot be denied, but appear to be easily forgotten.

So, if only for the sake of the record, I will essay, not to enter a flat wilderness of detail, but to pick out and describe some of the high spots in what was, for me, an exciting journey.

I must first make one thing clear which will be already clear to all who have sat in a Cabinet. As I have said earlier, no Prime Minister and no member of Cabinet may claim the sole credit for any particular Government policy or measure. It would be absurd and unfair to his colleagues if he did so. An individual minister may promote some idea, but it will be sterile unless his colleagues understand and support it, sharing the credit if all goes well, and the blame if it goes wrong.

There is a curious sort of legend in Australia that I was a dictator in Cabinet, that ministers accepted my views on pain of dismissal or disfavour. There are two obvious comments to be made on this piece of folk-lore. The first is that it does scant justice to my colleagues, who numbered among their ranks outstanding men of great skill, courage, and experience. The second is that the writers of such sorry fiction impale themselves on the horns of a dilemma. If only *my* word went, I should be given all the credit for our successful decisions; and this would be fantastic nonsense. If all Cabinet matters were fully and frankly discussed, as they were, with myself as *primus inter pares*, the legend is false.

For the benefit of students of political institutions, I will briefly describe my own Cabinet methods, which, as I have since learned, were those employed by S. M. Bruce when he succeeded Hughes in 1923. Bruce knew, for he had sat in a Hughes Cabinet for a time, that the fiery and unpredictable 'Billy' observed no order in Cabinet, but occupied the time by initiating some quite new scheme which he had got into his head, most of the real business being deferred or ignored.

Bruce insisted upon the production of a business paper and the previous circulation of ministers' submissions. This was my method also. The Prime Minister's Department, thanks to Chifley's appointment of Allen Brown as head of the department, had become in effect the Cabinet Secretariat. Individual submissions, except under very special circumstances, had to be put in three days before the Cabinet meeting. Brown, who had assembled some officers of great talent and devotion (one of them was Bunting, who succeeded him), fed out to two or three of them the submissions for comment or added information. They consulted the department or departments concerned, and provided Brown with notes, to which he attached some shrewd observations of his own. The day before the Cabinet, greatly aided by these labours, I studied all of the submissions and formed some tentative views or questions of my own.

This meant that, when Cabinet met, I was extremely well informed. Most of my colleagues had inevitably concentrated on their own submissions and had simply a general view of the others. With the exception of a couple of senior ministers, I was probably the only one who had been furnished with comprehensive notes on all of the submissions and had studied them. There was nothing odd about this. The function of the Prime Minister, as I understood it, was to be as well informed as he could be, to encourage exposition and debate, to question ministers on their submissions, sometimes very closely, and to be ready to come in at the appropriate time, usually late in the debate, with some proposition which would embody the general view.

Occasionally, a Prime Minister, on a great matter, will need to be a strenuous advocate of what he believes to be the right course, and do his best to convert his colleagues to his own view.

But such cases are exceptional. Ministers are not children, and it is offensive to their intelligence to think that they sit dumbly at the feet of their political schoolmaster. I have only to think of that fine South Australian Philip (now Sir Philip) McBride, my constant friend throughout my life at Canberra, to be reminded of his great willingness and capacity to challenge any proposition from any source whatsoever!

With these preliminary remarks, which may or may not be necessary, I will go on in later chapters to describe what I have referred to as some of the high spots on my political journey after the 1949 election. I say 'some', because a selection was necessary, if only for reasons of time and space.

If, in the course of my narrative, I appear to give to my Government any credit for developments which were, in an immediate sense, the product of other people's ingenuity in discovery and efficiency in production, I crave pardon. But the basic philosophy of Australian Liberalism is that the prime duty of government is to encourage enterprise, to provide a climate favourable to its growth, to remember that it is the individual whose energies produce progress, and that all social benefits derive from his efforts. That philosophy does not deny that there are many activities in a young and vast country which cannot be left and have not been left to private enterprise. Witness the railways, where only the State could in a country like Australia have laid down lines which could not be expected to be profitable for years, but which were essential to settlement and development. Witness the Post Office and its allied communications services. Witness power and light production and distribution, with their sometimes interstate ramifications. Witness the great irrigation and storage schemes, of which the Snowy Mountains is the most recent and conspicuous example. We do not regard such Government enterprises as inconsistent with our philosophy. On the contrary, we know that private enterprise cannot do its work without them. They provide in many ways a foundation upon which the efforts of private entrepreneurs can build.

I illustrate by reference to the great mineral revolution in Australia during the last fifteen or twenty years. That the skilled labours of the Commonwealth Bureau of Mineral Resources and of the State geological authorities did invaluable initial work in the field of discovery will not be denied. That the Government by its various fiscal measures contributed to and encouraged search and effort is equally clear. But the actual developments in the field required a combination of elements which no Government could provide. Those elements may be stated as: specialized skills, to an extent imported from overseas; vast sums of risk capital, a good deal of which clearly could not be generated in Australia; and powerful aid in the development of large and profitable markets overseas.

The best Government contribution to the obtaining of massive help from overseas was to create the favourable climate; to establish a reputation abroad for financial and economic stability, political integrity, and a high international credit rating. It is freely acknowledged by leaders in the overseas investing countries, and by industrial leaders and State ministers in Australia, that we made this contribution successfully.

5

Dissolving Both Houses of Parliament

In Australia, the Commonwealth Parliament consists of the Senate and the House of Representatives, the powers of each of which are set out in the Commonwealth Constitution. Except for money bills, which have to originate in the House, and which the Senate can reject but not amend, the Senate has equal legislative authority. It can reject bills of any kind originating in the House; it can, except for money bills, amend them as it thinks fit.

The party which has a majority in the House forms a Government; it is in the House that Governments are made or unmade.

But though the same electors vote for the election of senators and ministers, the methods of election are in some respects vitally different.

The House of Representatives is elected by a number of single constituencies in each State. Normally, it endures for three years, but may be dissolved after a shorter period on the advice of the Prime Minister.

The Senate is elected by States, the electors in each State voting as a single constituency. Except for casual vacancies, every senator is elected for a period of six years. Elections are so arranged that half the senators retire each three years. So it was that when my party, in 1949, won a handsome majority in the House and in respect of the retiring half of the Senate, it was confronted in the Senate by a hostile majority, the non-retiring half being mostly Labour senators, elected in 1946.

This, of course, made government very difficult. Ordinary legislation came almost to a standstill. I resolved quite soon that this log-jam must be broken if the Government were to succeed.

Now this is a state of affairs for which the founding fathers had made provision in the Commonwealth Constitution, Section 57 of which reads in part:

If the House of Representatives passes any proposed law, and the Senate rejects or fails to pass it, or passes it with amendments to which the House of Representatives will not agree, and if after an interval of three months the House of Representatives, in the same or the next session, again passes the proposed law with or without any amendments which have been made, suggested, or agreed to by the Senate, and the Senate rejects or fails to pass it, or passes it with amendments to which the House of Representatives will not agree, the Governor-General may dissolve the Senate and the House of Representatives simultaneously. . . .

This provision had been invoked only once before in Commonwealth history, in 1914, when the then Prime Minister, Joseph Cook, obtained a 'double dissolution'. The Senate had twice rejected a Bill on an industrial issue which nowadays we would think almost trivial. So Cook got his double dissolution, and his Labour opponents won the election.

Fresh from victory at the General Election as I was, and frustrated in the Senate, I decided that I would work towards a double dissolution on a lively issue. If I could secure it, I felt confident of victory. But I knew, and later so advised the Governor-General, that I could not get it as a mere matter of advised discretion on the part of the Governor-General; that it had to be established *in fact* that the conditions of Section 57 had been complied with. They were:

1. That the House of Representatives had passed a proposed law.

2. That the Senate had rejected or failed to pass it, or passed it with unacceptable amendments.

3. That after an interval of three months the House had again passed the proposed law with or without any amendments suggested or agreed to by the Senate.

4. That the Senate had then rejected it, or failed to pass it, or passed it with unacceptable amendments.

Now, the legislation we selected for the test was the Commonwealth Bank Bill, which contained a series of provisions including a very contentious one which substituted for one-man control of the Commonwealth Bank—which had been established by the Labour Party—control by a board of directors.

The bill was passed by the House of Representatives on 4 May 1950. The Senate passed it with amendments on 21 June 1950. The amendments deleted the provision for a board of directors.

On 22 June, the House of Representatives rejected the amendment, and so advised the Senate. The Senate insisted, and the House once again, for good measure, though there was no legal necessity, insisted on its disagreement.

So far, it was clear that, of the conditions above stated, numbers 1 and 2 were established. Over three months later, on 11 October 1950, the House of Representatives once more passed the same proposed law, and sent it to the Senate, where the second reading was moved on 17 October 1950, the debate being then, as usual, adjourned. On 24 October a Government motion in the Senate, to enable the bill to be called on for debate, was defeated. On 31 October, a similar motion was again defeated, the Senate thus refusing to debate the bill at all.

On 1 November, the second-reading debate was resumed, and continued through 2, 7 and 8 November. The debate was then, on the motion of the Opposition, adjourned, and was not allowed to be resumed before Parliament adjourned in December. Parliament having reassembled in March 1951, the second reading was further debated in the Senate on 13 and 14 March, and was carried. The Opposition then put forward, and the Senate passed, a resolution referring the bill for consideration and report by a Select Committee of Labour senators which was directed to report in four weeks' time; a time which the Senate had power to extend at the will of a majority of its members, that majority, of course, being opposed to the bill.

This manœuvre had, as was well known in the lobbies, been recommended by Dr Evatt, who had formerly been the Labour Attorney-General, and another legal senator, Senator McKenna.

It seemed to me that these moves, relating to a bill which had been discussed almost *ad nauseam* for many months, were nothing more than a delaying procedure, and that a point had been reached at which it could be concluded that the Senate had failed to pass the bill.

In order to test the accuracy of my own advice to Cabinet, I had two consultations with the then leader of the Bar, Garfield Barwick, Q.C. (now Sir Garfield Barwick, Chief Justice of the High Court of Australia), and also secured written opinions from the Attorney-General and the Solicitor-General. In the result, they all agreed that a case for a double dissolution was clearly established.

On the morning of 15 March, I sought and obtained an interview with the Governor-General, Sir William McKell, who had previously been the Labour Premier of New South Wales.

I told him that I would be making a submission to him about a double dissolution, but that I thought it would be useful if I were to set out in writing the principal arguments which I desired to advance to him. We then had a general conversation on the matter, in the course of which he told me that he had been following the parliamentary proceedings on the Commonwealth Bank Bill very closely, and that, as one familiar with parliamentary procedure, he thought he had appreciated the significance of the steps that had been taken. I told him that I realized this, but that as, in my opinion, it was necessary that I should clearly establish certain basic matters of fact, it would be proper if I were to set out the various steps that had occurred, accompanying my statement with an argument about the interpretation and application of Section 57. His Excellency agreed that this would be a proper course, and I left him with the promise that I would have my letter delivered to him on the following day.

In the course of our discussion, I had made it clear to His Excellency that, in my view, he was not bound to follow my advice in respect of the existence of the conditions of fact set out in Section 57, but that he had to be satisfied, on his own judgment, that those conditions of fact were established.

That afternoon, I personally drafted a long letter to the

Governor-General. I showed it to Barwick, who told me that, in his opinion, my submission was completely justified on the facts and in the terms of the Constitution.

I then met the Cabinet, read my draft letter to them, and obtained their approval. Next day, I forwarded my letter to the Governor-General for his consideration.

In that letter (to which I attached the written opinions of the Law Officers) I first of all set out the narrative of parliamentary events which I have already set out in this chapter, emphasizing that the Senate's whole purpose had been delay; that on the record the Senate had, on the second occasion, 'failed' to pass the proposed law; that the Governor-General now had power to dissolve the Senate and the House of Representatives simultaneously; and that I unhesitatingly advised him to exercise that power.

But I then went on to deal with another aspect of the matter, though I advised the Governor-General that it was, in my view, irrelevant. I referred to it only because, in my earlier discussion with His Excellency, he had recalled that, in the granting of a double dissolution in 1914, some importance appeared to have been attached to the unworkable condition of Parliament as a whole. Having rejected this consideration as a ground for a double dissolution, which in my opinion could be granted only by reference to the conditions specifically stated in Section 57, I went on to say that if, contrary to my view, the unworkability of Parliament were thought to be a relevant factor, it could be completely proved. I said that the then position in the Commonwealth Parliament was, for the reasons I set out earlier in this narrative, 'such that good government, secure administration, and the reasonably speedy enactment of a legislative programme are being made extremely difficult, if not actually impossible'.

It was easy to establish this. The policy on which we had been elected in December 1949, with a House of Representatives majority of 74 to 47—a large majority in a small parliament—had included a bill to extend social services by providing child endowment for the first child in a family, a bill to dissolve and

4

outlaw the Communist Party, and a National Service Bill, designed to introduce National Service training.

The hostile majority in the Senate had, by inserting amendments which it later abandoned, delayed the passage of the Child Endowment Bill for months. It had battered the Communist Party Dissolution Bill, first by making amendments which were rejected by the House of Representatives. The bill was then laid aside. After an interval of three months, the bill was re-introduced and passed in the House of Representatives. There were further amendments in the Senate, and further disagreements, after which the Senate thought that the risk of a double dissolution was looming up most ominously, and passed the bill without amendment, six months after its original introduction. In the case of the National Service Bill, it had passed through the House on 30 November 1950. The Senate majority did not like it, and postponed it until 1951. It then adopted the expedient of appointing a Select Committee, which in due course reported on some other matters, but made no real report on National Service at all. Having achieved this delay the Senate then passed the bill; but the commencement of our defence scheme had been grievously postponed.

But these, though powerful considerations if a Prime Minister were seeking a dissolution of the House of Representatives only, had, as I pointed out in my letter, no relevancy to the extraordinary constitutional remedy of a double dissolution.

I concluded my letter by placing myself at the Governor-General's service should he desire to discuss the matters set out in my letter, or any other aspects of the matter which seemed to him to merit examination.

On 17 March, I went out to Government House for an interview with the Governor-General. He indicated that he proposed to accept my advice, but, as is usual in the case of any dissolution, he would require an assurance that adequate provision existed for the carrying on of the public service in all its branches until the anticipated date of assembly of a new parliament. I was able to give him that assurance. He then sent me a letter saying:

I am prepared forthwith to dissolve simultaneously the Senate and the House of Representatives under the provisions of Section 57 of the Constitution of the Commonwealth.

Well, that is the story, which will have interest for students of constitutional history. There were loud howls of execration from the Labour Party, which had been badly advised. But the people voted, and the Government came back with a majority in both Houses. After that, it was up to us.

6

Pacific Policy

I am one of those old-fashioned Australian politicians who think that our nation's foreign policy should not be aimed at noisy demonstration or assertion. A little man waving a big stick is not only faintly absurd, but liable to lose his balance.

Situated as we are in the world, washed on our western and northern shores by potentially hostile seas, and numerically incapable—despite intense defence preparations—of defending ourselves for long against all-out attack by a great power without massive aid from our friends, it seems to me to be clear (and my Government acted on that belief) that our foreign policy should be to cultivate friendly relations with our neighbours; to do what we could to help their development and stability; to encourage every means of peaceful economic and financial co-operation; to avoid avoidable war; to play our part in helping to prevent tensions among our neighbours; to be loyal members of the United Nations while having no illusions about its present protective effectiveness.

But if, in spite of all effort to live at peace, a war comes, the business of foreign policy is to see that we enter it with great and powerful friends.

This last phrase, which I have frequently used, is now used in a sneering sense by some commentators of a highly isolationist colour; but I adhere to it. It is a completely realistic and honourable policy. I hope that nothing will be done in the future to impair our relations with those friends.

During my long term of office, some features of which I am now putting on record, I was fortunate to have a Cabinet which unanimously shared these views, and succeeding Ministers for External Affairs who laboured brilliantly and successfully to make our policy effective.

It is nowadays fashionable for slick commentators to say that Australia has only in the last few years discovered the problems and significance of the Pacific area and, in particular, of Asia and South-East Asia. This is a myth.

When I first became Prime Minister in 1939, I made a speech to the nation in which, for the first time in Australian political history (as I believe), Australia was put squarely into the Pacific rather than the Atlantic world.

In the Pacific we have primary responsibilities and primary risks. Close as our consultation with Great Britain is, and must be, in relation to European affairs, it is still true to say that we must, to a large extent, be guided by her knowledge and affected by her decisions. The problems of the Pacific are different. What Great Britain calls the Far East is to us the near north.

I have become convinced that in the Pacific Australia must regard herself as a principal, providing herself with her own information and maintaining her own diplomatic contacts with foreign powers. I do not mean by this that we are to act in the Pacific as if we were a completely separate power; we must, of course, act as an integral part of the British Empire. We must have full consultation and co-operation with Great Britain, South Africa, New Zealand and Canada. But all those consultations must be on the basis that the primary risk in the Pacific is borne by New Zealand and ourselves. With this in mind I look forward to the day when we will have a concert of Pacific Powers, pacific in both senses of the word.

This policy was put into effect. By 1940 we had opened a Legation in Washington, a High Commission in Ottawa, and an Embassy in Tokyo. As I recorded in *Afternoon Light*, I went to London early in 1941, the whole reason for this wartime visit being to discuss what my Government believed to be a serious menace from Japan (still at peace so far as we were concerned, but waging major military operations in China) and to urge the strengthening of the defences of Singapore.

Then came the Japanese attacks at Pearl Harbor and her South-East Asian drive. For Australia, throughout the rest of the war, the Pacific had become the overwhelming focus of interest.

Returning to office at the end of 1949, we very soon had to

face the need for a positive approach to the problems of the area. I will summarize what we did, in chronological order.

The Colombo Plan

I had appointed Percy (now Sir Percy) Spender, Q.C., as my Minister for External Affairs. He was (and still is) a man of great and intelligent energy, prepared to attack a problem, persistent, and not easily rebuffed. As soon as January 1950 he was off to a British Commonwealth Conference on Foreign Affairs, the main purpose of which was to consider plans to assist the countries of South and South-East Asia to stabilize their economies and raise their levels of production, thus improving the standards of living of their people. Spender took a prominent and constructive part in the discussions, never allowing his audience to lose sight of the central fact that local self-help must be assisted, promptly and generously, from outside. A Consultative Committee was set up, and met in Australia. From that and later meetings grew the famous 'Colombo Plan', which for some time was, in Australia, known as the 'Spender Plan', and can properly be regarded by him with pride.

He had, of course, and needed to have, the full backing of my Cabinet, for this was an international arrangement of the highest importance, and proved invaluable to the recipient countries. Money was given, and much-needed technical aid; in the course of time Australia was to receive, as a result of this plan, thousands of students from South and South-East Asian countries so that they could in due course return their acquired skills to their own countries. This is still the case.

Aid was arranged on a bilateral basis, the countries concerned indicating their own requirements. From first to last, our aid was given without strings or reciprocal obligations.

I am proud to record that, in addition to our large and growing financial obligations to support economic and social growth in Papua and New Guinea, which totalled over the same period £114,000,000, our total aid to the South and South-East Asian

46

countries during the next ten years amounted to no less than £40,000,000.

Before I leave this particular aspect of our positive Asian policies, I must quote a few words from Spender's principal speech on the Colombo Plan in the House of Representatives. He said, on 6 June 1950:

The House may also wish to know that some consideration was given to the problem of maintaining a uniform level of world prices for the export commodities of the countries of South and South-East Asia.

He was here foreshadowing an element which was never lost sight of by my Government, and on which, at subsequent Commonwealth conferences, my colleague the Minister for Trade, John McEwen, played a constructive part. For we saw quite clearly that one of the greatest underlying problems, which, until it is solved, will produce tensions which threaten the peace, is that of the gap between the living standards of the great industrialized nations with enormous physical and technological resources and therefore rapid growth, and those of the emergent nations with more primitive industry, limited industrial assets, and slower growth. Clearly, if this gap is to continue to widen, there will be much ill-will and frustration. New countries, having increased their export surpluses with technical and financial aid, must be provided with markets for their products at prices which will enable them to develop their capital resources and living standards.

This was the first major initiative of my new Government. It was a positive approach looking well into the future. It involved Australia closely with the countries and peoples of Asia. This association has persisted ever since and has been a major element not only in the policies and dealings of the Australian Government but also in helping to shape the background and attitudes of individual Australians. Australian ministers and officials, private firms, and universities are in frequent contact with their counterparts in Asian countries. Many thousands of Asian students had studied in Australia by the time I retired, and the process continues. The daily association of Australians with students and scholars from Asian countries has greatly widened the experience and understanding of our own people, and is a major achievement for which our Government can claim credit.

The Colombo Plan was also important in another respect. We wanted the industrialized countries of North America and Western Europe to give more attention to the economic needs of Asia. After the Second World War great economic aid had gone to Europe, primarily from the United States. The Marshall Plan which followed was a major and most generous programme by the United States to set Western Europe on its feet again economically. The justification for concentrating on Western Europe at that time was that it already had the skills and the basic economic capacity to enable it to become again a major element in the world economy and therefore to contribute to the economic well-being of all. At the same time, in the United Nations valuable work was being done in helping to promote and give practical effect to the idea of international responsibilities for economic development.

Australia supported these efforts, and President Truman's Point Four proposal of international technical assistance provided a substantial material base for United Nations programmes. Asia, unlike Latin America, had small representation in the United Nations in relation to the hundreds of millions of people living in that region. When the United Nations was formed, its only members from South and South-East Asia and the Western Pacific were the Republic of China, India, and the Philippines—only three votes in a United Nations of fifty-one. By the time the Colombo Plan Conference met in 1950, Burma, Indonesia, and Pakistan had been admitted to the United Nations, but the region still had far too little representation in proportion to its size. Australia was able, partly by its own initiatives and partly by working with its neighbours, to do something to direct the attention of the world to the Asian region and its economic needs. The

Colombo Plan was one such initiative. We kept up the effort, for example by our steady support for the United Nations Economic Commission for Asia and the Far East (ECAFE). Throughout my term as Prime Minister, and since, the Australian Government has always worked to get for the Asian region more of the financial and economic aid and trade of the developed countries of the world.

Peace with Japan

Our war with Japan, and the atrocious methods of the enemy, had produced much bitterness in Australia. Yet, on 8 September 1951, we were one of the signatories to a treaty of peace which was in many ways a 'soft' peace. Japan renounced many territorial claims; accepted the obligations of the Charter of the United Nations to settle disputes by peaceful means and to refrain from the threat or use of force; agreed to accept the judgments of war-crimes courts and tribunals; agreed to certain provisions for compensation for war damage and hardships suffered by prisoners of war.

The contracting parties realized that Japan's economic viability would be important for future world peace. Arrangements were made between the U.S.A. and Japan for the stationing by the United States of armed forces in and about Japan to assist in the preservation of peace and security in the Japan area.

We thought that the treaty and its ancillary agreements with the U.S.A. were economically favourable to Japan, since her budgets would be free of the large defence votes which the victors would need to maintain. But we were prepared to accept this, for we saw even then that an economically revived Japan would become a trading nation of much significance to us, and that a Japan not compelled to become introspective and bitter was much less likely to be drawn into the Communist orbit or to become once more an aggressor on her own account if she became an active trading member of the community of free nations.

The treaty itself envisaged the making of future commercial arrangements between Japan and the Allied Powers. It stated that 'Japan declares its readiness promptly to enter into negotiations for the conclusion with each of the Allied Powers of Treaties or Agreements to place their trade, maritime and other commercial relations on a stable and friendly basis'. Japan undertook that, pending the conclusion of such treaties or agreements, she would accord to each of the Allied Powers most-favoured-nation treatment with respect to duties and charges connected with the importation or exportation of goods; but the treaty went on to say that Japan should be obliged to accord this treatment only to the extent that the Allied Powers concerned accorded to Japan similar treatment. These provisions gave rise to various pressures in Australia. A series of negotiations occurred, and in 1957 we made a comprehensive trade treaty, the controversy about which was very great at the time, but the effects of which have turned out to be of great value to both countries. A little later I shall devote a special section to that matter.

The ANZUS Treaty

But from our point of view there were two factors, each of them involving national security, which gave rise to some apprehension. One was a long-range one: that at some time in the future Japanese militarism might revive and present a world threat. The other, more immediate, was the extreme and aggressive posture of Communist China, whose possible avenues of advance pointed in the direction of Australia and New Zealand, and which was already in conflict with the United Nations over Korea, where Australian troops were engaged.

We realized to the full the importance of maintaining and encouraging American interest in our corner of the world. Spender needed no encouragement from Canberra to get on with negotiations.

He kept us informed on progress, and showed a growing optimism. I remember saying to him on one occasion that if he could get an agreement on some sort of security pact it would be wonderful, but that he must not be too disappointed if the attempt failed. 'After all,' I said, 'America has a long tradition of reluctance to accept "foreign entanglements".'

But Spender, with our full backing, kept the ball rolling. At that time a Japanese peace treaty was not yet agreed upon; there had been differences at the Prime Ministers' Conference in London, and in the discussions which surrounded it. Some felt that if Japan was not to be brought within the Communist orbit, it must be defended, and that the burden of defending it should at least be shared by the Japanese people. We had clearly stated (and justified by reference to war history) our opposition to any resurgence of Japanese militarism.

Clearly, if a 'soft' peace were to be made, Australia would need to find some assurances or guarantees of protection. This aspect of the matter was closely followed up by Spender, to whose work I paid a tribute in the speech I made in Parliament on 7 March 1951, reporting on the London Conference. I said:

It is to the lasting credit of my colleague, the Minister for External Affairs, that he has, knowing the opinions of other nations on Japanese rearmament, continuing constantly to assert their strong opposition, been emphasizing in every appropriate quarter the problem of our own security in the Pacific. He has insisted that, particularly in face of any Japanese rearmament, there should be created such particular Pacific arrangements as will give to Australia some guarantee of friendly aid and protection in the event of a recurrence of threatened attack upon us.

Spender pursued his assignment with admirable vigour.

Following up the view which had been propounded by me in 1939, he told the House that 'the basic consideration for Australia is that, as a metropolitan Pacific power, it must achieve adequate security arrangements in this region'. He pointed out the significance of NATO in the Western world, and went on to say, 'It is therefore essential to establish, over and above the normal channels of diplomatic consultation, an organization in the

Pacific which will provide machinery through which mutual aid and political co-operation can be achieved.' He told the House of some discussions he had had, in 1950, as Australian Minister for External Affairs, with Mr Foster Dulles and with Mr Doidge of New Zealand, and was able to report distinct progress.

What came to be known as the ANZUS Treaty was signed in America on 1 September 1951; and I will, later in this chapter, summarize its contents and significance, without repeating the more detailed account which I gave in *Afternoon Light*. Meanwhile, in April, the Australian ambassadorship to the United States fell vacant. At his own keen desire, Spender was appointed, and resigned from the Cabinet. I had mixed feelings about the appointment, for though Spender was admirably qualified to advocate the views of the Cabinet and of myself, and in fact was remarkably successful in Washington, I valued him and did not want to lose him from Cabinet or Parliament.

He was succeeded in External Affairs by the widely experienced and distinguished R. G. (now Lord) Casey. But I arranged that Spender should sign the treaty on our behalf; he had done so much to bring it about.

Now, apart from our ancient and largely unwritten ties with Great Britain and the Commonwealth, the most significant feature of Australia's modern foreign policy was this mutually defensive treaty with the U.S.A. and New Zealand, ratified in accordance with constitutional requirements in all three countries. Its continued validity and effectiveness have been affirmed by successive American Presidents and Secretaries of State. It amply deserves some brief explanation in the context of this chapter.

At a period when it has become almost fashionable to make critical remarks about America and American policy, such remarks being made both at home and abroad, it is good for Australians to recall the provisions and circumstances of the ANZUS Treaty. Nothing can better demonstrate the role which the United States has accepted since the Second World War, and its willingness to match great responsibilities with great power, than this brief but significant treaty. The United States has seventeen or eighteen times the population of Australia and almost sixty times the population of New Zealand. Clearly what Australia and New Zealand could do to assist the United States would be a very small fraction of what the United States could do for Australia and New Zealand. But the Americans made the treaty and ratified it.

There are some statements made in the preamble to the treaty which I quote, for they should be remembered. One paragraph noted the American stationing of armed forces in the West Pacific; another recognized 'that Australia and New Zealand as members of the British Commonwealth of Nations have military obligations outside as well as within the Pacific area'. A further paragraph contained a declaration made publicly and formally of the sense of unity of the contracting parties 'so that no potential aggressor could be under the illusion that any of them stand alone in the Pacific area'. A final paragraph of the preamble looked to the future. It recited that the parties desire 'further to co-ordinate their efforts for collective defence for the preservation of peace and security pending the development of a more comprehensive system of regional security in the Pacific area'. (This glance into the future led, as I shall point out, to the making of the South-East Asian Treaty [SEATO]).

The principal operative articles of ANZUS, apart from the re-affirmation of the peaceful obligations under the Charter of the United Nations, were:

Article II: In order more effectively to achieve the objective of this Treaty the Parties separately and jointly by means of continuous and effective self-help and mutual aid will maintain and develop their individual and collective capacity to resist armed attack.

Article IV: Each Party recognizes that an armed attack in the Pacific Area on any of the Parties would be dangerous to its own peace and safety and declares that it would act to meet the common danger in accordance with its constitutional processes.

It has sometimes been said that Australia believes that under certain postulated circumstances the United States would be *automatically* at war. This view was dealt with by me in parliamentary debate on 21 April 1964, when I agreed that the phrase 'in accordance with its constitutional processes' excluded the idea of automatic and instant hostilities, since the parties to the treaty had their own constitutional requirements associated with the declaration of war. But I emphasized that the whole nature of the treaty had broad implications for each country concerned. It would, for example, be a strange thing if the parties under Article II had maintained and developed their individual and *collective* capacity to resist armed attacks, these words emphasizing the defensive nature of the treaty, and yet, at the same time, felt completely free not to resist armed attack.

The fact that the ANZUS Treaty does not produce an automatic result does not avoid the conclusion that between contracting parties of good faith it renders common action against a common danger substantially inevitable.

I concluded my speech by saying:

All I do is point out, as I am sure any member of the American Administration would, that there is a contract between Australia and America. It is a contract based on the utmost goodwill, the utmost good faith and unqualified friendship. Each of us will stand by it.

This statement, conveyed in full to Washington, was, I was informed, completely in line with official United States opinion.

Indeed, I had many discussions over the years with Mr Dean Rusk, who had become United States Secretary of State. We were always on common ground in our view of the great significance and substantive meaning of the treaty. On a visit early this year to Australia, Mr Agnew, the Vice-President, expressly said, 'We will keep our treaty obligations.'

That the ANZUS Treaty is the keystone of our Pacific structure I think I can justly claim. It is clear that it should be regarded as one of the major achievements of the period of administration about which I am writing. Without it, our modern apprehensions about the activities and aims of Communist China, great as they are, would be much greater and more oppressive.

SEATO

The South-East Asia Collective Defence Treaty (a very significant title) was negotiated and executed on 8 September 1954, by R. G. Casey on behalf of my Government. The other signatories were the plenipotentiaries of France, New Zealand, Pakistan, the Philippines, Thailand, the United Kingdom, and the United States. This was the year of the 'Geneva Accords', which led to the partitioning of Vietnam and made South Vietnam, in effect, a separate country. This defence treaty was, therefore, made under circumstances in which the source of danger was clearly recognized.

The Australian Parliament unanimously ratified the treaty. The Opposition sought some amendments to the bill, but on the desirability of the treaty there was no division. For example, in the Senate the Leader of the Opposition, Senator McKenna, said:

I can say at once that the Opposition supports ratification of it. I want it to be quite clear that we do support this treaty. That statement stands without qualification, despite the fact that we shall be critical of some provisions of the treaty and that we shall offer criticism of some provisions of the Bill, and even despite the fact that we shall propose certain safeguards for insertion in the Bill itself. The treaty is in line with the United Nations Charter, particularly with Articles LI and LII, which contemplated the making of regional arrangements.

My Government did not treat the debate in any perfunctory way. The Minister for External Affairs, R. G. Casey, made a long and careful analysis of the treaty in a statement opening the debate in the House of Representatives on 27 October 1954. I shall not traverse all the ground here now. One point which naturally attracted the attention of members, and which Casey dealt with fully, was the fact that the United States had entered a reservation to the effect that its commitment under Paragraph 1 of Article IV applied only to Communist aggression. Mr Dulles was of the view that the United States Senate would regard Communist aggression as being one arm of international Communism and therefore a threat to the peace and safety of the United States justifying greater discretion being given the President than would some other form of aggression. In the latter case the Senate would want to reserve more say to itself. The United States agreed that in the case of other forms of aggression it would continue to have obligations, but of a less automatic nature.

The consequence of all this was that, though the treaty was directed against all forms of aggression, the United States' automatic commitment was, in effect, limited. The other members accepted this because of the importance of having a treaty and particularly of having the United States as a party. It was accepted the more readily because the only form of aggression that was thought likely at that time was Communist aggression. Australia for its part also imposed a limitation because we had very much in our minds from the outset the question of possible fighting between India and Pakistan. Australia would have liked India to be a party to the treaty, and during the negotiation of the treaty Casey visited New Delhi to discuss the matter with Mr Nehru, first to see whether anything could be done to allow India to become a party, and secondly to ensure that, if India did not become a party, its Government would understand the motivations and actions of Australia. It was quite clear however that India would not adhere to any security arrangement. However, in signing the treaty in Manila, Casey made a statement which he repeated in the House of Representatives on 27 October. He said:

I wish to state categorically that the Australian Government would never regard itself as being committed, contractually or morally, to military action against any other member of the Commonwealth. I find it impossible to believe that either India or Pakistan would resort to force to settle any problem that might exist between them. The Pakistan Foreign Minister was informed of our position on this point before the treaty was signed.

Unfortunately the prophecy of 'no resorting to force' turned out to be inaccurate, for fighting broke out between the two countries in 1965. But Casey's statement about Australia's attitude was a wise one.

The preamble to the treaty said in terms that the parties 'declare publicly and formally their sense of unity, so that any potential aggressor will appreciate the parties stand together in the area', and went on to express their further desire 'to co-ordinate their efforts for collective defence for the preservation of peace and security'. The main operative Article then followed:

Article II: In order more effectively to achieve the objectives of this Treaty, the Parties, separately and jointly, by means of continuous and effective self-help and mutual aid, will maintain and develop their individual and collective capacity to resist armed attack and to prevent and counter subversive activities directed from without against their territorial integrity and political stability.

The phrase 'separately and jointly' should again be particularly noted. Some attempt was made in some quarters in later years to say that any decision to resist armed attack would require unanimity. It could be argued that for SEATO itself to act *as an organization*, unanimity would be required. My Government took the view that, the obligation of individual members being both joint and several, we could not avoid our treaty obligations by making our performance dependent upon the action of any other party. The United States had the same view and frequently expressed it through the mouth of Dean Rusk. Both our countries have, indeed, for some years been acting under it in Vietnam, the United States in a very large way. I find it impossible to doubt that the Vietnam fighting has been caused by armed attack by forces sent by Hanoi across or around the de-militarized zone which marks the point of partition, and that there have been, through the agency of the Viet Cong, admittedly organized from Hanoi, subversive activities against the territorial integrity and political stability of South Vietnam. This was expressly conceded by the Leader of the Opposition in Canberra,

5

an Opposition which opposes, and for a long time has opposed, Australian military participation in South Vietnam, who said in the Australian House of Representatives in 1965, 'That there has long been and still is aggression from the North and subversion inspired from the North, I do not for one moment deny.'

Article IV of this Treaty was also of great importance.

Article IV: (1) Each Party recognizes that aggression by means of armed attack in the treaty area against any of the Parties or against any State or territory which the Parties by unanimous agreement may hereafter designate, would endanger its own peace and safety, and agrees that it will in that event act to meet the common danger in accordance with its constitutional processes. Measures taken under this paragraph shall be immediately reported to the Security Council of the United Nations.

(This was, of course, done.)

South Vietnam was not one of the contracting parties, but it became entitled to the benefit of the treaty by virtue of a unanimous agreement by the contracting parties designating it as a 'protocol state' and so bringing it within the scope of the treaty.

No party to the treaty could take action on South Vietnamese territory except at the invitation or with the consent of the South Vietnamese Government. When the United States went into South Vietnam with armed forces it did so at the invitation of the Government. The same procedure was followed when Australia participated.

SEATO was by no means a purely military treaty. One of its leading provisions was as follows:

The Parties undertake to strengthen their free institutions and to co-operate with one another in the further development of economic measures, including technical assistance, designed both to promote economic progress and social well-being and to further the individual and collective efforts of governments towards these ends.

After SEATO came into existence Australia showed that it took this provision seriously and wanted it to have substance. In

58

doing so we had, of course, two qualifications very much in mind. In the first place, we did not want any economic activity to divert attention away from the primary purpose of the treaty, which was the preservation and defence of security. In the second place, we believed a very large amount of economic action in the region could better be taken in bodies that had a less restricted membership. Many of the South-East Asian economic problems concerned all the countries of the region and not simply those that were parties to SEATO. We did not want economic activities under SEATO to conflict with or draw resources away from United Nations and Colombo Plan efforts in the region. But Australia believed that nevertheless there was a role for SEATO in the economic field, and Casey went to the SEATO Council meeting in Karachi early in 1956 with concrete proposals. He said that Australia would give each year £1,000,000 for projects to help build up the defence capacity of member nations of the region. It was not to be military assistance, nor was it normally to be the ordinary form of economic aid of the sort that could be provided in other international schemes—it was to be aid that would increase the general ability of countries in the region to contribute to their own defence capacity. Australia hoped that other developed members of SEATO would also follow this example. This has not been the case, though of course the United States has had generous and substantial programmes outside the SEATO machinery. Up to 30 June 1969, Australia had given to the three Asian members and to protocol states under its SEATO aid programme $21,311,000, and this is a clear demonstration of the desire of the Government to make SEATO effective.

The programme has continued to grow quite substantially. I should perhaps mention some of the projects established by us under SEATO. We established in Bangkok a training school which provides comprehensive basic training to enable Thai tradesmen to become technical supervisors for men and instructors in the armed forces. Australian experts have worked in the Cholera Research Laboratory at Dacca in East Pakistan, an enterprise to which we have also given equipment and motor vehicles. A workshop was also established near Bangkok for vehicle rebuilding, to which we have contributed major items of equipment and materials, have supervised construction and provided training. We have also contributed to the Asian Institute of Technology at Bangkok which attracts students from Thailand, Pakistan and the Philippines. The courses are designed to lead to Masters' degrees in hydraulic engineering, public health engineering, structural engineering, and transportation and highway engineering. Contributions of men and materials have also been made to the Hill Tribes Research Centre in Thailand and to the Community Development Technical Assistant Centre in Thailand.

But above all, we recognized that unless aggression and subversion could be halted the opportunities for economic and social advancement, and for economic aid by us, would be restricted. That was why the treaty prominently included the military defence clauses to which I have earlier referred.

I mention these matters because many people are so forgetful of reality as to believe (or say) that SEATO as a military alliance was a mistake; that it should have been a purely economic association, on the assumption that the true defence against aggressive Communism was to be found in the building-up of the non-Communist standard of living upon the structure of some sort of democratic self-government.

That these political, social and economic factors are of vital importance nobody will deny. I, for one, affirm their enduring significance. But a country living under Communist military threat, harried at home by the murderous activities of organized bandits owing their allegiance to another country, is not in a position, or state of mind, to pursue steady domestic policies or to use effectively economic and technical aid provided by friendly powers. Until the independence of South Vietnam, and its freedom from military intervention, can be assured, the internal reorganization of that country must be gravely handicapped.

Australian–Japanese Trade Arrangements

After my Government won the General Election in 1954, we

60

gave some thought to how Australia should handle its relations with Japan during the three years of office that were ahead of us, and we approached this in a positive, considered way so that we would not be taking things simply as they turned up. Casey outlined to Cabinet the outstanding problems that existed between Australia and Japan, most of them arising out of the war, and after discussion we authorized him to try and settle each of them, either alone or in association with those of his ministerial colleagues who had responsibilities in regard to a particular subject. Our general approach was that Australia wanted to be on good terms with Japan and to bring it into the community of nations, so that it would have its self-respect and be a co-operative partner with full opportunities to develop and sustain its economy. I regard the outcome as one of the outstanding successes of my Government.

I turn particularly to our trade problems.

I shall not make reference to pre-war events since my prime purpose in this chapter is to show what my Government did. I might appropriately say what my deputy Prime Minister John McEwen did, except that, of course, he moved in close consultation with me and with our colleagues, particularly Casey, who was most active on the diplomatic front, and had our constant backing. There was still much hostility in Australia, among both manufacturers and the general public, to the making of any special agreement with Japan which might increase Japanese exports to Australia. Not only were war memories very strong, but most Australians viewed Japanese industry and its products with suspicion. Both had, before the war, been associated in the Australian mind with cheap labour; poor-quality goods; policies of price-cutting which unfairly competed with products manufactured within Australia and also imported from traditional suppliers; and, I fear, occasional dubious practices for the evasion of our Customs tariff.

Nevertheless, the long view needed to be asserted. Japan would be a growing Pacific power with a vast industrial population and she would need many of the things that we could provide and needed to sell. We, in turn, in all common sense, would have to recognize that, though the trade between us might never be expected to balance, Japan must have adequate means of earning foreign exchange if she were to become a big customer of ours.

So it was that in October of 1956 it was announced by the Government that trade negotiations between Australia and Japan would shortly commence and would be directed towards the conclusion of a trade agreement. Japan was already our second most important customer, particularly for wool, and the balance of trade leaned heavily in our favour. That imbalance could be expected to become even more serious at the time of our announcement, because domestic supplies of Australian steel were becoming sufficient to satisfy most internal demands, and Japanese exports to Australia of this item would substantially cease. This expectation proved correct, because the 1957 trade statistics showed that Australia had sold £139,000,000's worth of goods to Japan and had bought only £13,000,000. We had other considerations in our minds: development in Australia, which, even then, in the mineral field was very great, meant that we must expect a high rate of imports of capital equipment. This emphasized our need for additional export income. Our exports to the United Kingdom were not growing at anything like the rate needed and, in any event, London was looking eagerly in the direction of the Common Market as a means of ensuring her own trade development.

Our agreement with Japan was made in July 1957.

In August and September 1957 it produced a great debate in the House of Representatives. McEwen made a clear explanatory statement, tabled the agreement, and, following our parliamentary practice, moved that it be printed. Evatt, Leader of the Opposition, moved an amendment disapproving of the agreement. So the battle was clearly joined. If it had not been won by us, the whole course of our relations with Japan would have been drastically altered for the worse. Fortunately for Australia, the Labour Party's move failed.

I made an extensive speech myself, from which I shall make two brief quotations.

The first question, which emerges quite plainly from lots of speeches that have been made, is, should we have a trade agreement with Japan at all? What emerges from many criticisms is an apparent belief that we should not. This age in which we live is an age of trade agreements, either multilateral or bilateral—like the recent one that was negotiated with Great Britain. It is a common and proper expression of mutual arrangement between trading nations. Japan is a great trading nation—one of the significant trading nations in the whole Pacific area, and indeed in the world—and Australia is a significant trading nation.

We were reminded by my colleague, in his statement the other night, that in spite of our relatively small population, we are the eighth trading nation in the world. That represents a remarkable development—a remarkable development of export, a remarkable development of import and a remarkable development of internal production. The Government is as aware of that as is any critic and is as determined to preserve that position, and to improve it, as any critic. Could it be said that we could sensibly decline to make any arrangements for the regulation of our mutual trade with Japan? Do we prefer to be free to do exactly as we please with Japanese exports, leaving Japan free to do exactly as she pleases with Australian exports? Because unless that is our strange point of view we must have an agreement, and the first question answers itself. . . .

The agreement will play some part in assisting to create economic stability and growth in Japan. That is not to be dismissed as something unimportant. That is a proposition of the highest statesmanship if we know our position in the world and understand the problems of the Pacific. Indeed it ought not to take much to persuade us of the validity of that point because the economic recovery of Japan since the war has already given great benefits to us.

To say that the agreement was controversial is really an understatement. There was great hostility on the part of organized manufacturers and of important sections of the Press. I made speeches and national broadcasts. So did my colleagues. We

63

secured some good support from prominent ex-servicemen. We found ourselves facing a good deal of hostility. But we had made the treaty. It accorded to each party most-favoured-nation tariff treatment. Japan guaranteed more liberal access to the Japanese market for our wool, wheat, sugar and so on. Japan undertook not to impose a duty on wool during the first three years of the agreement. A very important provision of the agreement was one which enabled us to take immediate action to protect any Australian industry that was seriously disrupted by imports from Japan. Such action could be taken only after consultation with the Japanese; a consultation which was in any event provided for on a full and regular basis. The treaty was strongly opposed in Parliament by the Labour Opposition. Its Leader, Dr Evatt, urged that it should not be adopted, and said that from an Australian point of view it was a thoroughly bad treaty.

Well, admittedly the provision about emergency action was one which could give rise to differences of opinion. What assurance could manufacturers of goods which competed with imported Japanese goods have that their interests would be effectively protected? To meet this point the Government constituted a one-man advisory authority, M. E. McCarthy, who was Chairman of the Tariff Board and very well regarded in manufacturing circles. It was to be his duty to investigate complaints and to advise the Minister of Trade on the need for emergency action. The appointment of McCarthy was welcomed by both the Australian Chamber of Manufactures and the Australian Chamber of Commerce. In the result, although there were over a hundred items manufactured in Australia which were considered as sensitive to Japanese imports, in the first three years only fourteen complains and inquiries needed to be referred to the advisory authority, and only in five cases was action necessary. Apprehensions expressed at the time of the signing of the agreement were proving unfounded. The Japanese authorities turned out to be frank and co-operative. In some difficult cases conveyed to them, they voluntarily limited their exports to Australia. The general atmosphere improved all round. As the years went on, and as the manifold advantages deriving from the treaty and subsequent events became clear, various improvements were made. So that mutual understanding and fair dealing might be ensured, and after discussions with the major business groups in Australia, the Australia–Japan Business Co-operation Committee was formed in 1962. Its first President, interestingly enough, was a former President of the Australian Manufacturers' Association. At the same time a similar committee was formed in Japan, delegates from each of the committees meeting jointly once a year.

The only other major matter I need mention in this highly summarized account results from the famous Kennedy Round under the GATT. Australia finally got a 'binding' from Japan on the duty-free entry of Australian wool.

There are still, and of course there are likely to be for many years to come, problems which will crop up and which will need adjustment. But my colleagues and I look back with satisfaction on this great achievement in the trade field, the benefits of which to Australia (and, of course, to Japan) have been enormous.

The old controversies have, I think, largely died away because each country has found mutual advantages in the arrangements that have been made. I can best summarize the position by saying that in the year in which we came back into office our exports to Japan were four times as great in value as our imports from her, and represented seven per cent of our total exports. The figures have risen on both sides substantially during the years until last year Japan was taking twenty-four per cent of our total exports while our imports from Japan were twelve per cent of our total. It is clear, in short, that our trade with Japan has become a tremendously important factor in our national economy. She has become our best customer, and we are certainly one of hers.

7

Australia and New Zealand

The world interests of Australia and New Zealand are, properly
viewed, not identical but inseparable. There are great differences
of economic structure, for Australia nowadays has a highly
sophisticated and complex economy based upon great primary
industries, mineral resources developing at an astonishing speed,
huge industries such as iron and steel and aluminium, and manufacturing activities and production of great variety and growing
efficiency, while New Zealand still has a relatively simple
economy primarily based upon the farm and forest industries
which, being most efficiently conducted on a good soil and in a
drought-free climate, provide her with the bulk of her export
income, which in turn affords the means of importing manufactured goods mostly produced by others.

This comparison will not always be completely valid. For,
though New Zealand, so far as we know, does not possess anything like the mineral riches of Australia or her remarkable
facilities for the production of iron and steel, she does for example
have great resources of hydro-electric power of great actual and
potential significance to farmer and manufacturer alike.

But when we turn from these economic considerations to the
vital problems of national security in what is still a most insecure
world, to the considerations of international policy which have
such a bearing on the future, the interests of Australia and New
Zealand are identical and ought never to be looked at in isolation.
We are the same sort of people; most of us of the same stock and
traditions; separated by the Tasman Sea, but, I hope, getting and
feeling closer every year. And well we might: the distance from
the east of Australia to New Zealand is little more than half the
distance from Sydney to Perth, while, measured in time, distances grow shorter every year.

I have always felt that we in Australia have a special responsibility to our New Zealand cousins; a responsibility not always

easy to discharge because of our political separateness and economic differences, but in principle never to be forgotten. We are both active survivors of the old British Crown Commonwealth in a new Commonwealth which is becoming curiously addicted to republicanism. Our political institutions are for all practical purposes both inherited and identical. We both have an unshakable respect for the Rule of Law. In two wars our association has been both memorable and honourable. We are two of the three partners in the famous ANZUS Treaty. The name ANZAC is still, in spite of modern and minority sceptics, a name to conjure with. Who, then, shall separate us?

I am repeatedly told that a constitutional association between us in an Australasian Federation is not to be thought of. Yet its economic advantages to both countries would be considerable, for in our existing federation interstate free trade is entrenched, and is a great aid to fluidity of development.

But at my age I do not wish to engage in what would be regarded as an academic discussion. Constitutionally, we are separate, and, I suppose, likely to continue so.

This does not mean, however, that we are strangers. Personally, I have visited New Zealand on quite a number of occasions. I have always felt at home, as if I were among my own people. Whatever may be said on occasions of difference, Australians and New Zealanders can never be 'foreigners' to each other.

As my Government looked at New Zealand, we constantly had those considerations in mind, but we were conscious of the difficulties.

An outsider looking at the close proximity in which both Australia and New Zealand live, looking at two peoples of the kind that I have described, might readily suppose the trade relations between the two countries would be both intimate and easy. Nothing could be further from the truth. These relations have been almost as vexed as the tumbling waters of the Tasman Sea. They have presented an astonishing paradox, a paradox of two peoples genuinely anxious to help each other but unable to find simple ways and means of doing so.

Of course, history is more important than some moderns believe. There was a time early in Australian—or rather New South Wales—history when the Governors in Sydney liked to assume responsibility for and control of the New Zealand colonies. This, of course, proved intolerable to New Zealanders, but it had one important result. The ties between New Zealand and Britain were made direct, with no intermediary in Sydney. This tended to drive Australia and New Zealand apart and to induce New Zealand to look more and more to Britain for her trade and comfort. Many years later, the introduction of steamships and, later on, refrigeration reduced New Zealand's dependence on the Australian market and powerfully facilitated trade with Britain. The close trading and political ties so created have, even in my time, tended to give New Zealand a special place in the hearts of the people of Great Britain. In my own ministerial negotiations I have frequently been conscious of the fact that New Zealand has been looked on as a friend, almost as an unquestioning friend, while we Australians were felt to be more difficult and more critical.

It is one of my own fascinating recollections that on one occasion my late friend Sid Holland, for a long time Prime Minister of New Zealand, and I arrived in the same plane at London Airport. Presumably we were both pretty tired after a very long flight. Holland might indeed have been expected to be more tired than I was, for he had come from farther away. When we disembarked, some broadcasting man was on the tarmac with a microphone, while the photographers were as busy as usual. It was demanded of both of us instantly that we should broadcast a message to the nation. This had no appeal for me because I wanted to find my feet and then go, as I knew I would have to, into the Press and radio interview room. So I walked on. But Sid Holland had a different mind. He knew that he would be interviewed like myself later on, but he at once stepped up to the microphone and delivered in a clear voice what I was to find was his constant slogan: 'I just want to say to you good people of Great Britain that New Zealand stands with you. Where you go, we go; where you stand, we stand.' This, of course, was not to be wondered at, because from at least 1920 onwards the basic characteristic of Australian–New Zealand trade had been a marked imbalance in Australia's favour, and Britain as the main export market for New Zealand was therefore regarded with commercial favour in New Zealand while Australia, I fear, was regarded as a rather rapacious neighbour.

This state of affairs, I must say, was not the designed consequence of deliberate Australian policy, but was due to the nature and character of the economic development in each country. Australia was much larger and had, as I have said, a more varied economy. We had a broader range of exports, some of which New Zealand had to import. We had, particularly in later years, a much more diverse industrial development. Australia was self-sufficient in most of the products exported by New Zealand, for we had our vast wool and meat supplies, while at the same time we became, increasingly, exporters of manufactured goods to our sister country. New Zealand became increasingly conscious of this adverse trade balance and of the fact that we were in commercial competition for markets for similar exports. Some disputes, and occasionally a good deal of friction, were therefore inevitable. But after the Second World War, Australia, having regard to the vitally important political and defence association of the two countries, to which I have referred earlier, began to study this problem and to endeavour to find out how some of the undoubted grievances could be rectified.

True, the famous Ottawa Conference in 1932 had provided an opportunity to put trade relations between the two countries on a better footing, and one of the consequences was an agreement between Australia and New Zealand signed in 1933, mutual preferences being, of course, a central feature of the agreement. My predecessors had, in 1944, in what was known as the ANZAC Pact, agreed in general terms on mutual co-operation, looking to a development of commerce between Australia and New Zealand. Arrangements were made in 1948 between the two Governments for the exchange of visits by officials to permit of general and informal discussions on questions of economic development. When my Government came into office at the end of 1949, we began increasingly to pursue negotiations with New Zealand.

By the middle of the 1950s, both countries were experiencing severe balance-of-payments difficulties, and the imposition of necessary import restrictions by both countries had begun to have an adverse effect on trade in both directions. In 1956, there were discussions at Canberra between Holland and myself and McEwen, my Minister for Trade. New Zealand wanted some special import-licensing treatment for New Zealand commodities, particularly fish and timber, the export of which had been seriously affected by Australian restrictions. More, their new and growing newsprint and paper-pulp industry naturally needed markets if it were to develop. We, in our turn, wanted improved access to the New Zealand market for our manufactured goods, particularly motor vehicles, which were coming into large production in Australia. The result of our discussions, which was embodied in what was known as the 1956 Trade Understanding, was the provision by us of special licensing facilities for New Zealand exports, particularly of fish, newsprint, timber and frozen vegetables. New Zealand reciprocally undertook to encourage extra imports from Australia. This arrangement was of some material benefit to both countries, but it still left the balance of trade heavily in our favour. There was, in fact, a general dissatisfaction in New Zealand at what was thought to be a lack of reciprocity in the bargain. Indeed, some very severe comments were made which suggested that New Zealand had been very unfairly treated by Australia.

Lower export prices for New Zealand's main export commodities, meat, wool and dairy products, had rendered New Zealand's balance-of-payments position very precarious. The anxiety of New Zealanders was easily understood, particularly when a campaign was begun in Britain for entry to the European Common Market. New Zealand was a major food supplier to Britain and could obviously be in serious danger if the European movement gathered pace.

Discussions continued as the 1950s proceeded. In 1958, Walter Nash was Prime Minister of New Zealand, having defeated Keith Holyoake at the end of the previous year. He was confronted by great budgetary problems, some of which may have been of his own making. New Zealand's balance of payments, it was estimated, would be by the end of the financial year 1957–8 in the worst position that it had ever occupied. It was at this stage that Nash sent me a message and said he would like to come and talk to me in Sydney. I had a pretty good idea of what this would involve, so I had discussions with McEwen and with the Treasurer about the question as to whether any temporary assistance could be given to New Zealand. When I sat down to discuss the matter with Walter Nash in Sydney, and he told me his story, I was able to comfort him by telling him that we had decided that, through our Reserve Bank, a £10,000,000 credit to the New Zealand Reserve Bank would be made available. Nash was, of course, delighted, but as he and I were very old personal friends I thought I might permit myself a little bit of fun with him. So I said, 'Walter, you are supposed to be a Socialist. And I am a dedicated non-Socialist. Why did you come to me?' He gave me that delightful smile that he could call upon and said, 'Do you know why I came to you, Bob? Because you are my friend.'

But it was not all as simple as this. By July of that year our officials had gone to New Zealand to continue discussions. One thing they did find was that the average New Zealand businessman was beginning to realize that commercial considerations and not Australian Government policies were limiting sales in Australia of New Zealand products. But the members of our delegation were also satisfied that the New Zealand balance-of-payments situation was very grave and that they must therefore investigate the possibility of enlarging the market for New Zealand newsprint and allied products and in the field of industrial development. They agreed that they would bring to the notice of Australian manufacturers any industries which the New Zealand Government decided it wanted to see established

71

in New Zealand. The delegation recommended that a limited free-trade area was the one move that New Zealand could make to achieve a growing trade with us, and that we should take the initiative in this matter. In 1959, the New Zealand Minister, Mr Holloway, suggested a Customs union between Australia and New Zealand. (Curiously enough he also included Indonesia and Malaya.) Well, the idea of a Customs union, as McEwen pointed out in our Parliament at a later date, was not practicable; because a Customs union requires the members to introduce a common external tariff against imports from other countries. But a free-trade area was well worth investigating, though the difficulties in achieving one, having regard to the special interests of both countries, were very considerable.

The matter was further complicated when in February 1960 my Government made its decision to abolish import licensing. This, of course, rendered virtually void those provisions of the 1956 trade understanding under which special import-licensing facilities were granted to some New Zealand products.

Clearly, the matter of our trade relations must be brought to a head. An Australia–New Zealand Consultative Committee of Trade comprising senior officials, who would report to ministers, was established. It was to meet regularly in Canberra and Wellington and to investigate the possibilities of developing greater trans-Tasman trade. There was no doubt that New Zealand had derived less advantage than we had from the pre-ferential arrangements of the old 1933 trade agreement. In 1963 proposals for a free-trade area were actively canvassed by the Governments of both countries. There were many meetings of the Joint Standing Committee and in the result my colleague McEwen was able on 17 August 1965 to announce to Parliament that an agreement had been reached on the formation of a free-trade area between Australia and New Zealand. The name 'free-trade area' did not mean that there was free trade in all matters. But it did, on this occasion, mean that many items considered to be important on both sides had been brought within the scope of the agreement, which in fact covered some sixty per cent of the total trade between the two countries.

An understanding of the importance of a fair deal for New Zealand became fairly widespread. For example, the representative Australian organizations advised the Government that they would have no objection to our offering to abolish the duty on New Zealand lamb if such a concession could be used to secure some advantage for Australia as a whole. Similar things happened with relation to other commodities. The result was an increased access to Australia for some New Zealand farm products. Australia in its turn secured an important improvement on its exports of manufactures, particularly motor vehicles. This agreement was, I think, a great achievement for the Government and, of course, in particular for McEwen, who had carried the enormous burdens of the negotiations for some years. I will quote the final words of his statement to Parliament because I think they summarize the position.

The conclusion of this free-trade arrangement represents the culmination of intensive activity by both Governments extending over some two years. It constitutes an historic landmark in the development of trade relations between Australia and New Zealand. Although its immediate results in new trade will not be spectacular, the free-trade arrangement is expected to have far-reaching long-term effects on the welfare, development, and growth of the two countries.

All I need say, some years after my retirement from office, is that these negotiations and agreements laid a sure foundation upon which both countries can build and are building. For it is literally true that we stand or fall together.

6

8

Changes in Defence

In my policy speech of 1949, I said that we would introduce universal military and physical training for periods suited to our needs and by methods and on conditions as to call-up and numbers to be determined on the best expert advice. Compulsory national service training had been abandoned by my predecessors at the end of the Second World War, but we felt that a new start must be made. By 1950, when we were back in office, the possibilities of a global war, having regard to the cold-war tactics of the Soviet Union, appeared to be by no means remote, while a limited war had already broken out in Korea. We therefore propounded a compulsory scheme designed to provide a reservoir of trained men. At the beginning of each of the previous wars, expeditionary forces had been raised and in due course trained. In each case this meant that there was a substantial interval of time before trained and equipped forces could be put into the field. But in 1950, circumstances had changed. The nuclear weapon had been devised and used, and was in large production in both the Soviet Union and the United States of America. It had therefore become clear that in the event of the outbreak of another world war there would be no time to train 'raw' recruits. Clearly, a nuclear war would require instant action and would allow no time for any avoidable delay. In the result, the late Harold Holt, who was then the Minister for Labour and National Service, introduced our bill, a National Service Bill, to the House of Representatives in November 1950. The bill provided for the universal conscription of eighteen-year-old men into branches of the Armed Forces for training for a period of 176 days, which was to include 98 days' continuous service in the first year.

The Labour Party, which had a majority in the Senate, used that majority to impede the passage of the bill and succeeded in deferring a debate upon it until the next session of Parliament. In March 1951, at the Australian Labour Party's Federal

Conference, a great change was made, Labour voting in favour of the National Service scheme by a small majority. The bill was then passed by the Senate. Training began in 1951, but the scheme proved to be increasingly inefficient and relatively expensive. It involved a very great drain on the Regular Army, from which large numbers of officers and N.C.O.s had to be subtracted in order to train the compulsory trainees. After examination by a Committee headed by the late Sir John Allison, substantial increases in pay and conditions of service were announced by the Government, in order that more long-term volunteers might be attracted. But the effect on recruitment was only marginal. There was an abundance of civil employment at good and increasing wages, and it became clear that the voluntary system in relation to the Regular Army (which had of course been continued) and to voluntary service in the Commonwealth military forces would not produce the necessary results.

In any event, there was one fact of singular importance. Clearly the defence of Australia, on whatever basis it might be devised, would be in no small measure dependent upon the help of the United States under the ANZUS Treaty; while the American intervention on a massive scale in South Vietnam under the provisions of SEATO was almost without precedent for that country. Yet American conscripts were engaged in South Vietnam and, therefore, in the long view, in the defence of Australia. Great Britain then had National Service, which provided many of her troops in Malaya. How could we possibly take up the attitude that whereas conscription for military service might be all right for our allies and protectors, it was no good to us, for local political reasons?

We therefore decided in 1964 that we must produce a more rapid expansion of the Regular Army than we could hope to achieve by any efforts to encourage voluntary enlistment. We must introduce national training and service. Our new scheme provided that twenty-year-old men should be taken in by ballot in the numbers needed to build the Army to adequate strength. The scheme required, and continues to require, all

National Servicemen, in common with voluntarily enlisted members of the defence forces, to serve either within or beyond the territorial limits of Australia.

This was, of course, in time of peace and, having regard to long-standing Australian traditions, a revolutionary measure. The old tradition had been, as I said in an earlier book, broken by Mr Curtin when he was Prime Minister in order to enable the Government to send compelled trainees out of Australia, for combat. There were territorial limits imposed upon this, which do not matter for my present purpose. But we decided, as we were becoming increasingly uneasy about South-East Asian affairs, particularly the intransigent activities of confrontation under Soekarno, and the Vietnam war, that there should be compulsion to serve abroad.

Our involvement in the Vietnam war began in July 1962, when we sent thirty military instructors to South Vietnam at the request of the South Vietnamese Government. In June 1964, we increased the number of instructors to sixty and also sent some transport aircraft. In April 1965, I announced that the Federal Government would send the 1st Battalion of the Royal Australian Regiment, part of our Regular Army, to South Vietnam. Later in that year support units were dispatched including artillery, engineering and logistic elements and light aircraft. Troops sent to Vietnam were to be sent for a one-year tour of duty before being returned home.

At the same time we had established in Malaya (as it then was) certain troops who formed part of a Commonwealth reserve.

We had, therefore, acted contrary to two long-standing traditions. First, we had introduced compulsion for service in a fighting zone abroad, without territorial limit; second, we had established garrison military forces in Malaya and therefore outside Australia. The necessity for these changes seemed to us to be clear and irresistible. So far as the first change was concerned, we found it inevitable and realistic. We could not honour our obligations under SEATO (obligations to which I have referred in an earlier chapter) without some system of compulsion which would keep our forces up to strength. As for the second, there had been in Australian politics a quite clear issue disclosed. My Government's defence policy was one of forward defence: to keep any war as far away as possible from our own shores; to provide Australian defence in depth; to help to produce a secure environment for our neighbours, with whom we are bound to have a close association as the years go by. The other view, still I think warmly held by the Labour Party, was that Australian defence should be local; confined to our own shores; a sort of 'Fortress Australia' or Maginot Line concept.

During our period of office we, of course, pursued an active policy of improvement in the defence services; made, after competent investigation, substantial improvements in the pay and allowances of the armed forces, and provision for defence forces retirements benefits. A vigorous programme of equipment procurement and of munitions manufacture was carried out. A great deal of attention was given to naval shipbuilding and acquisition, and the needs of a modern air force were given, in effect, a high degree of priority. I do not propose to elaborate on most of these matters. But I do want to say a few particular things about the equipment of the Air Force, since there was (and still is) a good deal of political controversy about one aspect of it.

As we and our advisers saw the position, the Air Force needed to have modern transport aircraft (having regard to our long distances), long-range sea-reconnaissance aircraft, suitable surface-to-air guided weapons and air-to-air missiles, up-to-date fighter aircraft and, particularly for army co-operation, short-take-off and -landing army-co-operation aircraft. I was able in May 1963 to report to the Parliament that we were well on the way to meeting our requirements. We had purchased the great Hercules transport aircraft and the Neptune for sea-reconnaissance purposes, the Caribou for army co-operation, and the French Mirage, the last word in fighters, some of which we obtained direct from France, and many of which were being assembled or made in Australia. This great programme left us short of a long-distance strike-reconnaissance bomber. Fairly early in our term of office we had obtained the Canberra bomber, the first one of which to be demonstrated in flight I had christened in England in 1951. It was by no means obsolete in 1963 for it was still being used by overseas air forces, including those of NATO, but it was quite clear that we would soon need something more modern. I told this to the Parliament on 22 May 1963, saying:

Having regard to our special geographic circumstances, we must consider range, the capacity to perform both reconnaissance and attack and the ability to use existing runways and services. An on-the-spot evaluation by a team of qualified experts is necessary, as it was in the selection of the Mirage. Such a team will be sent overseas at an early date, under the Chief of the Air Staff, to investigate and report. Then, of course, the Government will consider the matter further in the light of the report.

We were not the only people in Parliament concerned about a replacement for the Canberra. Members of the Opposition were loudly demanding one, while in the Cabinet Room we were much of the same mind but wanted to take care that any decision would produce the maximum of benefit to our defence. So it was that after my May statement (and in May 1963 I don't think that anybody was thinking about an election) we sent the evaluation team overseas and in due course received and studied its report. The team had made a thorough investigation of the possibilities including a recently designed reconnaissance bomber, the TSR2, in England and what was then called the TFX in the United States. They were both in the developmental stage on the drawing-board, and it would obviously be some time before they could go into production. But if we were to get the best defence value for our money we must clearly strive to secure the best machine.

The evaluation team reported to us that in almost every aspect the TFX was superior to the TSR2. They said that it would have better speed and range, range being very important for our purposes; that it would carry a heavier bomb load; that it would have better electronic counter-measures; that it would be better fitted for reconnaissance; that it could take off from a shorter runway; and that it would be delivered at about the same date.

With all our sentimental attachment to Britain, my colleagues and I found this report irresistible. (Indeed, the Government of Britain itself ultimately reached a conclusion that it would not order the TSR2.) Before we actually placed an order, however, we decided to ask the Minister for Defence, the late Athol Townley, who had established close personal ties with the American Defense Secretary, to discuss in the United States the practical problems of cost and delivery. He reported to us from Washington, we made one or two further queries and had them answered and thus he came back, his mission having been successful; so successful that I found it necessary to advise the United Kingdom Government that we proposed to go ahead with the arrangements he had made.

On 24 October 1963, I announced these facts in Parliament. As it was common ground that we should secure as soon as practicable a modern replacement for the Canberra, and as the Air Force experts who had advised us were the same people as would have advised a Labour Government, I did not expect my announcement to be as controversial as it turned out to be. But I had recently announced that Parliament would be dissolved and that an election would be held at the end of November. The Government was at once accused by its somewhat baffled opponents of having made a snap decision for electoral purposes. All I can say is that a Cabinet decision which was the result of expert inquiries and ministerial discussions spreading over four or five months could not sensibly be called a snap decision. Indeed, where the defence of the country is concerned, decisions ought to be made after complete investigation but, when made, they ought to be announced and acted upon promptly.

With all the benefit of hindsight, it has turned out in later years that the TFX, now known as the F111, which is in production in America, has had some 'teething' troubles and that its delivery to Australia has been substantially delayed. But the Air Force still has great faith in it and regards it as the very plane for our purposes, particularly having regard to the fact that a strike-reconnaissance plane for Australia must be prepared to travel great distances outside our shores, and back again. In my present state of retirement I permit myself to wonder what would have happened if we had chosen the TSR2, for which the Opposition, after my announcement of October 1963, had conceived a great respect. The answer is, of course, that there is no TSR2, and therefore if we had rejected the F111 we would now presumably be looking around the world to find some alternative. There are always risks in ordering a complicated aircraft which is still in the developmental stage, but the risks have to be taken if proper aircraft are to be secured. It is a somewhat juvenile state of mind to believe that when a country like Australia wants a modern aircraft all it has to do is to go and order one ready-made over the counter, so to speak.

Summing it all up, I think that we had good reason to believe that what we had done during our period of office towards the re-equipment of the Royal Australian Air Force was, and will be, of the highest value to the defence of the country.

9

Developments in Education

One of the significant things about this long period of office, one that I recall with great pride and satisfaction, is the dramatic development of the universities and of some aspects of secondary education.

Since my own student days at Melbourne, I had maintained my interest in university education. As time went on, particularly after I entered politics, I saw its growing community importance and occasionally chided many of my business and banking friends for not giving it greater encouragement and recognition.

As Attorney-General in the State Government of Victoria I had, in the early thirties, put through a bill for the appointment, for the first time, of a full-time Vice-Chancellor in the University of Melbourne. But this was at a time of relative stability in the university world; when student populations were comparatively small, and costs were low.

The Second World War brought about great social changes. In the eye of the future observer, the greatest may well prove to be in the field of higher education.

Before the Second World War, a university training had been regarded as a kind of privilege to be enjoyed by students of unusual talent or of well-to-do or self-sacrificing parents, or of both. Scholarships were very scarce, and hotly contested.

The universities, six in number, were all state universities, most of them partly financed by students' fees and all by substantial subventions from the State Governments. As education was, constitutionally, a State matter, the Commonwealth having been granted no specific constitutional power in relation to it, the Commonwealth stood clear.

When the war ended, the picture changed dramatically. The Commonwealth Government and Parliament of the day properly made provision, as part of the repatriation of ex-service men and women, for help towards a university education. Substantial sums were paid by way of grants to the states for the universities under a Commonwealth Reconstruction Training Scheme. They were not grants for the assistance of university education in general, but were specifically related to repatriation. The amounts of money were not great: in 1950, my first full year of office, they stood at only £450,000, and, in the nature of things, were declining.

At this time, I looked over the scene, and became actively concerned. For a variety of reasons, the numbers of young men and women anxious to avail themselves of university training had increased beyond all anticipation. Student enrolments had doubled, and in some cases quadrupled, since before the war. The universities were naturally under great strain both in terms of capital resources and in terms of providing the necessary and adequate teaching facilities. State finances being considerably less flexible than those of the Commonwealth, which controlled the main sources of revenue like income-tax and customs and excise, it was, I thought, not reasonable that they alone should carry the university burden. Indeed, I did not see how they could!

So it was that my Government, as early as March 1950, appointed a Committee made up of Professor Mills, Sir Douglas Copland and Mr H. J. Goodes of the Commonwealth Treasury. Their terms of reference were:

To examine and report upon the finances of the universities having regard to their facilities for teaching and research, including staff, buildings and equipment.

To examine and report upon the requirements of the universities in relation to the work at present undertaken and to the need for their future development.

To make recommendations as to whether any, and if so what, action should be taken by the Commonwealth to assist universities.

While the committee was conducting its inquiries, I was informed that it was excluding from its consideration the residential colleges, on what I thought was the strange ground that they were luxuries, and that churches or people who wanted them should pay for them. I therefore instructed the committee that it should pay attention to the position of these colleges. The committee made an interim and a final report, after which the Commonwealth had consultations with the State Governments. In the upshot, I brought in a State Grants (Universities) Bill in November 1951, and saw it passed through Parliament. Looking at it now, the amounts provided seem almost niggardly: something over £1,000,000 in each of three years, with a small allocation to the colleges. But they had opened the door.

The bill was a 'State Grants Bill' because Section 96 of the Commonwealth Constitution, which empowers the Commonwealth to make grants to the States on such terms and conditions as Parliament thinks fit, provided, constitutionally, our card of entry into the general universities field. We could not make grants direct to the universities, for we had no direct educational power except the somewhat sketchy and undefined phrase 'benefits to students' introduced into the Constitution by the amendments of 1946.

In any event, as the universities (with the exception of the recently established Australian National University) were State universities, primarily financed by State Governments, co-operation with those Governments was essential; and this co-operation could be best achieved under a State grant.

But apart from these considerations, I confess that I have always believed in the truth of the French proverb, *Il n'y a que le premier pas qui coûte*. I had a strong feeling that the Commonwealth must be the saviour of the universities, and was glad that in this legislation we had created a precedent. We passed subsequent Acts in 1953 and 1955. The actual payments made by the Commonwealth rose to £1,517,000 in 1954, and by 1957 had reached £2,335,000.

But, in spite of this help, the position of the universities was continuing to deteriorate. It became clear that we needed a basic and far-reaching inquiry. Clearly it had to be basic, for all the facts indicated that our remedies so far had been superficial and inadequate. Also, I wanted it to have international

83

authority; for the more our universities achieve repute at home the more do they enter that international community of universities and scholars which is such a feature of the twentieth century.

So I decided to aim high. If I could get the Chairman of the British University Grants Committee, Sir Keith (now Lord) Murray, to preside, I would do well. As I was, in 1956, about to make one of my official visits to England, I spoke to the Treasurer, my colleague Arthur Fadden, and warned him that I was initiating an enterprise which could not fail, in the result, to be vastly expensive. Now Arthur (or 'Artie') Fadden was not a graduate of any university, nor would anybody (as he would be the first to concede) have taken him for an academic type. But he had a good Australian outlook; he knew that this matter was almost an obsession with me; and he was my friend. So he gave me the all clear; without which the subsequent events might well not have happened.

I went to England, attended my conference, and had an interview with Murray. He was clearly the man we needed, and was himself keen on the proposed assignment. But his 'master' was the Chancellor of the Exchequer, then Harold Macmillan. Well, Harold was and still is my friend, and promptly agreed.

And so, in December 1956, the famous 'Murray Committee' was set up. It was remarkably well balanced. Apart from Murray, the other members were: Charles Morris, Vice-Chancellor of Leeds University, who had been suggested by Murray; the late Ian Clunies Ross, who had a well-earned world reputation as head of the C.S.I.R.O.; Alexander Reid, a very able and eminent officer of the West Australian Government, and later to be Chancellor of the West Australian University; and the late J. C. Richards, assistant General Manager of the B.H.P. and a former Rhodes Scholar.

The terms of reference were very wide. I quote from my letter setting them out:

We would hope that the Committee would take a wide charter to investigate how best the Universities may serve Australia at a time of great social and economic development within the nation.

The Committee is invited to indicate ways in which the Universities might be organized so as to ensure that their long-term pattern of development is in the best interests of the nation, and in particular to inquire into such matters as

(1) the role of the University in the Australian community;
(2) the extension and co-ordination of University facilities;
(3) technological education at University level; and
(4) the financial needs of Universities and appropriate means of providing for these needs.

This list is not meant to be exhaustive and it does not set out to limit the inquiry to be undertaken by the Committee.

In brief I had in mind that the Committee might pay attention to what Australian Universities could reasonably be expected to do, how they might be organized to do this, and how their activities should be financed. Some of the specific topics which interest me include: numbers which should be kept in mind in determining whether a new University ought to be established, machinery for ensuring that the creation of new Faculties and Chairs is done in such a way that existing resources are used adequately and needless duplication does not occur, and an analysis of the adequacy of the Commonwealth Scholarship Scheme whereby some 3,000 new scholarships are available annually for students at tertiary institutions. These, of course, represent only a few of the large number of topics which could be listed, but I would prefer the Committee itself to retain a considerable measure of freedom in deciding which problems might be studied in detail to give the most useful type of advice.

The committee presented its report on 19 September 1957. It had enormous financial and other implications, and I was eager for a Government adoption as soon as possible, for the end of session was approaching. I circulated the report to ministers, notified them that I would like a Cabinet discussion in two or three days' time. The Treasury, of course, had a full opportunity of examining the proposals. When Cabinet met I said that I would like it to sit morning, afternoon and evening, and reach its conclusions that night. The Cabinet, knowing that this was an outstanding event in my life, humoured me, and I am still grateful to them.

The report was approved, and its recommendations were adopted.

On 28 November 1957, I tabled it in Parliament, and made a speech. As this chiefly consisted of a summary of the recommendations, I shall not quote it extensively, because I want a little later to explain, as briefly as possible, the novel and sometimes revolutionary features of this historic educational document. But I will venture to quote three passages.

The first is one which discloses my own emotions, which were deep and, for me, unforgettable.

Mr Speaker, if I may confess it, this is rather a special night in my political life.

The others are:

The social, scientific, economic and industrial complexities of Australia today are largely beyond the imagination of forty years ago. Great skill achieved after high training is no longer to be regarded as something to be admired in a few. We must, on a broad basis, become a more and more educated democracy if we are to raise our spiritual, intellectual, and material living standards. Viewed in this way, our universities are to be regarded not as a home of privilege for a few, but as something essential to the lives of millions of people who may never enter their doors. . . .

This new charter for the universities, as I believe it to be, should serve to open many doors and to give opportunity and advantage to many students. They will, I am sure, not forget that, under all the circumstances I have described, the community is accepting heavy burdens in order that, through the training of university graduates, the community may be served. This represents a challenge to the whole future student body to take the fullest advantage of the chances which come to them; to see that future failure rates are not their fault; to realize more than ever that the contribution that they have to make to this great social effort is to be willingly and effectively made. A university may look to Governments, and perhaps primarily to

Governments, for land and buildings and equipment. But its ultimate achievement will depend, as ever, upon the zeal and quality of its staff and of those who train under them.

The principal features of the Murray Report and our adoption of it can be stated quite briefly, though, as will be seen, they had a dramatic effect upon the development of university education in Australia.

I should perhaps first state the broad financial implications. Under our earlier novel provisions made through the states to the universities, the Commonwealth had found during 1955, 1956 and 1957 (continuing what had been done earlier) a total of £6,000,000. After the adoption of the Murray Report, the figure for the triennium 1958–60 was £22,000,000. It can be imagined how the announcement of these figures breathed a great feeling of hope into the universities.

One particular recommendation was that we should set up a permanent Australian Universities Commission. The Government agreed that it should not be called a Grants Commission, for this might narrow its significance. We desired, and in due course put into statutory form, a commission which would try so to organize the development of the universities as to produce the best results and avoid overlapping. (We did not instantly set up the commission because we wanted to consult the states, who would and did become involved in large financial responsibilities, before the actual creation of the body itself.)

We also made a large and growing provision for the Australian National University, the original estimates of the cost of which as primarily a research institution had been gravely underestimated.

Under the new scheme, the Commonwealth was for the first time to contribute to the cost of university buildings and their major equipment; equipment which particularly in the science and engineering departments was becoming increasingly complex and costly. The committee had examined and recommended a building programme, worked out in respect of each of the then

87

universities, to the cost of which both Commonwealth and State would contribute pound for pound except for West Australia and Tasmania in which the Commonwealth would contribute twenty-five shillings per pound. This item alone in the triennium 1958–60 was estimated to cost £6,250,000. I have used the word 'triennium' because a triennial provision by the Commonwealth was to become a great feature of Commonwealth university aid. It had proved most frustrating to the universities not to know from year to year how much they would have to spend in the future. This was, of course, inimical to long-range planning, and it clearly had to be put on a proper footing. The triennial provision has, I think, proved of great value to the universities, who may now think three years ahead. It has its difficulties, because circumstances can change so rapidly that what seemed adequate at the beginning might prove to be inadequate within a couple of years. But my own principle was that if some case could be put to the Australian Universities Commission which justified some supplementary provision during the triennial period the Government might feel willing, as it did indeed several times in my own time, to make additional grants.

The small beginnings of our earlier token payments to the residential colleges were powerfully supplemented by the recommendations (and our decision pursuant to the Murray Report) of capital grants over the ensuing three years for building and equipping of, or extensions to, residential colleges on a pound-for-pound basis. These represented a total of £600,000 over the three years and in subsequent triennia became much greater. These provisions for residential colleges, most of which were church foundations, encountered some criticism on the old sectarian basis to which I shall make some particular reference later in this chapter.

The committee also recommended that Commonwealth Scholarships (that is scholarships awarded to secondary-school students to enable them to take a university course) should be further examined. It was my Government that had actually started the system some time earlier with about 3,000 scholarships; the committee clearly thought that there was room for an increase in this number. In our adoption of the report we did not deal with this matter out of hand, but subsequently made extended provisions for such scholarships.

The committee did a great deal of work of a demographic kind in trying to project the future demand for university education. The total undergraduate population in the then Australian universities after the war was growing at unexpected speed. The Murray Committee found that the actual enrolment in 1957 was 36,465. Having considered the rate of natural increase and of immigration and the growing demand for tertiary education it estimated that in 1965 university enrolments would be 70,785. I think that it is conclusive evidence of the enlarging effect upon the university horizon which our revolutionary changes helped to bring about that the actual figures of enrolment for 1966 were 95,000.

This enormous growth has been, of course, associated with the modern doctrine that boys and girls who can pass the qualifying examinations have a right to university training. I can see the virtues of this, but I also see that the problem the doctrine presents to Governments and universities is a tremendous one. Governments may find that, with all the other demands both external and internal made upon them, they may reach a point at which some limitation must be put upon the demands of tertiary education. I hope not, but it would be foolish to pretend that the problem does not exist. As for the universities themselves, they have special problems. If they desire to maintain their standards of scholarship and the reputation of their degrees, they must maintain a large intake of highly qualified teachers and research workers. It is much easier to find bricks and mortar than it is to find highly qualified people of this kind. In my young days quite a few of the professors came from overseas. We cannot expect this any longer; we must, in the broad, produce our own, and this will demand such facilities for postgraduate and research work as have never been thought of before. Added to this, we have so great a duty to our neighbours, particularly our Asian neighbours, to assist them in the raising of their own educational, medical, scientific and technological development that we must take our part in finding or training our share of the expert minds that they need.

Ultimately, the Australian Universities Commission was established under the distinguished Chairmanship of Sir Leslie Martin. Two more triennial recommendations were made by it in my period of office, and adopted by the Government. For the reader to appreciate their immense significance in university history, I need only to set out the figures. For purposes of comparison, I set out all amounts in Australian dollars.

1955–7	$12,000,000
1958–60	$40,000,000
1961–3	$80,000,000
1964–6	$117,000,000

Of the total for these nine years, $249,000,000, no less than $76,000,000 was granted for capital purposes (i.e. buildings and equipment). The result of this is to be seen in the exciting building programme of the universities. As one who remembers the financially bleak character of the universities in the early days of my administration, I never fail to be thrilled by it, and hopeful for its continuance.

But there is more to be recorded. For the figures I have so far quoted do not include grants for residential halls and colleges, teaching hospitals, special research, and computers.

The Murray Committee had the same views as myself about the vital importance of the colleges and the halls of residence which were to come. In their report, their recommendations for grants for these bodies for both recurrent and capital costs totalled, over 1958–60, $2,400,000. In the next triennium, 1961–3, this figure rose to $4,000,000, and for 1964–6, to $8,800,000!

To these figures must be added grants for teaching hospitals, which after consultation with the commission we had agreed to include in the concept of university education, though of course there would be problems of separating out the teaching costs from the other hospital costs. These grants were at first for capital only, but later included some provision for recurrent expenses also. Over the second and third trienniums, the total grants were over $7,000,000.

Special research grants over the same period totalled $4,000,000, while computer grants totalled nearly $1,000,000.

To sum up, our Commonwealth provision for university education, historically novel in 1950, and almost nominal for some years thereafter and until the appointment of the Murray Committee and our subsequent actions, had amounted at the time of my resignation to a grand total of roughly $270,000,000!

There was a strong feeling that tertiary education should not be confined to the universities. There was, and is, a growing need for technological and other skills to be taught in post-secondary educational establishments which are not universities but provide an alternative to the normal academic training provided by a university. We set up a special committee under the chairmanship of Sir Leslie Martin to examine the broad problems of tertiary education, and in particular the possibility of devising some structure which would provide for what might be called a tertiary alternative, offering the prospect of advanced education to many students who had no desire (or opportunity) to take a university course.

In the result, proposals have been adopted in various States for the creation of Colleges of Advanced Education (or, in Victoria, an 'Institute of Colleges') which are providing splendid scope for tertiary but non-university students and studies.

I return briefly to the matter of church and independent schools and colleges.

My youth was lived in a period of Australian social history when there was much religious intolerance. Sectarianism was not engaged in solely by one side; but from my earliest days it nauseated me. The ecumenical movement had not been heard of (at least in my circle). There were bitter publications, masquerading as religious literature. Prelates and divines sought and obtained the courtesy of the Press to preach the gospel of love—with grave exceptions.

Even much later in my life, when I had become, in 1928, a member of the Legislative Council of Victoria, I remember vividly that, having attended the opening of a Roman Catholic church school in my electorate, I was rebuked by some of my older (and much-loved) relatives, and promptly replied that I represented in Parliament *all* of the electors of East Yarra, of all denominations or of no denomination, and not just some. I had no more family trouble, but the incident started in me a train of thought which was to contribute, during my Prime Ministership, to a quite revolutionary change in Government educational policy. The first episode concerned the financial position of the Roman Catholic schools in Canberra, in the Australian Capital Territory.

Now, Canberra was an artificial and Government city. It housed a great and growing number of Government departments, and its population was growing both in size and in demand. The civil servants who had been brought to Canberra in large numbers had arrived not by independent individual choice, but, in effect, by compulsion. The Commonwealth Public Service at that particular time, for a variety of reasons, had a higher percentage of Roman Catholics than the general community, and they, following the general rule of their church, wanted their children to attend church schools, where their education would have a religious background. In addition to the merits of their claim, they had one of the best-informed, mildest-mannered and persuasive of advocates, Archbishop Eris O'Brien, who soon recruited to his forces the Anglican Bishop, Dr Clements.

My then Minister for the Interior had the same views as I had, and the Cabinet concurred. The Government had a special responsibility, created by its own policy, to its Canberra employees for the education of their children. It could not ignore the fact that considerations of religion imposed a financial burden on the Roman Catholic authorities which they clearly could not sustain unaided. We should therefore help them, by assistance to secure loans, by interest subventions, or by other means.

All that I need say in this book is that assistance has been progressive and useful, and that, after the first small flurry when our first scheme was produced, there is, so far as I know, no local issue on the matter.

The time came when these views of mine about church and independent schools were able to achieve a further expression.

I had, in my own student days, had an all-round experience: a small country state school, a larger provincial state school, a privately owned secondary school, and a great church public school in Melbourne. I had no doubt that a religious background was of the greatest educational significance in the building of character.

In my declining years, witnessing a world in which moral values are treated with such complete contempt in some intellectual, or, more accurately, pseudo-intellectual circles, and in which the powerful influence of the Press seems to be, all too frequently, hostile to all received standards of social behaviour, I retain my belief in the ancient virtues, and value the services which the church schools and colleges render to them.

So it is that in going back over my long term of office I recall with pleasure other educational provisions made by my Government.

The first was a relatively small but quite important innovation in the income-tax assessment laws. In 1952 the Act was amended so as to make school fees up to an amount of fifty pounds in any one year an allowable deduction. This provision applied to (*inter alia*) church and independent schools. The amount was quite small, and was increased in later years.

The next thing was an important alteration in the taxation laws concerning gifts to schools for building purposes. Such gifts made to universities were already deductible, but not gifts made to schools. Years before, an incident had occurred which left a mark in my memory. Wesley College in Melbourne, my own old school, needed rebuilding, but where was the money to come from? The famous Nicholas brothers, George and Alfred, of Aspro fame, decided to come to the rescue, had plans prepared,

93

saw the headmaster, and, shortly thereafter, provided a vast sum for the rebuilding of the school. They could claim no income-tax deduction, so that in the result they made the gift and then paid income-tax on the amount. Indeed, the position was even worse. They had given to the school the whole profit shown on the profit-and-loss account of a proprietary company, and, because they had not made any distribution to shareholders, were made to pay penalty rates of tax!

Now, my colleagues and I believed that the independent and church schools had a valuable part to play in the secondary-education field. We looked into the possibility of encouraging building gifts. The Commissioner of Taxation naturally could give no estimate of what a concession might cost the revenue; but we decided that, whatever risk was involved, real benefits to these schools would result.

So in 1954 an allowable deduction was introduced in relation to a 'public fund established and maintained exclusively for providing money for the acquisition, construction or maintenance of a building used or to be used as a school or college by a Government or public authority or by a society or association which is carried on otherwise than for the purposes of profit or gain to individual members of that society or association'.

The result of this provision is to be seen in secondary schools all over Australia. It gave such relief to worried school councils that any remnants of the old sectarianism disappeared. It opened new horizons, and has justified itself a hundredfold.

The third great step was taken in early 1964, in performance of a promise made in my policy speech at the 1963 General Election. We provided an annual amount of £5 million for the provision of science buildings and equipment in secondary schools, Government or independent, without discrimination, and similar amounts of £5 million annually for State technical education. In each case the grants were made to the States, who had agreed to be the channels of distribution.

Each provision was, of course, directed to the need for improved science teaching in the secondary schools, a need which had been made quite clear by a too-high failure rate in first year at the universities, and to the urgent need, in a growingly technological age, for the encouragement and improvement of technical training. These schemes were and are a great success. Today, throughout the whole Commonwealth, new science blocks may be seen in an enormous variety of schools, and in the universities the first-year failure rate in scientific subjects has fallen sharply.

I should add that this scheme did not come entirely 'out of the blue'. My colleagues and I had been very much impressed by the voluntary work of a strong group of businessmen who had created a fund for this purpose under the enthusiastic chairmanship in Victoria of C. S. (now Sir Charles) Booth of the Australian Paper Manufacturing Company. We concluded that the Commonwealth Government, which of course commanded much greater resources, should enter this field, with the results that I have briefly described.

At the same time we gave statutory effect to another scheme for the provision by the Commonwealth of secondary-school scholarships. In the same policy speech I had made this announcement:

There are many good pupils in secondary schools who would benefit if they were helped to have the final two school years which they might otherwise miss through family circumstances. Those two years will make them much better equipped, whatever they do thereafter. There are many undergoing technical training. Any scheme which assists a student to carry through a course of technical study for an additional two years will have great national value in these times.

We propose to create special Commonwealth Scholarships, to be awarded competitively, at standards to be worked out with the States.

There will be in the case of secondary schools 10,000 such scholarships per year, tenable at a secondary school for two years. They will cover each year payments for fees and books up to £100 per annum, and a further maintenance allowance to the parents of £100 per annum. They will be open to students of all secondary schools, State or independent, without discrimination.

There will also be 2,500 scholarships, carrying the same benefits, open to students at technical schools.

When we were returned to office with a good majority, Senator Gorton (as he then was, now Prime Minister) was assigned by me to take charge of Commonwealth activities in education and research. In the Senate, in May 1964, he announced the introduction of these scholarships and their allocation between the States, with a lot of detail which he had worked out with the States, and with some improvements. The necessary legislation followed.

Now, the reader will understand that I have set down a record of which the long Menzies Government might feel reasonably proud.

But the chief criticism aimed at us by our political opponents was this: 'Oh yes, you have done pretty well for the universities and the independent schools, but why don't you do something for the State schools?' They have apparently made some headway with this propaganda, for now, in my retirement, I occasionally see stickers on the rear windows of cars, reading: *Commonwealth Aid for State Schools.*

This is no doubt a rather emotive slogan, but it reveals an abysmal ignorance of the facts. For, as I pointed out in my 1963 policy speech:

We have not overlooked the educational responsibilities of the States in the fields of primary and secondary education. The size of the school population is a large factor in determining the Commonwealth Grants to the States. These have increased from £165,000,000 in 1951–2 to £469,000,000 in 1963–4. On the capital side—which brings in school buildings—we provided, between 1951 and 1963, assistance to the States' programmes, over and above the yield of the Loan Market.

The whole of that yield, in spite of our legal claims under the Financial Agreement, we had conceded to the States.

I pointed out, as was the fact, that in the light of these facts it was pleasing but not surprising that the State Governments had been able to increase their expenditure on education from £60,000,000 in 1951–2 to £201,000,000 in 1963.

These observations are made in no derogatory sense. Without generous and enlightened co-operation by the States, our own record, particularly in the university field, could not have been achieved. But that it was achieved is one of my happiest memories.

10

Stability, Capital and Development

We inherited in 1949 a position in which prices were rising too rapidly and inflation was making its unhappy mark. We decided that we would get this under control as soon as possible. But the gods willed otherwise. In 1950 the Korean War was on, and the great wool boom got under way. In a sense this was due to some rather inexpert handling on the part of the State Department in Washington. Knowing too little about the complicated techniques of wool marketing, they simply gave orders that large quantities of wool for uniforms and the like should be bought in Australia in a limited period of time. The result was that the prices of wool at auction rose enormously until some special lines reached the price of £1 per pound of wool. The effect upon the wool industry and upon the wool-growers was quite dramatic. Comparatively small men who had been accustomed to an income of three or four thousand pounds suddenly found themselves in possession of an income of twenty thousand pounds. With the bigger growers the results were in proportion. It was not surprising that many of the 'newly rich' should forget about their taxation problems and began to spend their money with a light heart; new and expensive motor cars, trips abroad and the like.

Now, no country like Australia can suddenly add hundreds of millions to its export income without experiencing the results in terms of high and rising domestic prices and grave inflation of the currency. So far from our controlling inflation, inflation was getting out of hand. It was clear that we must take stringent action. We therefore produced our famous (or, as some people thought, infamous) Budget of 1952. Its two main features were, first, that we budgeted for a large surplus, which involved steeply increased taxation, and, second, that we took twenty-five per cent of the wool cheque and put it into a reserve to be made available to the wool-growers at a subsequent time. This was the most unpopular Budget in modern political history, though I have never doubted that it was dead right. The wool-growers showed their resentment at the next election by voting out several of the wool-growing members among our supporters, while the Gallup polls in 1953 showed the Government stocks at the lowest point in recorded history. But the Government stood firm and so did the Government members of Parliament.

I can recall making frequent exhortations in the party room to the effect that the medicine was undoubtedly harsh, but that as it began to show its effectiveness the people would come back to us. And so they did; but only just in time to enable us to win the 1954 election with a reduced majority. The best proof of the soundness of our policies was that, from that episode on, there has been in Australia, for the most part, a remarkable stability in the price level and in economic conditions generally, without which I doubt whether we would have proved such a source of attraction for business investors around the world.

Our broad policy, of course, was to ensure economic stability at home, not only for its domestic advantages but also because we knew that for the rapid development of our enormous resources, particularly mineral, which were being disclosed, we would need investment and expertise from overseas to supplement our own resources. I believed, and I still believe, that a nation which has any great need of developmental capital from abroad can attract it only if it exhibits to the world an integrity in which the world believes, a responsible attitude towards its obligations, a stable economic base, and political steadiness.

I should deal first with public borrowing as distinct from private investment. I have narrated in an earlier book the circumstances under which I was able to negotiate our first loan from the International Bank for Reconstruction and Development.* But there are one or two interesting points about that transaction which are worth recording.

Only twelve months before we came back into office, Mr Chifley had stated quite firmly that Australia could and should live within its means in relation to sterling and dollar income,

* *Afternoon Light*, pp. 141–2.

and that his Government was therefore opposed to overseas borrowing. Indeed, his attitude was that Government overseas borrowing was not feasible even if it were thought desirable. When I went to Washington and had my talks with Eugene Black, I had already learned something about the difficulties which confronted me. Undoubtedly the World Bank, as I shall call it for short, was the most hopeful prospect. But it had established certain general rules the effect of which was that it would lend money only for some specific project which had been put forward by the proposed borrowing nation and had been fully examined by the bank's economists and engineers. Experience had shown that the normal period occupied by these inquiries and subsequent reports was the better part of a year. I had no specific project to present; it would have been impossible in the time to work one out in consultation with States and municipalities. My task was to show that much developmental work had to be done in Australia, that for most of it at that time equipment procurable only in dollars was necessary, and that in fact Australia needed a line of dollar credit which would enable her to make a prompt start on these tasks. We were either persuasive or lucky or both because (I believe for the first time) the bank made us a dollar loan, after a consideration of days not months. It clearly trusted us to use the dollars to constructive advantage, and we did so. So interested was the bank in the emerging developmental prospects in various parts of Australia that it arranged for a mission to visit Australia in 1951 to assess our developmental requirements for dollars over a period of five years. This first loan was the first of seven granted by the World Bank during my period of office. They totalled $418,000,000 (U.S.). We effected further transactions on the New York market; over the period of which I am writing Australia raised $390,000,000 (U.S.) in loans which were listed on the New York Stock Exchange. The New York market had been, in effect, closed to foreign borrowers since the immediate post-war years, and our success therefore represented a real break-through.

We turned our attention to the London market, which had

been virtually closed to Australia for a long time, and in 1958 we raised a cash loan in London, our first since the war. This was followed by a series of cash and conversion loans which, up to 1966, brought our loan raisings in London to almost $460,000,000. In these operations we were greatly assisted by our friendship with Lord Glendyne, the then senior partner of the Commonwealth's underwriters in London (Nivison and Co.) and with the Bank of England. Apart from these, the major transactions to which I have referred, we borrowed Swiss francs in Switzerland, Canadian dollars in Canada and guilders in the Netherlands.

To sum up, during this period the Australian Government borrowed abroad the equivalent of $1,035,000,000 of new money.

These transactions, being on public account, were, I think, generally approved by the Australian people and, of course, were not subject to the criticisms, to which I shall refer later, which attended the inflow of private investment capital. We had built ourselves up from a little-known borrower on international capital markets to one that was able to obtain the best possible terms and conditions in all centres. No other foreign borrower was able to improve on the terms for new Australian loans, and in fact the securities issued were strongly sought after in the markets after they had been issued.

I now turn to private investment from overseas, which has undoubtedly been of major significance in the development of our resources. In our period it totalled over £2,000,000,000 or $4,000,000,000. A great deal of the money came from the United States, but even more from Great Britain. This great inflow, of course, had its critics, who felt that the ownership and control of some great enterprises were passing into foreign hands. We were conscious of this argument, but we were also acutely aware of the fact that Australia, with a small population, simply could not generate its own capital in sufficient quantities to support a great expansion, and that therefore the broad choice was between a rapid development with overseas contribution and a very much slower development based upon our unaided resources. We also remembered that whether businesses in Australia are owned and controlled by non-residents or not, they remain subject to the fiscal and industrial laws of the land and carry on their external operations subject to the over-riding constitutional powers of the Australian Commonwealth. We found no practical difficulty about this problem. We welcomed investment from overseas and indeed gave it encouragement and a feeling of security. But we also believed and said that we would encourage companies of overseas origin or control to admit Australians to some equity shareholding and to have as many Australians as possible engaged in the tasks of management. Some debate having publicly occurred, I took the opportunity in my last policy speech in November 1963, after consultation with my colleagues, to state our attitude in these terms:

This investment has produced great advantages, but under some circumstances produces problems which need to be handled with care and understanding. As, from a national Australian point of view, we would wish to see new capital from overseas employed for the great purpose of developing new industries or extending existing ones with all the benefit of overseas skills and experience, we will always have a particularly warm welcome for new capital designed to these ends. We also believe that fears and misunderstandings are least where there is an Australian participation in shareholding and management, and most when there is no more than a mere change of ownership without more. There is, we believe, a growing recognition of this in the minds of intending investors.

One aspect of investment from overseas deserves special mention. It was the fact that we normally had a deficit on current international trade, but managed to come out right on the balance of payments because of the capital inflow.

This, of course, had its dangers unless we could continue to develop our export trade, for any sudden drying-up of capital inflow from abroad would have left us in trouble with our balances. (This had happened in 1929, when the sudden and complete drying-up of our loan market abroad had materially contributed to the impact of the great Depression on Australia.) But our view as a Government was that any capital inflow which served to develop a new industry with a large export potential would itself make a handsome contribution to getting our balances ultimately into a healthy condition. As I write, this has proved to be quite accurate; for the export of minerals, either in their original or in processed form, is now becoming one of the major elements in our export trade.

As it will be clear that I regard the confidence in Australia displayed by overseas investors as a very great factor in our rapid economic growth, I think I should try to offer a few reasons for this confidence.

First of all, as I have previously indicated, the overseas investor was convinced, and with good reason, that the potentialities of the Australian continent were and are very great. But this alone would not have been sufficient if the nature and actions of the Australian Government had not been such as to give confidence to the investor. There are, of course, some speculators who will put their money into a country which has marked inflationary trends, on the prospect of a quick profit; but these were by no means either in the majority or a very considerable factor. Most overseas investors wanted to see stability in the Australian economy and in its political management, because they did not want to put their treasure into a leaky vessel. It must be remembered that the investment of risk or venture capital in any country is not usually designed to produce a quick profit and a quick exit but looks to the long-range prospects of both growth and profit. It therefore desires a stable domestic base and a feeling of security for the future, a future which may in a few cases be fairly immediate but in most cases will possess an essentially long-term character.

We wanted to encourage investment from overseas. We were conscious that it might give rise some day to problems which we thought could be dealt with; but we saw very clearly that if our economic growth was to be as dramatic as we thought it could be, having regard to our resources, and must be, having

103

regard to our future, we could not rely simply upon locally generated capital for the purpose.

I should say quite plainly that Australians produce a great deal of the capital they require. There is occasionally some suggestion that we are an improvident people, over-devoted to gambling. But the fact is that by one means or another we save a great deal. Capital generated in Australia for an immense variety of purposes both great and small, both governmental and private, represents in fact about eighty-seven per cent of all our normal capital needs. But the thirteen per cent makes a world of difference. It enables huge undertakings to be put in hand and makes the difference between a steady economic growth and a large and expanding one. It is quite clear that if we had been required to rely upon our internal resources alone, we should not have seen the great leap forward which occurred during our time and which is continuing with notable momentum.

The overseas investor also wishes to feel that, having put his money into Australia, he can reasonably expect to be able to take some or all of his profits out and, indeed, repatriate his capital if that seems to him to be necessary. In the period of which I am writing, exchange control was administered in a way that was consistent with the policy of encouraging overseas investment in Australia. All remittances abroad from Australia required exchange control approval, but in practice no restrictions were imposed on current (i.e. non-capital) transactions. Actually, the Australian trading banks were authorized to deal with the great majority of these transactions as agents of Exchange Control. In the result, all current net income after taxation accruing to firms or individuals resident overseas could be remitted without restriction. Moreover, approval was also normally granted for the repatriation of capital. We did not tie our hands by making any advance commitment to allow such repatriation, but in fact I know of no case in which approval was withheld. This was a good record of fair treatment and gave rise to a reputation which did much to ensure a maintenance of the capital inflow.

There was, of course, from time to time some criticism of the large profits earned by American-controlled companies in Australia. I take a notable example. One of the principal targets was a great American company which had started car manufacture in Australia for the first time. There would be no point in concealing its name: it was General Motors–Holdens. Superbly efficient, it not only produced a large proportion of the cars on the Australian roads and of those exported, but it also gave prosperity and employment directly to many thousands of Australians and indirectly to many more thousands employed by Australian businesses supplying parts and equipment to the main company. All of these overseas companies pay their proper taxes to the Commonwealth; most of them in fact plough back a substantial percentage of their profits for future development of the industry in Australia, and with it increased Australian employment. The net balance, I always thought, was heavily in our favour. I personally know of overseas companies who have established themselves in Australia and provided a fine market for Australian producers and who, during their initial years, sometimes for a long time, ploughed back all their profits into Australian development and remitted none overseas.

I have just read the latest Annual Report of General Motors–Holden's on its operations in Australia. It confirms the truth of what I have been writing. In 1969 its total sales were $415,000,000. To suppliers of materials and services it paid $230,000,000. To its direct employees it paid $103,000,000. To Government, for taxes and duties, it paid $29,000,000; to provide for depreciation $24,000,000; for use in the business to provide facilities and working capital $11,000,000. To the shareholders went $16,000,000, or 3·9 per cent of the total sum.

I have no doubt that, in spite of the fact that the parent company in the United States does not allow any equity shareholding in Australia, the balance of advantage from its Australian investment is heavily in our favour, and constitutes a real national asset.

True, we would like to see increasing Australian participation in the management of such enterprises, a participation which is steadily expanding, and some equity shareholding by Australians. But I for one was never able to see how cast-iron rules could be devised to compel these things without reducing, or running a grave risk of reducing, the flow of investment. There is a world-wide demand for capital, but the world supply is by no means inexhaustible. And investment in any particular country is not compulsory.

Our view was that a general exhortation might usefully be delivered to the overseas investor on these matters, but that strict and artificial conditions might well defeat their purpose by driving investors away from us.

Bearing in mind that one of the major consequences of this overseas investment in Australia, particularly in the mineral field, has been to add substantially to our national export income and to a material extent save imports, I think it could not well be denied that the net national benefit to Australia of such overseas investment has been enormous. I doubt very much whether we could have maintained and expanded our immigration programme, giving us a great increase in population, productivity and employment, which has been so important a factor in our advancement, had it not been for investment coming into us from other countries; to a great measure, in my time, from the United Kingdom (though this is occasionally forgotten) but in more recent years with a tendency to move in the direction of the United States of America and Canada.

In brief, although attention is often focused on the direct balance-of-payments aspect of overseas investment, with expressed apprehensions as to what the outflow of profits may some day be, by far the most important effect of capital inflow has to be looked for elsewhere. We looked for it and found it in the effect of overseas investment on the economy as a whole; on its capacity, diversity and efficiency, and its great export significance.

To sum up, the Australian economy undoubtedly underwent a marked expansion during our period. There has been enormous development of resources, particularly in the north and west of Australia. National income increased from about £2,000,000,000 (i.e., for purposes of later comparison, $4,000,000,000) to $16,500,000,000 in my last year of office. There was, of course, some decline in the value of money. The retail price index (and I quote the figures of the Statistician in the Year Book), which stood at 262 in our first year, rose sharply, under the special inflationary pressures to which I have referred earlier, by no less than 105 points in two years! Thereafter a considerable degree of stability was achieved, for over the next thirteen years of my term the total increase was 135 points. It will be seen that this still left the increase in the national income, in real terms, a quite phenomenal one. Undoubtedly, our net rate of economic growth was unusually rapid.

As the years went on and the financial position became stabilized on a high level, with a rapidly increasing population and full employment, we gave a lot of attention to northern and western development, in conjunction with the States concerned, for they had a vital interest in growth. By various financial measures we assisted in the making of important developmental roads and railway improvements in Queensland, South Australia, West Australia, and the Northern Territory, in the improvement of coal-loading port facilities in Queensland, and in other important ways.

We set up a Ministry of National Development, with a Northern Division, whose Bureau of Mineral Resources did invaluable work in mineral (including oil) surveys in Queensland and Western Australia. We gave special financial support to the search for oil, so vital for development.

With the discovery of bauxite in huge quantities, the aluminium age began in Australia. With the exposing of quite large deposits of uranium, particularly in the Northern Territory and Queensland, we began to approach the time when atomic power could be produced for commercial purposes. As a preparation, we established the Atomic Energy Commission, and the construction of an experimental atomic reactor at Lucas Heights, south of Sydney.

The northern part of Western Australia, once a lonely and

sparsely settled cattle area, has become the scene of great water conservation and irrigation works, the dynamic sponsor of which, in my period, was Charles Court, of the Western Australian Government, a remarkable man who would never take No for an answer (and still won't).

It has also become the scene of almost incredible mineral activity, with its invaluable attributes of processing and export, and a quite astonishing infra-structure of railways, roads, ports and housing. North Queensland has in a similar fashion shown remarkable productive growth, and can well claim that, with Western Australia, it is a 'State of the Future'. The Northern Territory is making its contribution. In short, the economic balance of Australia, once heavily loaded in favour of the great industrial States of the South-East, is being corrected, while men's eyes are increasingly turned towards those parts of the continent which were, not so many years ago, regarded as relatively thinly populated and unproductive tracts of land.

11

Reforms in the Australian Banking Structure

Thirty-five years ago, when I was Attorney-General of Australia, I was a guest at a dinner given by the chief bankers of Melbourne to a visiting banker from England. At a suitable time, I put a few questions to my hosts about their apparent indifference to politics, and received the then inevitable answer that 'we are so placed that we must keep clear of party politics'. My rather brash retort was that the day would come when politics, particularly Labour politics, would take an interest in them, and that they should prepare themselves for it.

The vital period of involvement began with a loud series of explosions in 1945 and 1947. The Chifley Government, stung by the High Court's invalidation of those provisions in its Banking Act (1945) which provided that without the consent of the Commonwealth Treasury no bank should conduct banking business for a State or a State-created authority, decided suddenly (I believe it was all done in one Cabinet meeting) to settle the argument with the banks by nationalizing banking and so putting the private banks out of business. I remember very clearly the circumstances. One Saturday afternoon I was at a lawn-tennis party at the home of a friend. When the news came on over the radio we all stopped to listen and heard the laconic announcement that, that very morning, Cabinet had decided to nationalize the banks, and that the nationalizing legislation would be produced at an early date. Now I confess that my first impression was that the move might have public support. I remembered how unpopular the banks had become during the Depression, when they were widely accused of restricting credit and of contributing to great hardship for hundreds of thousands of people. I thought that this unpopularity, though much had happened since the great Depression, would still operate to a perceptible extent. But my fears were ill founded. The announcement stung the banks and their staffs into unprecedented activity, while at the same time it transpired that whatever their past grievances may or may not have been, most bank customers liked to be able to choose their own bank and their own bank manager, and were determined to preserve that choice.

It is, of course, a matter of history that the widespread agitation which swept the continent did not prevent the scheme from going on to the statute-book in 1947. When the High Court of Australia and then the Judicial Committee of the Privy Council found the law to be invalid, a loud sigh of relief went up from most of the electors. The whole incident, as I said in an earlier book, made the issue of socialism of nationalization no longer an academic one for debating societies, but a live issue for the elector. No single factor did more to bring about our victory in 1949.

The Australian banking structure when we came back into office, a structure which we had undertaken to review, took this form. The Commonwealth Bank was not only a reserve bank, but also a trading bank with a duty to compete with the other trading banks and extend its business. It had once been controlled by a board of directors, but had, by our predecessors, been placed under the control of a Governor who was in turn directly responsible to the Treasurer of the day. These arrangements were felt to be grossly unsatisfactory by the 'private' trading banks for they felt, very properly, that competition by the General Banking Division of the Commonwealth Bank was in its nature unfair. In the second place the existence of the powers of the Commonwealth Bank over bank credit and banking policy generally meant that while individual trading banks had to observe the rules, the Commonwealth Bank ran free. My Government felt that this state of affairs should not be allowed to continue. So it was that in 1951, after the double dissolution, we repealed the invalid Banking Act of 1947 (to get it off the statute-book) and reconstituted a Commonwealth Bank Board in substitution for one-man control. We then began a long period of close study of the complex problems involved, and held many consultations with the parties. In the result, in 1953 we took our first major

110

steps. Under the original Banking Act (1945), trading banks were liable to deposit their reserves, or such portion thereof as the Commonwealth Bank might require, in 'special accounts' with the Commonwealth Bank. This meant that there was an 'uncalled liability' to pay money into these accounts, and that it was of such a volume that a complete calling-up might very well have wrecked the banks. We, of course, recognized that, in any system providing for a central bank, there must be some power to call up to special accounts and to immobilize some portion of the private banks' deposits so that the amount of available credit could be controlled. That was a quite legitimate central-bank banking technique. But clearly some proper ceiling should be provided for determining the future liability of the trading banks. In the second place, it was essential that the Commonwealth Bank's General Banking Division should be given a separate identity and be made subject to the same rules as those applying to the other trading banks.

And so, our Commonwealth Bank Act (1953) provided for the establishment of the 'Commonwealth Trading Bank' as a separate body to take over the business of the old General Banking Division of the Commonwealth Bank. It was to remain under the Commonwealth Bank Board but was to be managed under the Governor by a General Manager appointed on the recommendation of the Board.

A Banking Act was passed at the same time. It cancelled the uncalled liability of the trading banks to calls to special account and imposed limits on future calling-up. It also provided that the special-account provisions and other central-bank controls administered by the Commonwealth Bank were to apply to the Commonwealth Trading Bank just as they applied to the other trading banks.

But these steps, though they had some immediate importance, by no means solved the problems of the banking world. The important thing was to create a state of affairs in which there would be genuine co-operation between the central bank and the trading banks. In Great Britain, banks are much more accustomed to working according to co-operation and convention than we are in Australia; we have an inherent disposition to like to have things set down in black and white. The informal relations existing between the Governor of the Bank of England and the trading banks were not therefore easily to be reproduced in Australia.

But we looked at the problems one by one. Prior to 1956, the Commonwealth Bank group, which included the very powerful Commonwealth Savings Bank, had been the only one providing both cheque and savings accounts in the same building. This, from the point of view of the outside trading banks, gave the Commonwealth Trading Bank a facility denied to them to attract new accounts and deposits. From the savings-bank account to the cheque account was of course easy if it happened to be a simple matter of moving from one part of the building to another. We were approached by one of the major private trading banks with a request to grant it authority to carry on savings-bank subsidiaries. This request was supported by other banks, and we gave approval, subject to conditions. The conditions we attached were such as to ensure that the broad pattern of savings-bank investment in Australia, which had evolved over a period of many years in the Commonwealth Savings Bank and the State savings banks, would be preserved. In effect, that meant that seventy per cent of the savings-bank deposit balances should be held in liquid assets and public securities, with a provision that the balance be invested principally in loans to Government-guaranteed building societies and for housing and other purposes on the security of land. We made this stipulation all the more readily because at this time, and indeed throughout our term of office, we were greatly concerned to stimulate home-building and home-ownership.

In 1957, our studies and conferences had brought us to some important decisions. We felt that, though the Governor of the Bank, Dr Coombs, a man of outstanding ability and integrity, was personally well respected by the managers of the trading banks, it was difficult to secure the fullest measure of harmony and co-operation so long as the central bank was directly associated with the conduct of competing commercial banking operations. We also felt that we should work out some alternative to the special-accounts system, which had been criticized on a variety of grounds and in particular the not uncommon one that it was complicated and hard to understand! Shades of the income-tax assessment laws!

So in 1957 we produced two bills.

One was a Reserve Bank Bill, which provided for the setting up of a central bank to be called the Reserve Bank of Australia, whose functions, with one exception, would be related solely to central banking. The one special department of the old Commonwealth Bank to be left with the Reserve Bank was the Rural Credits Department, which had direct relationships with several 'orderly marketing' schemes for primary products. The existing Commonwealth Bank Board was to become the Reserve Bank Board. After a reasonable time after the legislation came into force, the Head Office of the Reserve Bank would be required to occupy buildings separate from the Head Offices of the other institutions theretofore attached to the Commonwealth Bank group.

A second bill, the Commonwealth Banks Bill, provided for the setting up of a Commonwealth Banking Corporation, to be under the control of a new board and separate management. The Commonwealth Banking Corporation would embrace:

(a) The Commonwealth Trading Bank
(b) The Commonwealth Savings Bank
(c) The Commonwealth Development Bank

This last was, in effect, an amalgamation of what had been the old Mortgage Bank Department and the Industrial Finance Department. The Development Bank was to have the main functions of providing finance for the purposes of primary production and for the establishment or development of industrial undertakings, particularly small undertakings, where the finance for either

113

would not otherwise be available on reasonable or suitable terms and conditions.

The charter of the board of the Commonwealth Banking Corporation was designed to ensure that the policies of the three constituent banks were directed to the greatest advantage of the people of Australia and, in particular, should have due regard to the stability and balanced development of the Australian economy.

We also put forward a *Banking Bill,* the main effect of which was to establish a Statutory Reserve Deposit (S.R.D.) system in place of the special-accounts system. The trading banks were still to be required to lodge sums with the Reserve Bank, provided that forty-five days' notice should be given if the proportion of a bank's deposits to be held with the Reserve Bank exceeded twenty-five per cent. A uniform proportion of deposits was to apply to all major trading banks. There were also other provisions, which I need not recite, which made it definite that regulations made in relation to savings banks should apply uniformly to the Commonwealth Savings Bank and the more recently established private savings banks.

All of these bills were passed by the House of Representatives but, having regard to the fact that, at an intervening election after the double-dissolution election, we had lost our majority in the Senate, they were twice rejected by the Senate in 1957 and 1958. At the end of 1958 we had another general election, from which we returned with a majority in both Houses. The banking legislation was re-introduced and passed in April 1959, and came into operation by proclamation in January 1960.

We had reason to believe that we had achieved a satisfactory result which would ensure a full and frank co-operation between the trading banks and the Reserve Bank. Certain things remained to be done. It became clear that the Commonwealth Development Bank, if it were to fulfil its important function, would need from time to time to have increased provisions of capital. In the time of my Government three contributions were made, raising the capital of the bank to almost £31,000,000.

One further matter remained. It was properly felt by the banks that they ought to play a more positive part in the growth of Australia and the expansion of our trade abroad. As a result of discussions between the Government, the Reserve Bank and the trading banks, it was agreed that the banks should expand their facilities for 'term lending' to meet Australia's growing developmental requirements and for the financing of exports. The arrangements were announced by the Treasurer, Mr Holt, who had played such a great part in the negotiations and formulation of policy, in April 1962. Briefly, they provided for the establishment by the trading banks, with the Reserve Bank, of special 'term loan' funds in amounts equal to three per cent of the trading banks' deposits. The term loan funds on this basis began with an amount of almost £57,000,000 and were subsequently augmented. These funds provided the trading banks with the sources needed for the making of loans for fixed longer-term periods, and for a range of developmental purposes including capital expenditure for production in the rural and secondary industries and the financing of exports of capital goods on extended terms. At the same time, Holt was able to announce that agreement had been reached on certain arrangements with respect to overdraft interest rates, which had the effect of producing a satisfactory degree of control.

In 1964, the establishment of an Australian Bankers Export Re-finance Corporation, Limited, was announced by the Chairman of the Bankers Association and the Managing Director of the Commonwealth Banking Corporation. This was welcomed by the Government. In addition, the Reserve Bank had, with our full backing, offered a substantial measure of financial support in bringing the new scheme into operation.

This brief narrative will, I think, show that, having inherited a somewhat chaotic condition in the banking world, we were able ultimately to look back on a most satisfactory and workable reform of the whole system, prime regard being paid not only to interbank justice, but also to the economic interests of Australia as a whole.

12
National Health

I begin with a little relevant history. The Labour Government passed Pharmaceutical Benefits Acts in 1944 and 1945. These were replaced by Pharmaceutical Benefits Acts in 1947 and 1949 providing free benefits in relation to specified uncompounded medicines and medical compounds. But before the Act of 1947 there had been important constitutional events.

The original Commonwealth powers were to make laws for the peace, order and good government of the Commonwealth with respect to:

51. (xxiii) Invalid and old-age pensions.
(xxxix) Matters incidental to the execution of any power vested by this Constitution in the Parliament . . .

There is also, in Section 81, a power to appropriate moneys 'for the purposes of the Commonwealth'.

Upon this somewhat precarious foundation successive Parliaments had built up a variety of social services going beyond invalid and old-age pensions.

In 1945 the Pharmaceutical Benefits Act (1944) was challenged in the High Court as having no visible means of constitutional support. It was argued that the appropriation power was limited to 'the purposes of the Commonwealth', and that such purposes must be confined to the specified legislative powers, the executive powers, and the judicial powers. The court, with one dissentient, held the provisions of the Act to be invalid for want of legislative power to support them.

The reasons given by the judges varied, but they gave no support to any belief that the appropriation power could be exercised without regard to the limitations upon the legislative powers.

Clearly, something would need to be done by way of an

amendment to the Constitution if chaos was to be avoided in the social-services field. Both sides of the Commonwealth Parliament, with only a solitary dissenting voice, voted for a bill to amend the Constitution in terms which would enable comprehensive social-services programmes to be validly enacted. In the ultimate result what is now Section 51 (xxiiia) of the Constitution was passed by Parliament and approved in 1947 by referendum and so became part of the basic constitutional law.

It gives power to the Commonwealth Parliament to make laws with respect to:

The provision of maternity allowances, widows' pensions, child endowment, unemployment, pharmaceutical, sickness, and hospital benefits, medical and dental services (but not so as to authorize any form of civil conscription), benefits to students and family allowances.

I well recall the debate on this amendment in the House of Representatives. When the amendment was presented to Parliament by the Government, the words in brackets about 'civil conscription' were not included. I will shortly explain how they came to be inserted. I was then Leader of the Opposition, deeply attached to the principles of private medical practice and the singular importance of the voluntary doctor–patient relationship. And so, in the course of the debate, I made two observations which I wish to recall.

The first was during the second-reading debate on 3 April 1946, when I said:

Very little doubt exists that not only the words of the proposed amendment but also the decision of the High Court will mean that under those words '(the power to provide medical and dental services)' the medical and dental professions could be nationalized by making all doctors and dentists members of one Government service which had a monopoly of medical and dental treatment. In that sense this power includes a power to nationalize medicine and dentistry.

In committee, on 10 April 1946, I dealt further with the

117

matter. I hope that I may be permitted to quote the terms of my speech, for it led to a result of great importance to the medical profession and, I believe, the people generally, I said:

I move: that in proposed new paragraph (xxiiia), after the word 'services' the following words and brackets be inserted: '(but not so as to authorize any form of civil conscription)'.

In my earlier remarks on the bill I advanced my reasons for thinking that the expression 'medical and dental services' could very well support a proposal for the nationalization of the medical and dental professions. I do not want to repeat the reasons which I then gave, but as the Attorney-General [Dr Evatt], in his reply, did not add anything to what he had said in his second-reading speech, I wish the position to be made quite clear. The matter could easily be put beyond question. In my amendment I have taken the liberty of borrowing a form of words in the Constitution Alteration (Industrial Employment) Bill [introduced by the Labour Government]. In that measure, the expression used is, 'Terms and conditions of employment in industry but not so as to authorize any form of industrial conscription.' Although we have heard very little about it, I have no doubt that those words were put in that Bill in order to allay any fears that a broad power might be used to produce conscription of a form to which the Government and its supporters object. I have merely adapted the same language to this bill. I would never object to medical and dental services being provided for the people under some proper Government scheme. I have no objection to the Commonwealth having power to make proper laws in relation to medical and dental services, but so long as there is doubt—and I entertain grave doubts on the matter—as to whether that power does not authorize the nationalization of these two professions, their members are entitled to be protected against conscription just as are industrial workers under the bill I have mentioned. This is a perfectly fair proposition; if industrial workers are to be put beyond the danger of industrial conscription, then what is good for them should be good for professional workers also.

The then Attorney-General, Dr Evatt, accepted my amendment. As so amended, the constitutional amendment was approved by referendum, and became law.

Acting under the new constitutional powers (or purporting to act under them) the Chifley Government, by the Pharmaceutical Benefits Act (1947–9), established a scheme under which medicine specified in a formulary could be obtained free by the public on compliance with certain conditions. One of these was that the medicine must be prescribed by a medical practitioner on a form supplied by the Commonwealth. Section 7A provided that a medical practitioner should not, under penalty, write such a prescription otherwise than on a form supplied by the Commonwealth.

The validity of this section was challenged by the British Medical Association. The High Court, by a majority, held (79 C.L.R., 201) that Section 7A amounted to a form of 'civil conscription' and was therefore invalid. Several of the judges made observations about the novelty of the expression; what did the draftsman have in mind? It would have had no admissible relevance to the judicial task of interpretation in Australia, but I think that I, as responsible for this particular phrase, could have produced a very good practical reason. My Opposition colleagues and I wanted the best amendment possible. As I have pointed out, the Government had used a similar phrase in its Industrial Constitutional Amendment, which gave me not only a precedent but also a good debating point. It was vital for the validity of Commonwealth social services that a constitutional amendment be made. The Government knew this, and the Opposition agreed. If a Government wants to amend the Constitution, it is practically essential to have the support of the Opposition. The rejection of our amendment relating to 'civil conscription' could have led to a division of opinion which would imperil the public acceptance of the constitutional amendment as a whole. So the Government accepted our proposal, and the private practice of medicine secured a real protection.

In December 1949 Labour went out, and a Government led by me came in. We began the labours of evolving an effective National Health Scheme which would have a wide cover but at the same time preserve the doctor–patient relationship.

Finally, after a variety of regulations had gone into operation, we produced the National Health Act (1953). This notable measure had provisions dealing fairly comprehensively with certain medical services and 'medical benefits'. These were based upon contributions made by individuals to a Medical Benefits Fund conducted by a registered medical benefits organization, supplemented by a 'Commonwealth Benefit', being a benefit payable by the Commonwealth in respect of a professional service rendered to a contributor.

There were also provisions for pensioner medical services, hospital benefits and pharmaceutical benefits.

The basic principle was that the individual doctor–patient relationship should be preserved and the disadvantages of a fully nationalized and Government-conducted scheme averted.

The Minister for Health was the late Sir Earle Page, who had been a busy practising surgeon and had strong views on the problems of medical policy. His second-reading speech on the bill, delivered on 12 November 1953, after extensive Cabinet and departmental discussions, contains an extraordinarily able and well-informed exposition of our philosophic approach.

I will quote some of the main points of his speech which bear upon my thesis.

Speaking of the character of medical practice:

It is the person with his idiosyncrasies, allergies and family heredity and personal and financial problems who must be cured. It is the individual with his physical and mental disease and his own peculiar symptoms who must be treated.

It is the personal, continuous contact of the doctor, with an interest in the patient and his family, that must be maintained. These results can best be obtained by *maintaining the position, prestige and fullest usefulness* of the general medical practitioner. . . .

In recent reports on the British service, the great complaint of that system relates to the *deterioration of the general medical practitioner, due to inadequate hospital contacts and lack of time for proper examination owing to the panel system under which each doctor often has several thousands of patients.* . . .

The most important point in medical treatment is *complete and early examination and diagnosis*, whether the treatment is later given by a general medical practitioner or a specialist. It is imperative to preserve this cardinal feature of complete and early examination and diagnosis. . . .

. . . *it is absolutely necessary for the doctor to have time to be the friend and confidant of the patient and his family, because illness is not only physical. It is frequently psychological.*

These statements need but little elaboration. They indicate vividly our approach, so basically different from that of the Socialists.

I do not employ the word *socialist* as if it were a term of abuse. We have, for example, socialist railways and a socialist Post Office, mostly to our great advantage. Whether it is a good thing to have some activity completely controlled by the Government, with a 'no choice' obedience by the citizen, seems to me to depend upon the nature of the activity. As one who receives and sometimes answers letters, I do not care who delivers letters to me, so long as they arrive. The dweller in the suburbs who commutes daily to the city has no desire to select the staff or the rolling-stock (coaching-stock, to be more accurate); he simply wishes to be carried safely and punctually.

But there are other activities carried on in our community which depend for their success and value upon personal choice and personal confidence.

Take my original profession of the law, and assume that it became nationalized. When a citizen wanted some advice involving not only technical competence but wisdom and experience, he would no longer go to the trusted family solicitor, but to a solicitor to whose panel he had been allocated by an all-wise Administration. If litigation became necessary, and a barrister had to be employed, the citizen would take what he was given, and hope for the best.

So far as I know, nobody has yet seriously proposed such a wretched development. It has, I hope, been realized that any

9

activity in which *choice and personal confidence* are essential is not an activity for which the socialist solution is appropriate.

It was, it will be remembered, this very consideration which led to the devastating rejection by the Australian public of the nationalization of banking.

Similar considerations apply *a fortiori* to the practice of medicine, and for the reasons so clearly stated by Sir Earle Page. Our family doctor knows us, our history and our oddities, sees us as individuals, and evokes a high degree of frankness which is based upon mutual confidence. There is no substitute for the diagnosis and therapy so produced.

True, we are entering the computer age, in which, I am given vaguely to believe, all the factual ingredients will be fed into a machine and out will come the diagnosis, the prognosis, and, doubtless, the cure. Yet, every time I read the forecast of such miracles, I am reminded of Jerome K. Jerome's *Three Men in a Boat*. You remember how the narrator, feeling a little 'poorly' (as we might say), goes to the library to consult some such masterpiece as *Every Man his own Doctor*, discovers, to his horror, that his symptoms are of a fatal order, and finally totters out, having learned that he has every known disease except housemaid's knee!

I would hate to see, in my own country, any Government scheme which lowered the importance of the doctor–patient relationship.

So far, I may have a considerable body of support from medical men. 'But,' some of them may say, 'what has this to do with voluntary health or medical insurance?'

My answer is that, as we saw it, and as I see it still, something had to be done to cope with the sometimes terrifying problem of a major illness in a family, particularly an illness of the breadwinner, which could involve complete financial disaster. True, a completely nationalized medical and hospital service could in a sense avert these disasters; but the price to be paid involves another disaster, the nature of which I have been endeavouring to describe.

And in any event, all Government schemes have to be paid for by the people.

So, we thought, let us have a scheme under which people can pay a premium—fairly modest, all things considered—to an approved health or medical benefit association, with supplementary payments by Government; the total benefit covering the great bulk of medical expenses—to the great benefit and relief of the householder—while at the same time retaining complete freedom of choice and the remarkable benefits of the doctor-patient relationship.

It was with these considerations in mind that we produced our legislation.

It is not my purpose now to discuss how it may be improved; I am now self-removed from such contentious matters.

Various experts have either devised or rejected compulsory schemes. During the 1969 election campaign, both sides managed to bewilder the electors with masses of statistics of a highly complex kind. Such exercises, in my opinion as an old campaigner, defeat themselves. The average elector, however intelligent, is neither an economist nor an advanced mathematician. His judgment is formed on broad views of social policy, and not on a detailed analysis of complicated sums.

No doubt the system we established is far from perfect, and will need amendment from time to time. But there would be nothing to amend or to improve but for what we did many years ago. That is why I include our health measures as one of the high spots of my period as Prime Minister.

13

New Social Services

Labour, having suffered heavy defeat on the Socialist issue, devoted itself in Opposition increasingly to the advocacy of bigger and better old-age pensions and the like. It set itself up as the true social-services party.

It is, therefore, interesting to recall and record that it was my colleagues and I who were responsible for all of the new social services, genuine innovations, of the next fifteen years.

Of our medical health scheme, with its outstanding feature of health insurance, I have already written in another chapter.

On pensions, both civil and military, we made substantial improvements from time to time and indeed over our term of office we made substantial modifications in the means test, but it is not my purpose to write about them in this chapter. I want to deal, in particular, with the innovations.

In 1954, over the dinner table at the Prime Minister's Lodge, my wife made a remark which took root in my mind. She said 'I hear a lot of talk about rates of pension and so on, but do you know, I believe that the greatest social need for old people is that they should have a place of their own to live in. Couldn't you think up some scheme under which the Government could subsidize the building of proper accommodation?'

The immediate result of this suggestion was that I began to think more closely about that aspect of the problems of old age. The next step was to devise a scheme in consultation with some of my colleagues. The result was the Aged Persons' Homes Act. It was designed to encourage the provision of homes in which aged persons could reside in conditions approaching normal domestic life. Provision was made for Commonwealth subsidy for the building of aged persons' homes on a pound-for-pound basis to non-profit organizations, particularly religious organizations, or organizations the principal objects or purposes of which were

124

charitable or benevolent, ex-service organizations and the like. Government organizations were not included.

From 1954 to 1957 the basis of grant was pound for pound (or dollar for dollar), but in the latter year the grant was increased to two dollars for one. The effect of this legislation was quite remarkable. I have personally seen a considerable number of the homes so established. I use the word *homes*, but I hasten to point out that each building, or set of buildings, contained a series of individual homes; each in effect a little flat, with toilet and kitchen provision, and a pleasant atmosphere. In this accommodation, old people can live to themselves as if in their own homes, but can mix with other occupants in common dining- and sitting-rooms provided for the purpose. I don't think that any of our schemes was ever more widely welcomed by the public or gave us a deeper satisfaction.

When I was a boy at school in the city of Ballarat, living with an old Scots grandmother in a cottage in Dana Street, there was a vast building just across the road called the Benevolent Asylum. It looked all right from the outside, but we soon got to recognize its terribly institutional quality and the rather depressed appearance of the old people who lived in it. For they knew nothing of private life and were, at that time, in a sense dealt with *en masse* and not as individuals. It was the recollection of this rather depressing neighbourhood no doubt that made my own mind receptive to the general suggestion made to me by my wife. I know that vast improvements have since been made in the Ballarat institution; but the new subsidized homes for the aged have an individuality and quality which really preserve the human dignity of the people who go into them. The best evidence of the popularity and usefulness of this scheme is that at the time of my retirement the amounts granted in the one year totalled over $11,000,000, providing 3,200 beds.

The pharmaceutical benefits legislated for by our predecessors had fallen into a state of disarray because, as I pointed out earlier, the Government had adopted methods of compulsion on the professions concerned and, in the case of the doctors, that com-

125

pulsion had been found to be invalid. When we came in, our policy was to create a partnership between the community, the Government, the providers of medical and therapeutic services and voluntary organizations; supervision being secured by advisory committees nominated by the professional organizations concerned.

One of the first steps we took for the prevention and cure of disease was to provide for free life-saving drugs. We wanted to concentrate upon drugs which were designed to be life-saving and disease-preventing. The vast development of the antibiotic drugs in particular had, of course, made a powerful contribution to shortening periods of stay in hospitals and to the alleviation of human suffering. But many of them were very expensive, with the result that a great number of people who needed them could not afford them. There was also some tendency to prescribe such drugs too freely. We therefore required not only that they should be subject to the ordinary rules of professional prescription but that the committees set up should have authority to name the drugs and to supervise their use by the medical profession. In the course of time, the range of drugs to be provided was extended, as the public demand grew. Life-saving drugs had, of course, been paid for by the Government and not by the patient. But, in later years, and as the list of drugs became enlarged, the demands upon this service became so great as to present a real problem to the Budget. It was, therefore, decided that a nominal charge of fifty cents should be collected for each dispensing of a prescribed drug. This measure helped to keep in check what was becoming an unexpectedly large burden.

We gave the position of old-age and invalid pensioners special consideration and established for them a free medical and pharmaceutical service. The value of this to people in advancing years was, of course, enormous.

It was my Government which in July 1941 had introduced child endowment for each child under sixteen in excess of one in a family. When we came back into office, we not only included the first child but, by various steps, increased the amount of the endowment. When I left office, not only had the payments been increased, but special provision had been made to include in the benefits of the scheme full-time students between sixteen and twenty-one years. This, of course, was in keeping with our policy, which I have described elsewhere, of encouraging higher education.

Another of our innovations was in the field of mental health. This had been regarded as a purely State function. Each State had its own institutions and methods of treatment, but was inevitably feeling the pressure of financial considerations. When in 1946 Commonwealth hospital benefits were introduced for patients in public hospitals, no provision was made for patients in mental hospitals. This was changed in 1948, when agreements were made between the Commonwealth and the States under which the States would cease to make charges for the maintenance of mental patients and the Commonwealth would pay the States a benefit based on the amount which had been collected by the States from the relatives of patients in mental hospitals. These agreements, which had produced very trifling results, terminated in 1954. At that time a leading authority, Dr Stoller, of the Victorian Mental Hygiene Authority, was commissioned to undertake a survey of mental health facilities and needs in Australia. His report directed dramatic attention to the capital problems. He found that most mental hospitals were seriously overcrowded and that the most urgent need was the provision of more beds. Many of the hospitals were old and out of date and seriously discreditable to the country.

When this report came out, my Government offered $20,000,000 to the States as part of a capital expenditure programme of $60,000,000 on increasing and improving patient accommodation. This was the Commonwealth's first intervention in the field of capital provision for mental patients. All the States accepted our offer. We subsequently converted this into an annual assistance until in 1964 we passed an Act providing for Commonwealth aid of one dollar for every two dollars for capital expenditure by the States on mental health facilities. Such a provision by the Commonwealth was quite novel, but undoubtedly the circumstances demanded it. In consequence, the physical condition of mental hospitals and the equipment used in them in Australia has very remarkably improved.

Housing is always a pressing problem in a growing country, and it has special financial implications in Australia, where over three-quarters of homes are owned or in process of acquisition by the occupiers. We dealt with two of the financial problems in my 1963 policy speech, in which we made two significant promises which in the new Parliament were performed. The first promise related to the special difficulty experienced by young married people, particularly in the age-group up to thirty-five, in financing the purchase of a dwelling. We dealt with this by providing a Commonwealth subsidy of one pound for every three (later two dollars for every six) which a person in this age-group deposits or shall have deposited over a period of at least three years in an identifiable account at an approved institution, to be released upon or after marriage for home-building or purchasing purposes. The maximum subsidy for one house is $500, a very material aid to the home-seeking young married. As we desired to help the most necessary cases, we made the grant payable in respect of a home not costing more than $14,000. This new scheme, though it is no doubt criticized today for being inadequate, was widely welcomed in the first two years of its operation, which were my last two years in office; about 55,000 applications were approved and $24,000,000 expended.

The other problem to which we directed our attention was becoming a very acute one. Many people found that, to fill the gap between available housing loans and the buying requirement of the purchaser, it was necessary for the purchaser to borrow money, frequently on oppressive terms. We therefore set up a system of housing-loans insurance, the insurance to be issued by a National Housing Insurance Corporation. The object of the scheme was to insure approved lenders against loss arising from the making of loans for housing. With the Government guarantee involved in this scheme, people would be able to

128

borrow, as a single loan at a reasonable rate of interest, nearly all of the money they needed. It was provided that in order to encourage the making of high-ratio loans the Corporation would insure loans of up to ninety-five per cent of valuation for houses valued at $15,000 or less; where the valuation of a home exceeded $15,000 the maximum insurable amount would be ninety-five per cent of the first $15,000 of valuation plus seventy per cent of the balance, or $20,000, whichever was the lesser. This scheme, of course, meant that many people could be assisted in this way to buy houses which were rather more costly. As I said in my policy speech, 'We must not encourage too much uniformity of dwellings in a refreshingly individualistic country.' The best evidence that this novel provision met a real need is that the Corporation commenced its operations in November 1965, and at the end of June 1968 the face value of current insurances amounted to $122,000,000. When I add that of all the dwellings in Australia over forty per cent were built during the term of office of which I have been writing, it will be realized that on the housing front we could claim a notable record of achievement.

14

Changes in Industrial Policy

The Communist Party Dissolution Act, passed after protracted debate in 1951, was successfully challenged in the High Court on constitutional grounds. We then sought to secure an amendment to the Constitution, but the popular vote was against us.*

This was naturally a serious set-back for us; but it did not dispose of the Communist problem.

As an organized political party, it commanded too few votes to become a parliamentary or even electoral force. But its strength, and therefore its menace, lay in its infiltration of the trade unions, particularly the key ones.

In the unions, the Communists seized upon every agitation about grievances, and frequently found their way into union office, not because they were Communists overtly pursuing the Communist objectives but because of their cultivated talents for opportunism and leadership.

Once in any union post, great or small, they would take steps to consolidate their position by very effective means. Union or branch meetings would be held at short notice, meetings at which open votes would be taken, anybody bold enough to express a contrary view being threatened and abused. Non-Communist unionists who saw the results of this Communist infiltration were almost helpless. When, in the earlier days of the Labour split which I shall describe in my chapter on the Petrov Case, they formed 'industrial groups' to fight Communism in the unions, they were roundly abused, even by the Labour leader in the House of Representatives. How could we help to restore true democracy in their unions?

We concluded that we should legislate for the secret ballot in union elections. This we did, in the teeth of Labour opposition,

* For a more detailed account of these matters, see my *Central Power in the Australian Commonwealth*, Cassell, pp. 18–20.

in 1951. We had specifically sought a mandate on this matter at the 1951 election.

Our secret-ballots legislation set out that the rules of industrial organizations must provide that elections of certain officials should be conducted by secret ballot. The term *official* included members of the committee of management of the organization or a branch and specifically included 'the office of President, Vice-President, Secretary, Assistant Secretary or other executive officer by whatever name called of the organization or branch'.

There had been considerable discussion as to whether provision for the secret ballot would go far enough. True, most unions would honourably observe the ballot procedures, but there had been some cases involving scandalous practices and there were therefore proposals put forward that ballots should be conducted officially, i.e. under the supervision of the Arbitration Court or the Electoral Office. Such a proceeding would have involved a great deal of unnecessary work because, in reality, it was only the exceptional case that needed to be catered for. We, therefore, set out to preserve the integrity of the secret-ballot system by giving to the committee of management of a union, and also to minority groups (such as the industrial groups) an opportunity to secure an official ballot. Our legislation provided that these elections should be conducted officially when the committee of management required it, or when a sufficient number of members thought that it was necessary. The rule laid down was that ten per cent of the total membership, in the case of elections to the central body, or twenty per cent in the case of a branch election, should be able to apply to the Industrial Registrar requesting him that an election should be officially conducted. The Industrial Registrar would make such inquiries as he thought necessary and decide whether or not to accede to the request. If he decided to accede to it, then an election could be directed under the Registrar or some officer employed in the Registry, or pursuant to arrangements with the Chief Electoral Officer for the Commonwealth. There can be no doubt that these provisions, which have been not infrequently used, represented a large step towards the establishment of genuine democracy in the organizations.

I now turn to the question of the enforcement of awards.

In 1956 the High Court presented us with an entirely new problem by its establishment of the legal proposition that the Arbitration Court as such was not a judicial body and could therefore not itself exercise any part of the judicial power of the Commonwealth. As a result of this decision, we performed a surgical operation by setting up a separate court called the Commonwealth Industrial Court, which had clear judicial powers, and separating out what became the Commonwealth Conciliation and Arbitration Commission, which exercised purely arbitral functions. The Commonwealth Industrial Court has power to deal with cases in which it is alleged that there has been a dismissal or injury of an employee on account of industrial action, questions relating to the interpretation of awards, questions concerning the eligibility of somebody for membership of an organization, disputes between an organization and its members. To avoid any suggestion of too much legalism, the parties are able to elect whether to appear personally or to be represented by lawyers or officials.

One of the earliest complaints about the conciliation and arbitration system, many years ago, was that though employers were bound to observe awards and could of course readily be compelled by court proceedings, the unions were not bound in the same simple way, and would sometimes disregard an award regarded as inadequate. To meet this anomaly the Conciliation and Arbitration Act, as amended twice in our time, empowered the court (i.e. the Industrial Court) to order compliance with an award proved to the satisfaction of the court to have been broken and not observed; and to enjoin the organization or person from committing or continuing a contravention of the Act itself or a breach or non-observance of an award. In the same Act the court was given a full power to punish contempts of its power and authority, not only contempts committed in the face or hearing of the court but also a contempt arising out of a failure to comply with an order of the court made under the provisions that I have just referred to. Substantial penalties were provided for in the case of both organizations and certain officers of organizations. These provisions have come to be known as the 'penal provisions' of the arbitration system and have excited great opposition on the part of a growing number of trade unions.

Any proceedings taken under these provisions, of course, involved proof to the satisfaction of the court of perhaps a complicated series of facts. This could involve a great deal of time and litigious activity. It therefore became a common practice for employers in particular to approach the Arbitration Commissioners in order to secure the inclusion in their awards of clauses designed to promote obedience. This has not uncommonly been done. In particular, a 'bans clause' can be inserted prohibiting the calling of a strike or imposing restrictions on work against the terms of the award. If, in the face of a bans clause, a strike is called or some other restriction imposed then the organization concerned can be brought up before the Commonwealth Industrial Court for contempt of court and fined. Many such cases have occurred, and though I fear that the fines have not always been paid, I think it will be agreed by most people that the overall effect of the creation of this power has been good.

Ever since its establishment sixty-six years ago, the system of compulsory conciliation and arbitration in industrial disputes has enjoyed great public support in Australia. So great was that support, particularly by the trade unions themselves, who found in the awards of the arbitrators a valuable protection against exploitation, that when Bruce in 1929 put forward proposals for the abolition of the Commonwealth legislation so that the parties might be entirely remitted to State institutions his Government went out, and Labour came in under Scullin. I have no doubt that the system has justified itself in terms of industrial peace and productivity. I have never thought that the collective-bargaining processes which go on, without compulsion, in Britain and in

133

America have produced comparable results. So it will be understood that nowadays, as I am writing this book, I am surprised to find that the Australian Council of Trade Unions, the most significant union body in Australia, is beginning a campaign criticizing the compulsory-arbitration system and urging a wider recourse to collective bargaining, with its inevitable sequels of strikes and industrial dislocation. I doubt whether the average unionist really desires to turn about face from the attitude he took up in 1929.

I take a look at the official statistics.

Australia was once widely advertised around the world as a strike-infested country. In our term and under our industrial laws this charge could no longer be validly made. The number of man-days lost by industrial disputes was in that time never more than about 900,000 and was usually little more than half that number. When it is considered that the total work force in our country was of the order of three and a half to four million, it will be seen that the time lost in this fashion per head was almost nominal. This is the more noteworthy because, after the great flurry of inflation in the early 1960s, the price level had tended to stabilize, and full employment had become an established fact; so complete in itself there were in many industries problems arising from over-full employment and therefore a too rapid turnover in the labour force.

In addition to making the general conciliation and arbitration law more effective, we paid a great deal of attention to some industries which had been rather more strike-prone than others. I take coal-mining by way of example. When we came back into office there had been so much disorder in the coalfields, a disorder which the Labour Government itself had been compelled to deal with by uncommon and drastic measures, that Australia was actually importing black coal. Inadequate production in Australia, which actually possesses very extensive and high-grade coal measures, had been contributed to by two elements in particular. One was that the coal-miners were addicted to having Communist leaders and officials. The other was that, largely influenced by these people, the unions had great objections (on what might be called 'Luddite' grounds) to the introduction of mechanization into the coal-mines. In the absence of mechanization, and with individual production kept artificially low by union rules, output was inadequate. In our time great work has been done by the Joint Coal Board set up by our predecessors just before their defeat, in co-operation with the State of New South Wales; while a special Coal Tribunal under one of the judges of the Arbitration Court has, by giving special consideration to the problems of the coal-miners, achieved remarkable results. The improvement in the coal-mining industry has been dramatic. Stoppages due to industrial disputes have declined. Instead of a starved domestic market supplemented by imports, a significant export market has been established. Increased mechanization has meant a much greater output with a smaller labour force, the miners displaced having largely been found alternative employment. In the year before my retirement, to take the example of New South Wales, the major black-coal-mining State, a thirty-seven per cent smaller labour force than was employed in 1949–50 (our first year of office) produced seventy-eight per cent more black coal. Australian annual production went up from 11,300,000 tons to 20,200,000. Exports increased correspondingly to just on 3,000,000 tons.

We paid some special attention to other industries, notably those on the waterfront, which had a sorry record of strikes and disturbances. After careful investigations, we set out to regularize the industry, adequate authority being given to the Australian Stevedoring Industry Authority and provisions made for the setting-up of industrial-relations committees on a national and ports basis, and, as far as possible, the regularization of waterfront employment so as to give greater security on the job. I do not go into particulars of these matters for they would require a highly detailed piece of history. But I can sum up the results in the period between 1955 and 1964. Fifty per cent more tons were handled by ten per cent fewer employees. The growing use of bulk handling installations and mechanization, and nowadays the expanding use of container ships, have all had much to do with this result. But the most important factor has been the improvement in industrial peace, greatly reducing the number of days lost in industrial disputes.

The characteristics of our employment position have become a matter of great national satisfaction. There is relatively less unemployment in Australia than in Great Britain, and very much less than in the United States and Canada, where in recent years over five per cent of the work force have been registered as unemployed. Our figure, towards the end of the period about which I am writing, was little more than one per cent; while even then there were almost as many unfilled vacancies. In substance, therefore, we had no unemployment over all, with over-full employment, i.e. a shortage of labour, in many important industries.

15

Internal Airlines Policy

Australia, with its immense distances and widely separated capital cities, increasingly employs air transport.

After the war, a marked development occurred in both interstate and intrastate air travel, pioneered and conducted by private enterprise. The principal interstate operator was the A.N.A., controlled by Sir Ivan Holyman, whose family business was shipping.

In 1945, the Chifley Labour Government, which believed firmly in nationalization of industry wherever possible and was, a couple of years later, to make its ill-starred attempt to nationalize the banks, decided to take over the commercial airlines. For this purpose it passed an Act to create a National Airlines Commission with power to conduct air services, and then, by a series of statutory devices, gave it a monopoly, thus eliminating the private services. A.N.A., as the pioneer of this branch of aviation, challenged the validity of the Act in the High Court. Broadly, there were two grounds of attack. One was that the Commonwealth had no power to establish an authority to conduct air services under its trade and commerce powers. This ground of attack failed. But the other ground was more formidable. It was that the monopoly provisions, which in effect would exclude such enterprises as A.N.A. from interstate operations, violated the provisions of Section 92 of the Commonwealth Constitution, which provided, in language that has given rise to a vast mass of litigation, that interstate trade and commerce should be absolutely free. The High Court acceded to this argument, and declared the monopoly provisions invalid.

The validity of the existence of the new commission and its power to conduct air services was thus established, but competition was kept open, and before long was very active. The commission styled its enterprise Trans-Australian Airlines (T.A.A.) and, under the driving chairmanship of A. W. (now Sir Arthur) Coles, a well-known merchant and former member of Parliament, made great headway. T.A.A. has been most efficiently conducted, modern, and successful. No Government, of any political colour, would wish or be allowed by public opinion to destroy it.

But A.N.A. also succeeded in getting its share of a remarkably expanding industry, both before and after it was acquired by the irrepressible Reginald (now Sir Reginald) Ansett, and became 'Ansett–A.N.A.', and now usually 'Ansett'.

So the state of affairs when we came back into office was that interstate air traffic was 'free for all'. Before long it was becoming evident that, if the highest standards in the fields of aircraft, maintenance, safety and service were to be maintained (and from the enormously increasing traffic it was essential that they should be), there should be some attempt at rationalization. This indeed was urgent, but the difficulties involved were obvious. I put in many hours studying all the relevant papers which my then Minister for Civil Aviation made available to me. We then conferred, and the matter went to Cabinet for decision. The result was what became known as the Two Airlines policy. This policy was based upon the view that a free-for-all would be contrary to the maintenance of the standards I have just referred to. We should therefore aim to secure a position in which there were two, and not more than two, operators of trunk-route airline services, each capable of the highest level of service and of effective competition with the other. Clearly the two airlines concerned would be T.A.A. and Ansett, the Government airline and the private airline.

To make this policy effective, there would need to be Commonwealth control over licensing for interstate operation, which we had; and financial and equipment support for the selected competitors.

The airlines equipment problems of T.A.A. and Ansett were first dealt with by the Civil Aviation Agreement Act of November 1952. The act ratified an agreement under which specific provisions were made in respect of both capital provision and aircraft, so as to produce, not necessarily an equal share of the traffic, but equality of opportunity, i.e. fair competition.

The objects of the agreement as set out in the agreement compendiously expressed the Government's policy.

In order to facilitate trade and commerce among the States, provide for the efficient carriage of mail by air within Australia and assist the defence of the Commonwealth it is expedient in the opinion of the Commonwealth to make provision for the purpose of ensuring:

(a) the continued existence of the Company as well as of the Commission, as an operator of airline services within Australia;

(b) the maintenance of competition between the Commission and the Company; and

(c) the efficient and economical operation of air services within Australia.

The agreement then provided for a Commonwealth guarantee of a loan of £3,000,000 to be made to the Company for the purchase of modern aircraft. (The Commission, of course, was the financial responsibility of the Government.) There was to be a sharing of airmail business, and Government business was made open to both. There were provisions for rationalizing the services so as to avoid unnecessary overlapping.

Another Act in 1957 ratified an agreement between the Commonwealth, the commission and Ansett. The agreement, in conformity with the policy, recited that one of the objects of the parties was to secure and maintain 'a position in which there are two, and not more than two, operators of trunk-route airline services, one being the Commission, each capable of effective competition with the other'. The actual provisions of the agreement related chiefly to provisions for rationalization of services.

The matter was brought into final shape by the Airlines Equipment Bill of 1958, when Athol Townley was Minister.

The commission's position was first dealt with. It had a re-equipment programme estimated to cost £10,000,000. Its own capital, plus an amount by which the Government was to supplement it, would enable it to do a good deal, but it would still need £5,000,000. The additional funds it needed and the securing of the aircraft it planned for, were assured to it by the Government.

The company was also helped to a broadly corresponding extent, money provided by the Government being of course not a gift but repayable over a period of years.

As it had been freely said that markedly favourable treatment had been given to the company, the Minister pointed out that:

It is most important to appreciate that while the commission—that is, T.A.A.—receives the greater part of its assistance in hard cash, in the form of capital or the proceeds of loans negotiated by the Commonwealth on its behalf, the assistance proposed for the private operator is limited to guaranteeing repayment of loans which it negotiates on its behalf. Unless there is a default the Commonwealth will at no stage be responsible for providing any funds for the private airline. If there were default, the Commonwealth has an adequate security over the aircraft which will ensure that, in any event, it will not be involved in loss as a result of the giving of the guarantees.

Townley fairly pointed out that these arrangements would intensify rather than reduce competition.

He concluded:

The measures proposed in this bill are fair and non-discriminatory, and stand or fall as a related whole. They are consistent with this Government's established domestic air transport policy. The new equipment will give the Australian travelling public a first-class air transport system. The rationalization of fleets will eliminate excess aircraft capacity and, at the same time, retain the competitive incentive which has contributed so greatly to the efficiency of the domestic air transport system.

This policy has, I believe, justified itself by experience. It was stoutly defended and applied by one of my West Australian Ministers, the late Shane (subsequently Sir Shane) Paltridge, who had become Minister of Civil Aviation and had a remarkable administrative capacity. But it has an increasing number of critics, particularly among people engaged in interstate transportation, especially in goods, which now constitutes a fairly large and growing element in the business of the two major operators.

But looking back over the period of office of which I am writing, I believe that our policy produced very good results for Australia and the travelling public. Our airlines have a record of efficiency and safety and good service which is not bettered and seldom equalled in any other country in the world.

16

Canberra—The Making of a City

Every nation needs a capital city of which it can be proud. Old nations have old capitals, rich in history and the beauty of age: London, Paris, Rome. But for a new nation the problem is different, for it must consciously create a capital with all its history to come. Where, as in the case of the United States and Australia, the nation is created as a federation of States, each with its own capital city, the new Federal Government and Parliament must be established in an area and city acquired and established for federal purposes. In America, it was Washington and the District of Columbia; in Australia, it was Canberra and the Australian Capital Territory. As the new capital will inevitably have small beginnings it will begin by being looked down upon by its elder State brethren, and later, as it grows at the centre of power, be looked at sometimes with envy, but ultimately with pride.

Such things are inevitable at the outset of a federation, for the local patriotisms of the former colonies, now constituent States, are both strong and vocal.

In Australia, before federation, there was great jealousy between Sydney and Melbourne, each fearing that the other would become the federal capital. Before they would vote for federation, New South Welshmen needed to be satisfied on this point. So a famous compromise was made which found its place in Section 125 of the Commonwealth Constitution. This section provided that the seat of government of the Commonwealth should be in the State of New South Wales 'and be distant not less than one hundred miles from Sydney'. To soothe the feelings of Melbourne, it was provided that until it should meet at the seat of Government, the new Federal Parliament should sit at Melbourne.

A Parliamentary Committee was appointed to investigate suggested sites in New South Wales outside the prescribed radius.

142

The choice fell upon Yass-Canberra, which was a stretch of pastoral country through which there meandered a quiet little stream called the Molonglo, on its way to the not very distant Murrumbidgee river. An area of just under a thousand square miles was surrendered by New South Wales and accepted by the Commonwealth in 1909, the final vesting of the area taking place as from the beginning of 1911.

Later on, in the time of Hughes's Prime Ministership, a foundation stone was set on a hill, and the name of the proposed city, Canberra, announced.

A world competition was held for the best design of the new city. It was won by an American architect and town-planner, Walter Burley Griffin. The design, which has been substantially followed in subsequent years, was that of a garden city with tree-lined circuits and crescents and not too many straight lines. The central feature was to be a lake in part of the area traversed by the straggling and intermittent waters of the Molonglo.

But it was not until after the First World War that building began, and with it the gradual transfer of Government departments to the new city. In 1927 a new Parliament House was opened, Parliament House in Melbourne being returned to the State.

When I went to Canberra in 1934 to become Attorney-General in the Lyons Government the total population was about nine thousand; one could walk around it without undue discomfort on a Saturday afternoon. In the great centres of population it was referred to as the 'bush capital'. Facetious people would suggest that it be used as an insanity-treatment centre. One wit referred to it as 'six villages in search of a city'.

I cannot honestly say that I liked Canberra very much; it was to me a place of exile; but I soon began to realize that the decision had been taken, that Canberra was and would continue to be the capital of the nation, and that it was therefore imperative to make it a worthy capital; something that the Australian people would come to admire and respect; something that would be a focal point for national pride and sentiment.

Once I had converted myself to this faith, I became an apostle; though years were to elapse before major success.

In 1934, of course, we were handicapped by the fact that the country was just beginning to emerge from the great Depression. There was very heavy unemployment, but the prevailing economic doctrine was that deficit budgeting must be avoided. We now see the errors in this doctrine, and that Canberra's development might well have been accelerated. But the fact was that the Government saw good financial reasons for not going on with the lake scheme; these reasons became inevitably intensified during the Second World War.

There was another slightly amusing reason for delay: it was that the Canberra Golf Club was in possession of much of the land around the Molonglo and had established a pleasant golf course. Canberra being at that time a predominantly Civil Service town, it is not surprising that there was a good deal of passive or active resistance by the golfers and their committee men.

However, when I came back into office at the end of 1949 I began to think that I could see some renewed opportunity of doing something. Canberra was still a scattered town, with sections separated by the Molonglo and its river flats, crossed only by two narrow low-level bridges and one narrow high-level wooden one. Though the river would run in spate and flood its adjoining fields every year or two, it was for the most part a relatively small creek (as we say in Australia). The opponents of the lake used to say that if we put a dam across the Molonglo near Government House and created, by these artificial means, a substantial and permanent lake, we would divide Canberra irrevocably. But I never did believe this.

My contrary view was that, well done and with its surroundings properly landscaped and planted, it would become the real centre of a united city. It would lend itself to the construction of splendid bridges which would provide easy road communications, would be a great attraction to tourists; and would, therefore, build up Canberra as a capital in the eyes and minds of the Australian people.

144

While this argument was rumbling around, we kept bringing in more and more departments, principally from Melbourne (which had been the temporary capital), and had therefore to engage in an extensive building programme, with new problems of design and lay-out to be encountered. There was no single authority responsible for the development of Canberra; at this time, two departments, Interior and Works, divided the responsibilities, and to divide responsibilities over one topic is the wrong way to secure prompt decision and effective action. In the homely phrase, I thought that the buck was being passed too frequently. I therefore proposed in 1957 to Alan Fairhall, then Minister for the Interior, and Cabinet agreed, that we should set up a National Capital Development Commission, get as good a man as we could find to be the Commissioner, and give the commission authority which would not be subject to normal departmental control, and something in the nature of an annual budget.

This having been agreed to, I went off to London on one of my Prime Ministerial errands. When I returned I found that a bill had been drafted but that in effect it made the proposed commission subordinate to the Department of the Interior. That it should be responsible to some minister was essential; and that minister must plainly be the Minister for the Interior. But in all other respects I thought, and so did Fairhall, that it had to be a substantially autonomous body if the previous confusion in responsibility were to be ended. This view was agreed to, and the re-drafted Bill was passed and became law in October 1957. The statutory functions of the commission were splendidly comprehensive: 'to undertake and carry out the planning, development and construction of the City of Canberra as the National Capital of the Commonwealth'.

The one limiting instruction contained in the Act was that the commission should not depart from or do anything substantially inconsistent with the basic plan, which, though there had been various modifications, was essentially that of Griffin, though he of course cannot be taken to have visualized so large a city as Canberra was to become.

J. W. (now Sir John) Overall, an experienced architect, had been suggested as a suitable chairman. I met him in Melbourne and had talks with him and was left in no doubt that we could not possibly secure a better man. So he was appointed, has with his assistant commissioners a great record of achievement, and is still with us.

The Commission had a great job on its hands. Departments were being steadily transferred to Canberra, with thousands of officers, their wives and children. Areas were laid out and provided with necessary services, thousands of homes were erected, a great National Library created, office blocks constructed and shopping-centres set up on what were once empty fields. The growth was spectacular.

But one matter which I particularly asked the commission to look into was the possibility of carrying out the lake scheme. This required a great deal of work by the commission and its technical men. Some people had said that the lake would produce mud flats and mosquitoes and look like the Thames at low tide. So the commission conducted research into problems of flow and erosion and water levels until it was completely satisfied (and so were we) that it had the answer. So the year arrived when, for the annual estimates which preceded the Government Budget, they included, through their Minister, an item of approximately one million pounds for the beginning of the lake work, the marking and preparation of the lake's boundaries, the landscaping and so on.

I went away to England once more very happy, because the estimates had been accepted; my dream had been given shape; but when I returned I found that the Treasury (which in any country moves in a mysterious way its wonders to perform) had induced ministers to strike the item out. At the very first meeting after my return, and when I had completed a survey of the matters which had been discussed abroad, I turned to the Treasurer, who was my good friend and ultimate successor, the late Harold Holt, and said, with what I hoped was a disarming smile, 'Am I rightly informed that when I was away the Treasury struck out this item of one million for the initial work on the lake?' The reply was yes, and that Cabinet had agreed. I then said, 'Well, can I take it that by unanimous consent of ministers the item is now struck in?' A lot of laughter ran around the Cabinet room; there were some matters on which they reasonably thought that the old man should be humoured; and, needless to say, Overall's men were on the job next morning.

Well, in due course, the dam at Yarralumla was built and the lake was completed. Two splendid bridges, I think of great architectural distinction, had been built, and we were able to gaze over an irregularly shaped three square miles of water shining like a jewel in the middle of the city. Before long, we were to see boating clubs established; we could see the white gleam of sailing-craft. There was, and is, a setting of parks of great beauty and, looking from the university end of the lake, the splendid backdrop of the blue Murrumbidgee Ranges. All fears were dissipated. Canberra had emerged as a lovely city. Departmental officers would no longer feel it a hardship to go to live there. It had become a university city and a city of schools, with unrivalled facilities for water sports and a unique charm of its own. Nowadays, of course, its population has grown apace. It already exceeds a hundred thousand and may well exceed a quarter of a million by the turn of the century. Thousands of people from Interstate come to visit it and admire it. When I remember how every penny spent on Canberra used to be grudged and how many arguments I had to engage in when travelling from State to State, I am delighted in my old age to think that Australia's capital has now become an object of pride and pleasure. This was always a national conclusion devoutly to be wished.

When the time came to give the lake a name, I remember my then Minister for the Interior, Gordon Freeth, coming to me and saying, 'There is a widespread feeling that, as you have been in a material sense the father of this lake, it should be named after you.' My reply was prompt. 'Gordon,' I said, 'that is a characteristically pleasing thought on your part, but the lake is not going to be named after me. Do remember that the original designer of this city and the original creator of the whole notion of a lake was Walter Burley Griffin. So far as I know, he has no memorial in this place. He must have one. I want to have the lake called Lake Burley Griffin.' It was so named and has given Griffin a memorial which no man ever more handsomely deserved.

17

The Morale of the Civil Service

I include this topic among the high spots because I believe that our treatment of the Civil Service and, in particular, the terms of mutual confidence which we enjoyed with the senior Civil Servants were such that the morale of the Service was never higher. I use the words 'Civil Service' and not the more statutory phrase 'Public Service', not only because I have always been in the habit of doing so, but because public service, I believe, extends far beyond employment under the Crown.

Before I went to Canberra in 1934, I had been a minister in the Victorian Government for some years, and learned something of the function and significance of the Civil Service. Indeed, an old political friend of mine had reason to say to me one day that 'in any department the civil servants provide a level below which no minister can reasonably fall'!

At Canberra, I had a fuller and richer experience: five years as a Cabinet Minister, over eighteen years as Prime Minister. When I came in, towards the end of 1949, for my long second term as Prime Minister, there was a feeling around that Labour had attached significance to the political views of senior public servants; that the service was becoming somewhat political.

Whether this was true I have always taken leave to doubt. But the very existence of the rumour made me quite determined that my own administration's record should be clear. At the very outset I was told by people in my party organization that certain men in the Prime Minister's Department were or had been officers or members of the Labour Party. I recall my reply with some satisfaction. 'So long as they are competent and honest men, what of it? Kissing will not go by political favour in my department!'

At least two of the officers my party official had referred to were relatively senior, and in a position in which they might be required to offer advice. Each in his turn did so on occasion, and always with complete objectivity and integrity. I have no doubt that they discontinued their political activities for, being men of quality, they realized that a senior civil servant who is called upon to inform and sometimes to advise his Minister is on terms of strict confidence with him, giving and receiving confidence, and must therefore avoid all occasion of embarrassment.

In Australia, all employees under the Commonwealth Public Service Act have a full right to have their own political views. This is as it should be. After all, a member of the service is presumably an educated and intelligent citizen. We even provide that he has certain rights of reinstatement if he resigns to become a candidate for Parliament and fails to be elected.

But I firmly believe that the position of the senior civil servant in relation to both his Minister and Parliament is quite special and should be clearly understood and zealously guarded. When, in Australia, we decided on permanent tenure for the Public Service proper, we wanted to avoid the evils which had been prevalent in the United States when a presidential election determined the fate and future employment of many thousands of holders of public office, great or small. This changeability of advisers leads to some curious results in America. As America does not have responsible government as we understand it, with ministers sitting in Parliament and answerable to Parliament, they have in America created a great system of congressional committees with wide inquisitional powers and no particular hostility to publicity. These committees will summon before them, in an appropriate case, senior members of the administrative departments and question them as a rule quite publicly about matters of policy in their particular departments. All too frequently, if they agree with the policies which have been expressed by their particular Secretary, they are condemned as mere 'stooges'; and if they offer a contrary view to that of their chief, the headlines become damaging to him.

I know that there are quite a few members of Parliament in Australia who would like to see this committee system instituted. My own view has been and is to the contrary. I do not mean that

I object to parliamentary committees, of which we have a considerable and useful variety in the Federal Parliament. What I do object to is the idea of senior civil servants and senior people in the armed services being called before a committee to offer their views on matters on which they are the chief and confidential advisers of the Government.

It must be clearly understood that the Chief of Staff of any armed service is the man to whom the minister looks for advice of a technical kind; advice which he is not bound to accept but which he is bound to treat with considerable respect. If the Chief of Staff were liable to be hauled off before a committee with the Press cameras flashing and the reporters writing, he would find himself in a very painful position. He would be compelled to set out on oath his views on various aspects of his service, so that what should be properly confidential between him and his minister would become a matter of public notoriety. Under these circumstances, what mutual confidence could there be between the minister and his Chief of Staff, or in civil matters between the minister and those senior men in his department whose job it is to give and to receive confidence? If the confidential relationship between ministers and the senior men in their departments were torn to pieces in this way then not only would the standard of administration decline but the efficiency of the minister would suffer.

To put this matter in another way, in our system a political minister must face the music in Parliament; that is his duty and his privilege. He must take responsibility for his department and its administration. When I was Attorney-General I had a fixed rule that advice given to me by the Solicitor-General (who, in Australia, is an official and not a politician) was given to me for my consideration and if adopted by me became my advice for which I must accept responsibility. If his views were rejected by me, I would, of course, substitute my own opinion and the Solicitor-General's advice would find a resting-place in the files. This practice indeed represents the whole principle in action of ministerial responsibility; ministerial responsibility is of the essence of responsible government. This rule was not always followed by at least one of my successors who had, I thought, a bad habit of naming and quoting the Solicitor-General where the advice given by the Solicitor was favourable to the view that the Minister was presenting to Parliament.

Civil servants ought not to be dragged into parliamentary debate. They have great responsibilities which, in my experience, they discharge with outstanding honesty, and it would be deplorable to have their names and views bandied about in Parliament, thus involving the civil servant much against his will in party political controversy.

In brief, I firmly believe that Parliament by violating those principles could do lasting harm to the whole structure of public administration. A couple of years back there was a great hullaballoo in the Federal Parliament about the use of what are called V.I.P. aircraft. I had long since retired and therefore took no part in this controversy, which seemed to me to be curiously unreal. But I did prick up my ears when I found that there was a proposal in the Senate to call the Secretary of the Air Department before it as a witness and to give evidence which, it was presumably hoped, would discredit his Minister over this matter and advance the interests of politicians who, oddly enough, already used V.I.P. planes themselves and had high hopes of using them more and more in the future. I therefore came out of my retirement sufficiently to write a newspaper article explaining my views. I pointed out that it would be curious and alarming if an anti-Government Senate could undermine the objectivity and non-political integrity of the Public Service by exposing its senior and most responsible officers to a Parliamentary inquisition from which they had a right to be immune and compelling their entry into a field of political debate.

For it must be remembered that somebody summoned before either Parliament itself or one of its committees and compellable to make answers will be questioned on anything that occurs to the questioner, with none of the normal legal rules on the admissibility of evidence or of relevancy to a particular issue. Such a position would be disastrous.

I concluded by saying:

The permanent head of the Air Department is, let us suppose, ordered to attend before the Senate to be questioned.

He will, presumably, not be represented by counsel. He must look after himself under the questioning of not a few lawyer Senators.

He is asked to recount conversations or exchanges between him and his Minister in relation to some matter. If he refuses to answer, feeling that to answer would be to transgress a confidential relationship, he may be punished for contempt of the Senate.

If he answers, under this pressure, he knows that one of two things must result.

Either he agrees with his Minister about the order of events and the nature of the communications, and is then, by hostile questioning, put into the highly political position of defending a political Minister in a matter of political controversy—a position into which no responsible public service officer should ever be put—or he disagrees with his Minister, who, if he is a Minister in the House of Representatives, cannot be summoned to the Senate and will therefore not give evidence in rebuttal before that House!

What sort of a trial would this be? What would its effect be upon a relationship between Government and public service long since established and of long-proven value to Australian public administration?

My own ministers and I adhered very closely to this conception of the status of the senior civil servant. I am sure that this adherence meant a great deal to the service and contributed in a large degree to its high standard, its morale and effectiveness.

18

The Petrov Spy Case

This chapter sets out the strange eventful history of what followed the defection in 1954 of a man named Petrov, and his wife, from the Soviet Embassy in Canberra, and their securing of political asylum in Australia. There has grown up a legend that the whole affair was a cleverly timed political scheme. This charge was made by Dr Evatt, the Leader of the Opposition, time after time, and was shown to be false time after time. But, as so frequently happens in life, the picturesque slander outlives the sober answer. In the interests of the people involved, and of accurate history, I have now decided that the full story shall be told.

The establishment of a royal commission of inquiry brought many dark and sinister matters to light. Its disclosures not only established that the Soviet Embassy had been used as an espionage base but also exposed its methods so successfully as to render future activity of this kind extremely difficult. It established the reputation and proved the efficiency of the Australian Security Intelligence Organization (ASIO).

Moreover, much of the information provided by the Petrovs to ASIO related to the activities of people outside Australia and was therefore not within the scope of the royal commission; but it proved of immense value to security intelligence services abroad.

In the course of the inquiry the names and shameful activities of many Australian Communists were exposed.

True, the final report of the royal commission disappointed those who were hoping for the levelling of charges against some leading political figure or figures; a dazzling climax of a sensational trial and juicy evidence. To some people, it was an anti-climax. Towards the end of this chapter, I shall devote some particular attention to the results, which were very great; in the meantime I shall narrate the events.

The story begins with the establishment, by Mr J. B. Chifley,

Labour Prime Minister, and Dr Evatt, his Attorney-General,* of the Australian Security Intelligence Organization.

It will be remembered that in the late 1940s there was great international tension. The Soviet Union, which had, under German attack, become our wartime ally, became, after victory, our potential enemy, with a great 'colonial' domination over Eastern Europe, and a proselytizing spirit all around the world. The cold war began, promoted by Moscow. Its technique was to encourage subversive Communism in selected parts of the world. Australia, with its long tradition of free speech and tolerance, was one of the targets.

So the Labour Government decided, very properly, to set up an intelligence organization to counter espionage and subversive activities. The Government saw that this was not a matter of party politics; it concerned the security of the nation and its entire system of parliamentary self-government. The Prime Minister appears to have been particularly concerned about some mysterious leaks that had occurred in the Department of External Affairs. He laid down a rule, which I subsequently strictly observed, that ASIO must work in secret (since it was trying to counter an enemy who worked in secret), and that the details of its activities should not be exposed in Parliament or to the public at large.

The first head of the organization was Mr Justice Reed, of South Australia, who, some little time after I came back into

---

* As a great deal of this narrative will revolve around the personality and actions of Dr Herbert Vere Evatt, I should at once make some explanatory remarks about him. He had been a Justice of the High Court of Australia, a post from which he resigned in order to enter the Commonwealth Parliament as a Labour member. When his party went into office in 1941, he became Attorney-General and Minister of External Affairs in the Australian Commonwealth Government and President of the General Assembly of the United Nations; and, at the time of which I write, Leader of the Labour Opposition in the Commonwealth Parliament. He was a scholar of great attainments and a well-furnished lawyer, but, oddly enough, a poor advocate. He was a strange and controversial figure.

office at the end of 1949, indicated his desire to return to his important judicial work. We then appointed, from the Intelligence side of the Army, Colonel (now Sir) Charles Spry, who has recently retired.

Spry was ideally qualified for the post. He was a distinguished professional soldier, a graduate of Duntroon and of the Middle East Staff College. He saw active service in India in 1935–6.

Later, he was with the 7th Australian Division in the Owen Stanleys and on the Kokoda trail. He was wounded there. He was decorated with the Distinguished Service Order. He was Director of Military Intelligence in Australia from 1946 to 1950, for most of which time he was a trusted Military Intelligence adviser to the Labour Government in which Dr Evatt was most prominent.

But later on, as we shall see, nothing could save him from a violent attack by Evatt himself.

Technically, ASIO was attached to the Attorney-General, but from time to time the Director-General would have an interview with me in order to report general progress and any important matters affecting the security of the Commonwealth. He did not, as a rule, go into detail. I had great faith in Spry's activity, organizing skill and judgment, and at no time had any reason to lose it.

On 10 February 1954, Spry consulted me, told me that a defection was possible, and that the possible defector was probably a member of the M.V.D. (the Soviet Ministry of State Security). It is his memory that he for the first time mentioned the name of Petrov to me. There was no particular reason for me to remember an individual name; and in fact I did not.

On 3 April 1954, Petrov left the Soviet service and voluntarily sought political asylum in Australia. Naturally, I was informed at this stage and, after consultation with the Law and External Affairs Department, approved of the granting of the application. But I said nothing publicly, since the formalities of diplomatic communication had to be attended to.

On 13 April, the Department of External Affairs, following

diplomatic practice, by official Note informed the Soviet Embassy of these facts.

The Embassy's first suggestion was that Petrov had been kidnapped. Without seeing the documents handed over by Petrov, they found no difficulty in saying that they had been forged. Within eight days they felt able to assert that Petrov had stolen Soviet funds.

These allegations turned out to be stock-pattern in the Soviet technique. External Affairs requested detailed particulars of the alleged embezzlement, but obtained none. I say 'stock-pattern' because in the famous Gouzenko case in Canada similar charges of embezzlement had been falsely made.

On 13 April, after the Soviet Embassy had been notified, I convened Cabinet, told ministers of these dramatic events, and secured their approval of a statement to be made promptly to the Parliament, and to the setting-up of a royal commission of inquiry.

That evening I spoke to the House, recited the above-mentioned facts and said (*inter alia*):

M. Petrov, who has been carrying out in Australia the functions of the Russian Ministry of State Security—the M.V.D.—has disclosed a complete willingness and capacity to convey to our own security people a great number of documents and what may turn out to be much oral information and explanation. In the examination of all this material, involving as it does a great deal of translation and comparative research to establish the meaning of particular expressions and code-names, much time will necessarily be spent. I am therefore not in a position to make a full statement. . . .

Enough material has been examined—though only a small fraction of the whole—to show that there are matters affecting Australia's security which call for judicial investigation. These matters concern not only the activities of M.V.D. agents in Australia, but also the position of some Australian citizens named in the documents, under 'cover' or 'code' names or otherwise, as contacts or co-operators.

As would be expected, I do not propose to mention names of people until the investigations have so far proceeded that a coherent case, of proper probative value, can be prepared. . . . The Government therefore proposes to set up a royal commission of investigation into what I may call espionage activities in Australia. This will be done as soon as possible. Naturally it may take some little time to secure the services of a suitable royal commissioner and prepare the precise terms of reference. Moreover, as I am informed, much detailed work will have to be done on the material provided to us before the commissioner could proceed with his investigation. But the Government thought that an announcement of the central fact and our intentions should be made at the earliest possible moment.

I then said:

While it would have been agreeable for all of us to defer an appointment of such importance until after the new Parliament has been established, there can, as I am sure all parties here will agree, be no avoidable delay of investigation into what are already beginning to emerge as the outlines of systematic espionage and at least attempted subversion.

When the House met on the following day, 14 April, Dr Evatt made a statement on behalf of the Australian Labour Party, in which he said that it would support the fullest inquiry into the matters to which I had referred, and all relevant matters. 'If any person in Australia has been guilty of espionage or seditious activities a Labour Government will see that he is prosecuted according to law.'

He then went on to say that there should be consultation with the Opposition about the royal commission and its terms of reference.

On the same day, which was the last sitting day of the Parliament before the General Election, I introduced a bill for an Act to set up the foreshadowed royal commission.

I said that the matter was certainly not a party one, and, as far as I knew, involved no party considerations.

I added that I would be happy to consult with the Leader of the Opposition about the terms of reference.

Dr Evatt thanked me for having shown the text of the bill to the Opposition. He said that they had studied it, and would give it their full support. The bill was carried without further debate.

The terms of reference of the royal commission, approved without division by Parliament, were that the commission should inquire into and report upon:

(a) the information given to the Commonwealth by Vladimir Mikhailovich Petrov as to the conduct of espionage and related activities in Australia and matters related to or arising from that information;
(b) whether espionage has been conducted or attempted in Australia by representatives or agents of the Union of Soviet Socialist Republics and, if so, by whom and by what methods;
(c) whether any persons or organizations in Australia have communicated information or documents to any such representative or agent unlawfully or to the prejudice or possible prejudice of the security or defence of Australia; and
(d) whether any persons or organizations in Australia have aided or abetted any such espionage or any such communication of information or documents, and, generally, the facts relating to and the circumstances attending any such espionage or any such communication of information or documents.

The choice of a commission presented difficulties. I agreed with Evatt that more than one judge should be appointed. It might be thought by some that the judges should be drawn from the highest court in Australia, the High Court. But the High Court is *the* court in Australia which decides cases under the Commonwealth Constitution. 'Is this law within the powers of the Commonwealth Parliament? Is this Act, passed by a State Parliament, invalid, having regard to the Constitution?' Now, such questions arising for decision, the High Court, though, I am proud to say, a great non-political body of fine lawyers, gives decisions which inevitably have a political effect. The court knows that this is inevitable, but so long as my memory runs has followed the practice of not making its judges available for royal commissions.

For, in human experience, royal commissions arise from political issues.

The same tradition does not extend to the Supreme Courts of some of the States, who, on application to the State Premier and with his approval, will make a judge available. I am glad that this is so because I have always believed that, so great and proper is the respect of the Australian people for the judicial office and the integrity of its holders, a report of a royal commission constituted by a judge or judges carries more weight than one made by a lay tribunal.

So I turned to the State Premiers and secured the services of three Supreme Court judges of the greatest eminence. Their appointment was, without division, approved later by the Commonwealth Parliament; but since they were later on attacked in a strange way by Dr Evatt, I should, for the record, say something about them.

Mr Justice Owen, who was not the first judge of his family in New South Wales, had been at that time for seventeen years a Justice of the Supreme Court of that State, and is now, as Sir William Owen, a Justice of the High Court. He enjoyed an impeccable reputation among both lawyers and the general public. So highly were his ability and character regarded that Mr Curtin appointed him from the Bench during the war to be, in succession to Sir Owen Dixon, chairman of the Central Wool Committee, a great national undertaking. Mr Justice Owen held that office from 1942 to 1945, when Mr Chifley, himself no mean judge of men, sent him abroad to lead the great wool-disposals mission. He served his country in two world wars. He served in the second in the way I have described, and in the first as a member of the Australian Imperial Force. He had and has a reputation as a judge which will survive.

The second member of the royal commission, *Mr Justice Philp*, had been for fifteen years a Justice of the Supreme Court of Queensland. He also was a soldier of the First World War. He stood very high in public and professional esteem in that State. He was a genial, shrewd judge of men. The third, *Mr Justice*

Ligertwood, had been for nine years on the Supreme Court of South Australia. He also had served Australia in war. He was president of the Law Society of South Australia several times, and *on two occasions he was appointed a royal commissioner by a Commonwealth Labour Government*—no doubt upon the choice of the Attorney-General, Dr H. V. Evatt. I had never heard any suggestion whatever against him of political bias or judicial incompetence.

The facts leading up to and surrounding the defection first of Petrov and then of his wife were clearly established before the royal commission and set out by them in their unanimous reports. It appears that ASIO used the services of one Michael Bialoguski, a man born in Russia of Polish parents, who had emigrated to Australia and completed a medical training, and was willing to supplement his professional earnings by acting as a part-time secret agent, while professing extreme left-wing sympathies.

I cannot describe him, for I never saw him, and heard of him for the first time when the royal commission's sittings were on. The part he played in Petrov's defection was fully examined by the royal commission, and has been described by him, within the sharp limitations of his knowledge, in a book entitled *The Petrov Story*.*

Bialoguski clearly achieved friendship with the Petrovs, and considerable influence over Petrov himself; and also appears to have maintained discreet contacts with officers of ASIO, particularly G. R. Richards, who was Spry's deputy. Richards is a man of responsibility and character, and was later to be honourably acquitted by the royal commission of wild charges made against him.

Petrov was Third Secretary and Consul in the Soviet Embassy at Canberra and thus had ready access to the diplomatic and social life of Canberra. Among other functions, he was a temporary M.V.D. Resident in the Embassy. He had many friends and enjoyed an extensive social life which took him from time to time to

* Heinemann, 1955.

Sydney, and to the celebrated King's Cross. It is clear that he enjoyed the freedom of Australian habits and had developed a real attachment to the country. But, of course, his job was to undermine that country, and he appears to have done his best.

Bialoguski was, in due course, able to report that Petrov was seriously contemplating leaving the Soviet service. To this state of mind the Soviet Embassy made its own powerful and indeed conclusive contribution. Petrov had been accused by the Soviet Ambassador (Lifanov) of trying to form a pro-Beria group among the Embassy officials. This was a false accusation, but it left Petrov with an acute sense of danger. For all these matters were, as he knew, reported to Moscow.

Towards the end of 1953 a new Soviet Ambassador (Generalov) arrived in Canberra, and, no doubt, on the basis of what had been conveyed to him by Lifanov, continued to be critical of his Third Secretary.

An incident then occurred at the Soviet Embassy which brought the matter to a head. Petrov was under notice of recall to Moscow, and was due to leave, with his wife, in a couple of weeks' time. His M.V.D. successor was on the way to Australia (and was, in fact, met in Sydney by Petrov, on the very day on which Petrov finally decided to defect). On 1 April 1954, the Ambassador officially accused Petrov of dealing with a secret document 'in a manner contrary to the administrative regulations. The charge was technical, but nevertheless serious, and if established, could have resulted in a term of imprisonment.'* The hitherto hesitant Petrov, dithering about between wind and water, was driven by these events to make his final decision. He communicated with Richards, Spry's chief lieutenant, showed him on 2 April some documents which he had abstracted from the Embassy, most of them being in Russian, and said that he would hand them over on 3 April. He thereupon signed his application asking for political asylum.

* Unless otherwise stated, quotations in this chapter are from the reports of the royal commission judges. The italics throughout are my own.

162

On 4 April, there was a conference at the Prime Minister's Lodge at Canberra, at which Spry, Richards, an interpreter, and I were present. No attempt was made to conduct an exhaustive examination of the documents. Such an exercise, with so many documents in Russian requiring interpretation, would have taken many hours and in any event was unnecessary at that stage. What I needed was a general understanding of the nature of the documents, and this I obtained.

This almost bald narrative of the events of early April, a narrative which is drawn principally from the unanimous judicial findings, contains the conclusive disproof of the political charges. The charge that Spry and I 'timed' the defection so that it would influence the approaching election obviously depends upon establishing that Spry and I were masters of the timetable, that we decided the date of the Petrov defection, and that Petrov complied with our directions and accommodated himself to our wicked plans.

That is why it has been, in my opinion, relevant and necessary to show that the date of defection was decided by the action of others. That is why the actual events of 1 and 4 April are so important and, indeed, conclusive, unless, of course, somebody is prepared to say that the Soviet Ambassador was my ally, or even my servant!

Should I, this defection having occurred, have concealed it until after polling day, when I would be properly accused of keeping from the public all knowledge of an unusual, and indeed startling, event of international significance? Should I, in breach of all diplomatic courtesy, have concealed it (I don't know how) from the Soviet Embassy? And later, when the Soviet Embassy had been formally notified, should I have concealed it from the Cabinet and Parliament?

Nobody in Parliament thought or said so at the time.

Now, at the time of the making of the application and the handing over of the documents Petrov knew, and ASIO knew, that from a Soviet angle his life was at risk. He would certainly lose his house and money in Russia. He was entitled to some

163

assurance of protection and of having some means of living while he established himself in some place or other in what was to be his new country. Richards thereupon, very properly, as the royal commission was to find, paid him a sum of £5,000 towards his future maintenance.

Petrov's wife appears to have been unaware of these events until the Soviet Ambassador dismissed her from her positions of accountant and secretary to the Ambassador and ordered her to leave her home (they had not lived in the Embassy) and go to the Embassy where she was then 'placed under guard night and day subject to indignities and hardships'. She herself was no negligible person. She had become an active Communist in Russia. She was an accomplished linguist and, by the time she was twenty years old, had become a member of the Soviet military intelligence organization and worked for it as a cipher clerk. Having married Petrov in 1940, she went with him to Sweden where she worked for the M.V.D. Resident. 'Her work was mainly concerned with Soviet espionage activities in Sweden.' In 1951 she accompanied her husband to Australia, where certain espionage duties in Australia were allotted to her. She had a competent knowledge of English, Swedish and Japanese. She was deeply attached to her native country, where members of her family still lived, and was, no doubt, shocked at her husband's decision to seek political asylum. She appears to have believed that he must have been forcibly taken and put under very harsh duress.

On 16 April the Department of External Affairs sent a note to the Ambassador enclosing a letter written to Mrs Petrov by her husband in which he denied that he had been forcibly seized and said that he was alive and well and was being treated well. He further said that he had written to the Ambassador asking him to arrange a meeting with his wife as soon as possible. This desire was frustrated, the Ambassador compelling her to write to her husband a letter refusing to see him. It was, of course, clear to the Soviet Embassy that she must leave Australia. So, on 19 April she was driven to the airport at Sydney to catch a plane for Darwin en route for Moscow, under the guard of two armed couriers. The news of this got about and there was a demonstration by a crowd at the Sydney airport who called to her not to go back to Russia. But, closely attended by her custodians, she was virtually hustled up the gangway. She spent an unhappy and sleepless night on the plane, filled with fear and uncertainty.

ASIO, at this time, in consultation with me at my house at Canberra, got into touch with the captain of the aircraft and asked him to have her talked to in order to find out whether she was going to Moscow against her own will. She was in fact spoken to by a steward and an air-hostess. The captain formed the impression from their reports that she desired to stay in Australia, but was afraid. She told her questioners, with much anxiety, that her guards were armed. When the plane arrived at Darwin, Mr Leydin, the Acting Administrator, under instructions from Canberrra, interviewed her. The guards were informed that it was unlawful to carry arms in an aircraft. Upon being asked if they were armed, they assaulted their questioners. They were then disarmed, a loaded pistol being taken from each of them.

In Leydin's conversation with Mrs Petrov, he found that she was distraught. She saw dangers in everything. She told him that she feared for her relatives in Russia if she remained in Australia against the will of the Embassy. She also said that she doubted whether her husband was alive and well and asked if she could see him or speak to him. Canberra being informed of these matters, a telephone call was arranged and, just before the plane was due to resume its flight, Petrov spoke to her from Sydney. He told her that he was well and free; that he had been forced to leave the Embassy on account of the lies told about him; and that when she arrived in Russia she would not be allowed across the threshold of her home and would never see her relatives. He urged her to remain.

After this conversation she said to Leydin, 'I will stay.' So the plane resumed its flight without her, and the guard went with it. Mrs Petrov then returned to Sydney where she joined her husband and made a formal written application for political asylum, which was granted.

Before the royal commission sat for the first time, I had a consultation with Mr Windeyer, Q.C. (now Sir Victor Windeyer, a Justice of the High Court of Australia), who had been briefed to assist the commission. We agreed that in opening the matter to the royal commission no individuals' names should be mentioned, and that no mention of any individual names other than the Petrovs' should be made until after the election.

I went further, to avoid any party political implications. Early in the election campaign it appeared that some political references had been made to the Petrov matter by one of my candidates on a public platform. I at once communicated with every Government candidate in Australia, and said that this was not a party political matter, and that as it was under judicial investigation I wanted it kept right out of the political campaign. This request of mine was scrupulously observed.

The royal commission secured the services of Mr A. H. Birse, C.B.E., whose proficiency and integrity were well vouched for. Birse was born in Russia of Scottish parents, and spent twenty-six years in Russia. During and after the war he acted as the official interpreter for Churchill in conferences with Soviet leaders, and was, in fact, the official British interpreter at Teheran, Yalta and Potsdam. The commission formed the highest possible opinion of his character and intelligence.

The royal commission opened the proceedings on 17 May, at Canberra. Mr Windeyer, conformably to our agreement, said:

The premature publication of *the documents* and of any names of persons mentioned in them might, I feel, seriously prejudice those investigations which are now proceeding. . . . Therefore, we suggest that there should be no immediate publication of those names, and that whether at any time publication be allowed should be a matter for Your Honours to consider later.

If the names which were disclosed and discussed in the royal commission's interim report months after the election had been disclosed before the election, their impact upon the voting would no doubt have been tremendous. But throughout the campaign they were known only to the royal commission and to counsel assisting them.

It thus appears that if, as was later to be claimed, I designed to use the Petrov case for electoral purposes, I went about it in a most remarkable fashion.

My announcement in Parliament was, of course, sensational news for the Press both in Australia and overseas.

There was nothing I could say publicly that I had not already said; but I finally agreed to have a Press conference and give them a chance to put questions. Seeing that I had announced that there would be a royal commission, they could not expect to get any information from me on matters which would fall for judicial investigation. Three times the usual number of journalists crowded into my office at Parliament House. I knew most of them fairly well, and they, particularly my 'regulars', knew me even better; so they had no great expectations, but were good triers.

Suddenly a little man burst into the room, elbowed and pushed his way into the very first row, announced himself as having flown from America as the representative of a world-famous journal which enjoys, I am told, great authority, and promptly fired his first shot. Referring to the Petrovs, he barked out, 'Say, are those people married?' I said, 'Yes, they have been married and have lived and worked together for many years.' His face fell. He had been balked of a 'sex angle', as I believe it is called. So he promptly elbowed his way out, and was never seen by me again. His first shot had turned out to be his last.

I tell this short story because it was the only bit of fun we were to get out of this matter for a long time.

The Press, of course, and from their point of view quite naturally, wanted to interview the Petrovs at once. But we had a security duty to the Petrovs, who had become the mortal enemies not only of the Soviet and the Soviet Embassy but of all their myrmidons; so I refused.*

* A few weeks later, we did develop the proposal for a limited Press interview so that the Petrovs could show that they had acted voluntarily and that they wished to become Australian citizens. This suggestion was

167

The papers handed to ASIO by Petrov not only provided the basic material for the initial inquiries of the royal commission, but opened up a wide field of subsequent investigation.

These papers were:

1. A document typewritten in English and marked by the royal commission *Exhibit H*. This document was clearly proved to have been composed and typed by one Fergan O'Sullivan in 1951, when he was a journalist employed in the Canberra Press gallery by the *Sydney Morning Herald*. He had been procured to write it by a Russian overtly representing the Tass news agency, but covertly a temporary M.V.D. Resident. The document was photographed, the negative being sent to the Moscow centre.

O'Sullivan became Dr Evatt's Press Secretary in April 1953. When after the 1954 Elections O'Sullivan admitted to Dr Evatt that he was the author of the document, Dr Evatt at once and properly dismissed him.

Exhibit H itself played a large, though perhaps not a very important, part in the inquiry; as will appear.

2. A document typed in English, marked by the Royal Commission *Exhibit J*, composed and typed by one Rupert Lockwood, a self-confessed Australian Communist, at the request of the Tass representative, who was also an M.V.D. worker. It also was sent to the Moscow centre. It was a long document of thirty-seven pages, closely typed. It covered a wide variety of matters deemed to be of interest to the Soviet Union. I will come back to it. All

---

discussed with the Chairman of the royal commission, who indicated his disapproval of the idea on the ground that the proposed interview might raise the question of contempt of the commission; which would be clearly undesirable. After some negotiations with the editors of the leading newspapers, I decided to abandon the proposal not only because of the question of contempt but also because an interview might raise political issues which in my opinion should not be raised, if at all, until after the election. In the result, the Petrovs gave all their evidence before the commission itself.

that needs to be said at present is that it was later described by Mr Windeyer, of all advocates the most restrained, as 'a farrago of fact, falsity, and filth'.

3. The next papers, written in Russian, were letters sent out from the M.V.D. Moscow centre to Petrov. These, of course, had to be translated. For this purpose, the royal commission secured the services of the highly qualified A. H. Birce.

4. A miscellaneous group of documents which were marked G by the royal commission and consisted chiefly of letters from Moscow to Canberra.

As the 'Petrov papers' attracted the early attention of the royal commission, which, after careful investigation, found them to be authentic, I should at once say something about their nature and contents.

Exhibit H was as I have said, the product of Fergan O'Sullivan. It contained short and sometimes pungent reports on no fewer than forty-five journalists. These were of value to the M.V.D., which well understood how a willing or unaware Canberra journalist might be used as a source of information. Canberra was, and still is essentially, a city in which Parliament and the administration provide the centre; while there is a substantial diplomatic colony. Press representatives move quite freely in this *milieu*. They claim access to ministers, and frequently achieve it. They have been known, I am sorry to say, to prise out Cabinet secrets. In the course of their news-gathering they are frequently to be found in the departments where information may be obtained; sometimes officially. At social receptions ('National Days') and the like, leading journalists are to be seen mingling with diplomatic and other guests. Many a secret has been spilt, or perhaps a slurred hint given, under the influence of a cocktail party.

For all these reasons, which are, I suppose, common to all official government cities, it was important for the Soviet Embassy, if its espionage were to be efficient, to know about the press-men: one might have a weakness which would make him susceptible to pressure; another might be a communist sympathizer; one might be warned against on the ground that he was a strict Roman Catholic who would be unlikely to have any communist leanings at all; several of those mentioned in Exhibit H were 'believed to be Security Agents'.

The reason for and the value of H were thus apparent. O'Sullivan must have known this, and of course knew that the value was one, not to Australia, but to Australia's potential enemy. Further, as the commission found, the fact that O'Sullivan gave the document made him susceptible to pressure to perform further tasks for the Soviet. The spies had a hold on him.

Exhibit J was a different kind of document. It was very long, running into thousands of words. It covered various topics. Some of its sub-headings were: *Japanese interest in Australia*; *American espionage in Australia* [sic]; *War contacts in Australia*; *Notes on the Australian Workers' Union*; and *Dr Evatt*.

'Amongst many other matters, the document contains personality reports on a great number of persons—politicians of every colour, newspaper proprietors and journalists, businessmen, etc. Many of the reports are scurrilous and grossly defamatory (some of the allegations are of a filthy nature), in some cases pointlessly so, since they refer to persons long dead.'

Before the commission, the authenticity of the document was fiercely contested. It was claimed that it had been fabricated 'as part of a conspiracy to injure Dr Evatt and the Labour Party'. The royal commission rejected this astonishing charge, and found that the document was authentic Lockwood.

But the commission's findings in its interim report will be given special attention later in this narrative.

The other documents making up the Petrov papers consisted of letters and memoranda containing instructions from Moscow, assigning and using code-names, including code-names for various Australians, many of whom were later called before the commission. These documents, which it would be tedious to quote from (many of them were set out by the commission in its final

170

report), had little to do with the ordinary processes of diplomacy, but were part of the fabric of a carefully organized espionage.

Proceedings Leading up to an Interim Report, and What the Report Said

After the General Election the royal commissioners sat in June, July, August, September and October in Sydney and Melbourne and heard a mass of evidence about the documents and the people named in them. About the authenticity and circumstances of birth of Exhibit H there was no doubt, since O'Sullivan admitted that he was the author. About the authenticity of Exhibit J there was a dispute. The Petrovs had stated that it was typed during three successive days in 1953, at a time when Petrov himself was in the Canberra Community Hospital; that it was typed in the Soviet Embassy at Canberra; and that it was typed by Rupert Lockwood.

The commissioners examined a mass of circumstantial evidence all of which indicated that Exhibit J had in fact been typed in the Soviet Embassy, that Lockwood was in Canberra at the times, which proved to be 23, 24 and 25 May 1953, and that Lockwood was the author. Lockwood had stayed at the Kingston Hotel opposite the Soviet Embassy during the days in question. When called as a witness during the Melbourne sittings, he refused to answer any questions concerning the authorship of Exhibit J.

It transpired in the course of evidence that one Grundeman, a member of Dr Evatt's staff, had been in Canberra at the relevant time, though Dr Evatt was absent abroad. Lockwood, O'Sullivan and Grundeman were proved to have been in company in Canberra for some hours on either 22 or 23 May. The records of the External Affairs Department showed that Grundeman had been in Canberra on these dates, and the commission found that the contents of these records were known to Dr Evatt before the next Sydney sittings (well after the General Election) began. It was at this stage that Dr Evatt apparently decided, though he had not been practising at the Bar, to seek leave to appear to represent

171

two members of his Secretariat, Grundeman and one Dalziel. It is curious that he should have sought to represent Dalziel because his name had been mentioned only as appearing in Exhibit J as a source of some quite innocuous information. However, leave was granted and Dr Evatt appeared. As the commission pointed out in its interim report, there was nothing in Exhibit J which materially reflected on Grundeman and Dalziel. It is clear that the real element which drove Dr Evatt to take up the cudgels was the fact that three members of his then Secretariat had been named in Exhibit J, and that it had been shown that there was a meeting at Canberra between Lockwood, O'Sullivan and Grundeman at the very time when Lockwood was said to have been typing Exhibit J.

Dr Evatt thereupon cross-examined the witnesses for a long time and with some ferocity. We had observed in Parliament for some little time that he appeared to be very ready to believe that he was a victim of 'conspiracies'. But his conduct before the royal commission was concisely described by the commissioners.

Dr Evatt conceived the theory that he and the political party which he leads had been the victims of a political conspiracy and he proceeded to cross-examine the witnesses before us with that in mind. . . . Charge followed charge with bewildering variations. Suggestions were made of blackmail, forgery, uttering, fabrication, fraud and conspiracy and—upon the repeated assurances of Dr Evatt that his examination of witnesses was directed to these matters and would prove them—we felt constrained to permit him great latitude in his questioning. . . . As day followed day and all that we heard was constant reiteration of vague charges of infamy, we demanded of counsel (he had two juniors appearing with him) on 1 September that they formulate with some exactitude their allegations. Dr Evatt then charged that Exhibit J had been fabricated by the Petrovs as part of a political conspiracy with the enforced aid of O'Sullivan who, he alleged, had been blackmailed into collaborating in the fabrication of the document and into inserting therein as sources the names of himself, Grundeman and Dalziel. The political conspiracy was alleged to be one to injure Dr Evatt and the Australian Labour Party by procuring

172

the false insertion in Exhibit J of the names of three of his secretaries as sources with the intention that the Petrovs should so nicely time their actions that Exhibit J could be produced and published on the eve of the Federal Elections in 1954. [*Remember that it was not!*] He further charged that at least one senior officer of the Australian Security Intelligence Organization, Richards, had been guilty of serious derelictions of duty in that, without proper care and inquiry, he had accepted from Petrov fabricated documents, had paid him large sums of public money for them, and had 'uttered' these documents, presumably to the Prime Minister of Australia.

Then came the culminating points in the Royal Commission's narrative.

Although, in the result, all the charges turned out to be fantastic and wholly unsupported by any credible evidence, they were grave and necessitated patient judicial inquiry by us.

It was apparent from the outset, and it was ultimately conceded by counsel for Grundeman and Dalziel and by counsel for Lockwood, that if Exhibit J had, in fact, been typewritten wholly by Lockwood, then and for that reason alone, all the charges of conspiracy and the like against the Petrovs and O'Sullivan, and those made against Richards and the Security Service, would fall to the ground.

Many witnesses, including the Petrovs, Lockwood, O'Sullivan, Dr Bialoguski and Richards were examined and cross-examined at great length but, except for one portion of the evidence of Lockwood, no evidence emerged to support these grave charges. Indeed, the whole of the evidence led the judges irresistibly to the conclusion that Lockwood did type Exhibit J. It is interesting to note that Lockwood, during the Melbourne sittings, had not denied the authorship; but, on the contrary, had refused to answer any questions concerning it. He was a little more communicative when recalled in Sydney. He then admitted that he had given to one Antonov, in the Soviet Embassy, some typed material; that part of this material was typed by him in the Embassy over a period of some fifteen to twenty hours on 23, 24 and 25 May, 1953; and that the subject-matter of the material so

173

given was almost identical with the subject-matter of Exhibit J. But he would not admit that Exhibit J was the document which he had given to Antonov.

The story on which he ultimately settled after much prevarication was that he had left at the Embassy about a hundred and seventy pages of his typewritten material, and he suggested that Exhibit J, which comprised only thirty-seven pages, must have been recast from that material and typed by somebody else. But the royal commission, which had exhibited almost superhuman patience, and was made up of judges highly skilled in the evaluation of evidence, had no doubts. Their words deserve quoting.

We had ample opportunity of evaluating Lockwood's credibility. His repeated prevarications and evasions and his general demeanour were such that no reasonable man, who had seen and heard him for the fourteen hours during which he was in the witness-box, could accept him as a witness of truth where he was in conflict with the only inferences to be drawn from the circumstantial evidence.

The remarkable and ill-balanced activities pursued by him in court Evatt took with him into the public arena. He publicly attacked the members of the royal commission and some of the witnesses appearing before it in such violent terms that the chairman felt it necessary to reprimand him; telling him that if any other counsel appearing in the inquiry had made such statements about the commission and witnesses giving evidence before it, the commission would have committed that counsel for contempt.

Evatt was quite unmoved by this. Most barristers would have understood the characteristic delicacy of the judge in thus obliquely reminding Evatt of the obligations which arose from his earlier judicial eminence. But Evatt was the kind of man who, if he thought about it at all, thought that the law of contempt which applied to other men could not and did not apply to him. His legal capacity and his political capacity had become muddled in his own mind. But the end had to come, if the royal commissioners were not to find their public investigations degenerating into a forum for unsupported charges, garnished with the kind of comment made by Evatt outside the court-room; comment which could give aid and comfort only to the Soviet Embassy, Australian Communists, and such people as would wish to cripple and destroy the vitally important Australian Security Service.

So the day came when the royal commission, who had earlier— weeks earlier—given him leave to appear, felt compelled to cancel that leave. The chairman, speaking for all three of the judges, said:

On more than one occasion during the past three weeks we have pointed out to you, Dr Evatt, that a position seemed to be developing in which you, as counsel for Mr Grundeman and Mr Dalziel, were really appearing for yourself, since you have claimed that a conspiracy has been entered into to injure you politically. We had hoped that you yourself might have come to realize the embarrassing position which was gradually becoming more manifest. A climax has been reached by the statements made by you.

This is a reference to an intemperate attack Evatt had made on the French Government and the French Ambassador in Australia with reference to one Madame Ollier, an employee of the French Embassy, who had been cultivated, under instructions from Moscow, with a view to obtaining cipher information and had some secret meetings with Soviet Embassy officials. Except that the whole matter was further proof of Soviet espionage methods, she was not of great importance. But of her I shall say more later in this chapter.

The chairman, after referring to the Ollier incident, said, 'It has become apparent that you cannot dissociate your function as an advocate from your personal and political interest.' His leave to appear was thereupon revoked. Such a humiliation was without precedent in Australian legal history. But all it did to Evatt was to persuade him to transfer his advocacy to the floor of Parliament where, as the debate which he demanded on the interim report will show, he heatedly reiterated all of the arguments which had been, after a complete examination, completely rejected by the judges.

In the course of an intensive legal and political experience, I can recall no similar instance.

The Debate upon the Interim Report

On 21 October 1954, the royal commission presented their interim report to the Governor-General, who, following the usual practice, forwarded it to me on 25 October. On 26 October, again following usual practice, I tabled the report in Parliament, so that it would become a matter of public knowledge.

In the interim report, having disposed of the charges which had been put forward, chiefly by Dr Evatt from the Bar table, and having affirmed the complete authenticity of the Petrov papers, the judges went on to explain why they found it necessary or desirable to take the unusual course of making an interim report.

These reasons were that grave charges had been made against the integrity of the Security Service and, as they were made in open sittings, had received very wide publicity. Such charges were calculated to cause grave disquiet in Australia, whose security was involved, 'but also to shake the confidence of other friendly Nations in the integrity of that Service', as the interim report pointed out. The judges thought that these charges clearly needed to be dealt with as a matter of urgency, and reported upon forthwith. I will quote the last three operative paragraphs of the report. They leave no room for doubt, and are, of course, by implication a dreadful condemnation of Dr Evatt's conduct before the commission.

We heard the evidence of all persons who, so far as we could see, would be able to throw any light on these allegations, and there were placed in our custody and examined by us the contemporaneous Security reports and records, including wire recordings of certain significant conversations relating to Petrov's decision to leave the Soviet service and to the receipt of the documents handed by him to Richards.

The evidence of these persons, supported as it is by the contemporaneous records, entirely disposes of all suggestions of improper or negligent conduct on the part of Richards or any other officer of the Security Service. *Indeed, we think that these officers acted with high intelligence and complete propriety in difficult and delicate circumstances.* Whether Exhibit J was an authentic document or a fabrication, the undisputed fact is that it was one of a number of documents brought by Petrov from the Soviet Embassy. Immediately those documents were handed by Petrov to Richards, the latter showed them to his superior officer, the Director-General of Security, who forthwith placed them before the Prime Minister, as was his plain and only duty.

Other assertions, which were constantly reiterated by counsel for Lockwood and by counsel for Grundeman and Dalziel, that Richards had improperly bargained with Petrov, and ultimately paid him £5,000, for fabricated documents designed for some ulterior political purpose, *are entirely disproved.*

In fact Petrov, when he was contemplating leaving the Soviet service and seeking asylum in Australia, necessarily required assurances as to his physical protection and the provision of the wherewithal to start a new life in Australia since otherwise he would be penniless. The Director-General of Security rightly instructed Richards to give assurances to Petrov on both these points. Richards did so and paid the £5,000 in pursuance of explicit instructions from his superior officer. Richards's evidence, confirmed as it is by contemporaneous reports and by wire records secretly taken of his conversations with Petrov during February, March and early April 1954, *establishes beyond question that the 'bargaining for documents', to which reference was made so often by counsel, existed only in imagination.*

Before tabling the report, I told Evatt that I thought that a debate on an interim report could serve no good purpose. I suggested that he might prefer to await the final report and then have a full-dress debate on its contents. 'The interim report,' I said, 'contains trenchant criticisms of your own activities before the commission. You might prefer to discuss these as part of the total subject-matter rather than have a debate which would give sole prominence to criticism of yourself.' He at once said, 'I want a debate at the earliest possible moment, and I will insist upon it!'

177

'Very well,' I replied, 'but if you force me to it I want to make it plain that our past association will not inhibit me from dealing with you in the plainest possible terms. Your blood be on your own head!'

And so it came about that, on 28 October, he moved, pursuant to leave, 'that the paper be printed'; a motion which, under Australian parliamentary practice, permits of a general debate on the contents of the report.

But before this happened, the Speaker, Mr Archie Cameron, a somewhat testy but emphatic man, gave a ruling in these terms:

The interim report arose out of the findings of a royal commission appointed by this Parliament to inquire into certain things. I have previously stated from this chair that it is my considered opinion that a member of this House, having spoken and voted on a measure before this House, is thereby precluded from taking part in any court action arising out of that act of the House. In this case, the Leader of the Opposition appeared as a barrister for some time before the royal commission. I hold the view that a member of this House has no right to appear before that royal commission, except in the capacity of a witness, and it is my further view that, having so appeared, as the right honorable gentleman did appear, he should not discuss in this House any reports or matter that arose out of the proceedings of the royal commission at the time when he was there as a barrister. I leave the matter to the judgment of the House.

I said that as the Leader of the Opposition was eager and insistent, I would move the suspension of the Standing Orders, to enable him to proceed with his motion. My motion was carried, and at 8.5 p.m. Evatt began a highly emotional and attacking speech which lasted for two hours. The Press galleries were crowded; the House of Representatives chamber was full.

Though he was later on to speak contemptuously of what he called the 'trivial results' of the investigation, he took an early opportunity of saying, 'I desire the House to bear with me tonight, because this in one of the greatest cases in the history of

Australia, as that which is involved in it is fundamental to our lives.'

He first, not unexpectedly, attacked me. He accused me of having announced the Petrov defection and the appointment of a royal commission in a dishonest and successful attempt to win the then approaching election. As I have, in other parts of this chapter, dealt with this latter-day and false allegation, I need say no more.

He attacked the royal commissioners, whose appointment he had originally approved. The commissioners had 'failed to hear the case'; they had failed to hear relevant evidence; they had rejected Evatt's application to call another expert on handwriting, because they called only those who were 'suitable', presumably those who would agree with the judges' own notions. They had not shown a proper competence or understanding of their judicial duties.

He attacked the security officers. They had acted 'with gross and culpable neglect'. What was worse was that they had 'dangled five thousand pounds in notes before Petrov' as an inducement to hand over the documents. 'I think that the heads of security acted negligently and did not act with justice and propriety, as they should have done.' To cap it all, 'the disclosures which took place on 13 April were not recent but old disclosures, and that the time of making the disclosures was fixed so that they would give electoral advantage. The security people must have known that it would assist the Government, as it did, in the election.' In short, he was clearly charging the security service with party political bias amounting to corrupt practices.

Evatt had said nothing to the House that he had not said, with much reiteration, in his other capacity to the royal commission.

I was therefore already prepared to reply at once, and very willing to do so. I thought that Evatt's conduct before the judges had been grossly improper, that he was out to destroy the security service, that his antics were giving pleasure only to the Communists and the Communist Press. And these people, though the electors had denied us a constitutional amendment which would have enabled the Commonwealth Parliament to outlaw them, I regarded and still regard as the enemies of democratic self-government, the orderly processes of the law, and the freedom of the individual in a free country. Evatt lost the 1954 election because he had made in his policy speech extravagant promises. He had, as it turned out, made these wild promises without consulting several of his senior colleagues. I had found little difficulty in publicly exposing their unreality and irresponsibility, and the Australian people, whose judgment and common sense I had always respected, rejected them, and him. As earlier Gallup polls had prepared him for a victory, and had over-excited him, the blow of defeat was both heavy and bitter. He became obsessed by a sense of grievance; he began to exhibit delusions of persecution; the word 'conspiracy' was frequently on his lips. His party became divided, and a process was clearly developing which led to its political disintegration and has kept it out of office for many years.

So, and I do not seek to conceal the fact, I was not only prepared but eager for the debate.

The points I set out to make will appear most clearly if I do something which is normally repugnant, make a series of literal extracts from my own speech:

The House has had a very uncommon privilege tonight. It has heard counsel who has unsuccessfully advanced certain arguments before a tribunal have the opportunity to advance them for the second time before a tribunal which has not heard the witnesses and has not read the detailed evidence. That is something that I cannot remember in my fairly long experience of public affairs. I listened very carefully to the right honourable gentleman in his capacity as the Leader of the Opposition. I read very carefully, day by day, the transcript when he was acting in his other capacity as Dr Evatt, one of Her Majesty's counsel, and I am bound to say that he has tonight said nothing to this House that he did not say to the royal commission. . . .

He elected to make this a great case of conspiracy. *Conspiracy against his clients? Oh dear, no! They were of no moment. Conspiracy against himself!* And from that moment the royal commission found

180

itself compelled, against every sensible instinct it had, quite obviously, to devote weeks and weeks to investigating this document and its authorship.

Now the right honourable gentleman has invited this House and the country to prefer his judgment on the facts—facts which, for the most part, have not been studied by one of his listeners—to the considered and impartial judgment of three of the most distinguished Supreme Court judges in Australia! Because all this is, properly considered, an attack on the royal commission, and amounts to saying to us and to the people, 'Don't take the view of the royal commission. Take my view, the view of the defeated counsel,' I feel compelled to say something about the royal commission. I did not feel compelled to say it before.

I then proceeded to speak of the acknowledged eminence and integrity of the three judges (as I did earlier in this chapter) and continued:

Here we have three Supreme Court judges of great experience, of unquestioned ability and of untarnished character, who have heard every word of the evidence, seen every witness and every document, and listened to tape-recordings to which the right honourable gentleman has never listened. Having had all this material before them, they have made an interim report—a calm, cold, logical, judicial report, in which they find the facts without hesitation. In the result, they are treated with hysterical abuse and their findings are submitted to examination by an audience which, I very respectfully submit, has no material before it on which it could dare to disagree with those findings. . . .

I am old-fashioned enough to prefer the cold judgment of the judge to the heated allegations of the advocate. . . .

The fourth charge was that there was a political conspiracy against him and the political party of which he was the leader. . . . This conspiracy, for some weeks, remained quite unformulated. In the long run, having been formulated, it involved, as the royal commission records, *blackmail, forgery, uttering, fabrication and fraud.* . . .

The royal commission has found all those charges—and I again use the commission's words—to be fantastic and wholly unsupported by any credible evidence. . . .

181

The fifth charge made . . . was that, as a result of the conspiracy, the production of document J was to be so timed that it should be published on the eve of the 1954 general election. The royal commission did not need to find on that charge, because every honourable member knows that document J was never published before the general election and that no portion of it became known until it was revealed in the proceedings of the royal commission long after the election had been concluded. . . .

Charge No. 6—and this, if I may say so, was a particularly wicked charge—was that Mr Richards, of the Australian security service, was guilty of a serious dereliction of duty in accepting from Petrov the 'fabricated' document. The royal commission has found that that charge was fantastic, because it was conceded by all counsel who appeared before the commission that *if document J was typed wholly by Lockwood, the charges of conspiracy and dereliction would fall to the ground.* The royal commission found, without doubt or hesitation, that document J clearly was prepared and typed by Lockwood. As I have just said, the only evidence to the contrary was given by Lockwood himself, and the royal commission found him to be a prevaricator, an evader and not a witness of truth. Yet, as it turns out, he was the entire sheet anchor of the case of the Leader of the Opposition. . . .

I feel bound to say that there can have been few instances in the whole history of judicial investigation in which charges so wildly made have been found to be so utterly without foundation. *Therefore, they were presumably made without real instructions, wantonly and recklessly.* . . .

In short, ever since his inglorious and discreditable performance before the royal commission, he has engaged, to use his own favourite words, in a smearing campaign, a campaign in which he has had the enthusiastic support of the Communist Press. Why has he attacked these judges? Because they disagree with him, because they do not share his own curious, excited, ill-balanced view on these matters. That is the only reason, unless, of course, he has come back to the good, simple, old-fashioned ground that you always should attack the judge when you have lost. Nothing could do more harm to the safety of the people of Australia than attacks on the security service. I would not have believed it possible, until the last few weeks, that *the leader of a political party in Australia should have worked so hard to destroy the confidence of our people in these men, who are our guardians and our friends.* That the Communists should engage in such attacks is, of course, elementary, as the security service is their enemy. But I cannot help wondering how many of the great army of Labour supporters in Australia, who fear and dislike Communism, and who are its pledged enemies, have enjoyed the spectacle of their leader, in his dual capacity, playing the Communist game on a public platform, and therefore with public influence, to a degree that the Communists, by their unaided efforts, could not have reached in a hundred years.

The debate was then adjourned.

The Final Report

On 22 August 1955, after examining many witnesses and documents, the royal commissioners made their final report.

They found that for many years the Government of the Soviet Union had been *using its Embassy at Canberra as a cloak under which to control and operate espionage organizations in Australia.*

They described those organizations.

They named the five Russian M.V.D. Residents from 1943 to 1954, and also twelve of their principal Russian M.V.D. collaborators in Australia.

They described the methods and purposes of the M.V.D. activities, and their techniques of approaching and influencing Australian 'prospects'. They went on to make what amounted to a warning to the Australian people by saying:

The evidence clearly shows that it was only amongst Communists (in which term we include Communist sympathizers) that the M.V.D. could expect to find in Australia willing helpers. The only Australians who, so far as the evidence shows, knowingly assisted Soviet espionage, directly or indirectly, were Communists.

We believe that the Soviet deliberately refrained from using the Australian Communist Party, as a party, for espionage purposes lest exposure should lead to its serious political embarrassment and, possibly, to its outlawry.

Without Communism Soviet espionage could have no hope of success in this country, and the existence here of Communists who were and are willing to act to the prejudice of Australia was the fundamental cause of the formation of our Security Service and necessitates its retention in its present role as a 'Fourth Service', essential to the security and defence of Australia.

They reported that their inquiry disclosed no trace of any significant leakage of information from the Department of External Affairs since 1949 (when ASIO was established), though, as they reported, it was *evident from the Moscow letters that penetration of that department remained throughout a principal aim of the M.V.D.*

These were, of course, disclosures and findings of the highest value to those countering espionage, not only in Australia but elsewhere. They would have remained unknown to the Australian Parliament and people but for this defection of the Petrovs and the appointment and labour of the royal commission.

The whole process was therefore abundantly justified. But Dr Evatt had claimed in Parliament that the appointment of a royal commission was, in effect, a bogus stunt and a waste of public money, since no prosecutions were recommended!

The commissioners dealt with this matter quite clearly. In Chapter 20 of their report they examined the legal position, in clear terms which deserve special quotation. Having found that no Australian *organization* had been implicated, since the Australian Communist Party as an organization had taken care to keep clear, though leading Australian Communists had been active, they proceeded to examine the legal positions of individual persons. They therefore considered 'whether any persons have communicated information or documents to any Soviet agent' either 'unlawfully' or 'to the prejudice or possible prejudice of the security or defence of Australia', and went on:

The pattern of secrecy followed by the M.V.D. is such that seldom is a communication made directly to a known Soviet agent. The communication is usually made to a person who appears not to be a Soviet agent but who in fact is a conduit of the information to the Soviet.

Whether or not an act is unlawful is a matter to be determined by reference to the substantive law. Whether an act alleged to be unlawful can be proved in a prosecution in a court of law is an entirely different question, the solution of which depends upon the law of evidence.

As we have pointed out earlier, *the technical rules of the law of evidence do not apply in an investigative inquiry such as ours*, with the result that all relevant material is admissible before us, and it is our duty to consider it, *although much of it would be inadmissible upon a prosecution.*

Particularly is this so because Section 14 (1) of the Royal Commission on Espionage Act 1954 requires a witness to answer questions even though the answers may incriminate him, but Section 14 (2) provides generally that *the answers cannot be used in any civil or criminal proceedings against him. Accordingly, even a clear confession by a person before us that he had done acts which amounted to a criminal offence would be inadmissible in a prosecution of him for that offence.*

It is thus apparent that we might conclude upon material before us that a particular person has, in fact, committed an offence, although it would be impossible to produce in a court of law admissible evidence to convict him.

They therefore, in their general conclusions, said:

In Chapter 20 we have dealt with the law in Australia relevant to the matters set out in the Letters Patent. The substantive law is such that, when considered in conjunction with the technical legal rules governing the admissibility of evidence in courts of law, it would appear that prosecution of none of the persons whose acts we have considered in our Report would be warranted.

The Debate on the Final Report

And so it might have ended; but the report had to be tabled in Parliament and, later on, debated. It was tabled on 14 September 1955, a year after the interim report. On 19 October Dr Evatt opened a debate upon it. He spoke for two hours. He repeated his political charges against me and others with considerable fire, though he could get no comfort from the report. He then decided to concentrate on the Moscow letters and other documents, the authenticity of which the judges had clearly and conclusively established.

All of a sudden, he produced the most sensational and fantastic statement most of us had ever heard.

I communicated with His Excellency the Foreign Minister of the Soviet Union. I pointed out that most of the Russian-language documents in the Petrov case were said to be communications from the M.V.D., Moscow, to Petrov, M.V.D. Resident in Australia. I pointed out that the Soviet Government or its officers were undoubtedly in a position to reveal the truth as to the genuineness of the Petrov documents.

I duly received a reply, sent on behalf of the Minister of Foreign Affairs of the Union of Soviet Socialist Republics, Mr Molotov.

[Honourable members interjecting.]

Dr Evatt—Honourable members may laugh, but they have to face some facts tonight. They will not put me off by their organized opposition. They have to listen to this because this is the truth of the affair. The letter to which I have referred informed me that the documents given to the Australian authorities by Petrov 'can only be, as it had been made clear at that time and as it was confirmed later, falsifications fabricated on the instructions of persons interested in the deterioration of the Soviet–Australian relations and in discrediting their political opponents'.

I attach grave importance to this letter which shows clearly that the Soviet Government denies the authenticity of the Petrov documents.

It was a dramatic occasion. Great gusts of laughter came from both sides of the House. What an absurdity this was; to ask Molotov, who had none of the exhibits before him, to pronounce on their authenticity was too ludicrous for words. One could almost hear members saying to themselves, 'What the devil did he expect Molotov to do? Why is Molotov's inevitable denial, couched in the usual Communist jargon, to be preferred to that of the judges, who had seen and read all the exhibits, had had them translated by one of the world's great interpreters, and had

186

examined a mass of evidence about them? The whole thing is an insult to our common sense!'

So the derisive laughter rolled on. The obvious reactions of members of the Opposition themselves boded ill for Evatt's future as their leader.

(The absurdity of this appeal is increased when it is recalled that in 1947–8 the Soviet Union had tried the experiment of combining the major Soviet espionage agencies, those of the armed services and the Foreign administration, into a single body, *of which the first head was Molotov!*)

But, although flushed with anger, Evatt was not to be deterred; persistency had always been a notable characteristic of his advocacy, whether legal or political.

So he went on to propose solemnly that an 'International Commission should be established by agreement with the Union of Soviet Socialist Republics to settle the dispute once and for all'. The Soviet Union, he said, 'was not represented at the hearing'. This was a strange complaint, since they had never applied for leave to appear, but had, on the contrary, closed their Canberra Embassy, removed their Ambassador, driven our Australian diplomats out of Moscow, and washed their hands of the whole inquiry. Yet one had only to read what Dr Evatt himself had had to say both before the Judges and outside to realize that the Soviet's presumed views were not entirely neglected.

But Dr Evatt had his revenge, in a parliamentary sense, on his merry-making fellow members. For the better part of two hours he did two things. He repeated what he had said back in August of 1954 about the circumstances of the Petrov defection, about the activities of the security service, about the payment of £5,000, with great vehemence. He concluded that phase of his speech by repeating his belief that the Petrov case would outrank in history the famous Zinoviev letter in England thirty years earlier.

At great length, and with much citation of reported cases. he asserted that the three judges neither understood nor applied the laws of evidence receivable by a royal commission.

Turning from me reluctantly, he dealt with a previous statement by the then Minister for External Affairs (Mr R. G. Casey, later to be Lord Casey and Governor-General of Australia) and convicted him of 'bluster' and 'evasion'. Leaving Mr Casey, he returned to the royal commission. Words and phrases like 'deliberate frame-up of the worst description', 'manufactured and fabricated', ornamented his speech. From the point of view of members present, his speech was not easy to follow. He appeared to speak from notes written on a vast quantity of scraps of paper. These he picked up and discarded at a great rate, so that his vehement words appeared to issue from a veritable snowstorm of papers.

He went to pains to clear the names of several individuals who had already been cleared by the royal commission, and then turned to a long and detailed examination of the documents and their authorship. Why he did this I did not know, for the judges had spent weeks and weeks on this examination, assisted by sworn evidence, and with long judicial experience of assessing the credibility of the many witnesses. His end conclusion was that 'there is a grievous doubt about the documents. The Soviet Government says that they are not authentic.' He seemed to think, and in fact actually said, that the House should itself investigate the documents and try the issues which had been raised before the commission concerning handwriting. In short, there should be a rehearing of the case by Parliament itself. How many weeks or months of Parliament's time this task would occupy may be imagined. The proposal was so absurd as to defeat itself.

He then went on to endeavour to prove, *à propos* of the amount of the £5,000 payment which the judges had found was properly made to Petrov, that Petrov was a comparatively poorly paid officer. He had been so advised by an anonymous economist! He said nothing about Mrs Petrov, who drew her own salary, or about the house which had been provided for them and which they had inevitably lost. All of these things were properly in the mind of Petrov, and combined to make a single payment of £5,000 extremely modest.

Towards the end of what must have been an exhausting speech, his logical faculties broke down. One self-contradictory paragraph will demonstrate this:

This M.V.D. organization, or whatever it is called, is supposed to be ruthless, centralized and efficient. Over and over again it gave instructions to Petrov. *There is no dearth of instructions in these documents.* Let us assume for a moment that there is no doubt about their authenticity. It is very difficult to find any case where instructions given to Petrov were carried out. He is told to do something. He simply treats the instruction as though he had never received it, and I think that is the answer. He did not carry out any instructions *because there were no instructions to carry out.*

After two members had spoken, the debate was adjourned until 25 October. That evening, I rose to make my concluding speech. Normally, a fairly brief speech would have sufficed. But Evatt had, in spite of his experience before the judges, and in spite of their findings in both of their reports, decided to make his last desperate throw, and had sprinkled his charges with recklessness and violence, including charges against me which, if they were only partly justified, would have unfitted me for the high office of Prime Minister or, indeed, for public life.

So I decided that I must dispose of the charges once and for all without any mercy for the man who had made them. I began by reminding the House that it had, with approval from both sides of the house, referred the Petrov disclosures to a royal commission, which had reported on them; and that Dr Evatt had now indulged himself in the luxury of being the advocate in Parliament of causes which he had unsuccessfully advocated before the judges.

I then referred in detail to the charges he had made in his long speech just concluded. For clarity, I will deal with them *seriatim.* I beg the reader not to be deterred by this apparent formality, which I design merely to reduce to order the most astonishing and irresponsible and confused outpouring of abuse which I ever heard. I quote from my speech:

Against the judges he makes the charge that they were incompetent, that they acted without proper evidence, that they culpably failed to discover a great conspiracy, and that they have, in the result, made a false report.

Against the Australian Security Intelligence Organization, which I shall refer to as the security service—the service set up by the late Mr Chifley in 1949 after there had been a serious leakage from the Department of External Affairs between 1945 and 1948—the Leader of the Opposition unleashes a volume of hatred which I have never seen surpassed. He concentrates his venom upon Brigadier Spry, the head of that service, but, through him, he charges the service with being corrupt, oppressive, conspiratorial and actuated by party political motives. He even goes so far as to say, as I remind honourable members, that for people like Brigadier Spry, peace is a dangerous word—the very words used by the right honourable gentleman were 'peace is a dangerous word'—a strange allegation to be made against a man who has been decorated in the service of his country, and who was wounded on the Kokoda trail.

Against Mr Victor Windeyer, Queen's Counsel, who appeared to assist the royal commission, he makes the charge—which would be damaging if it came from any other quarter—that he lent himself to a conspiracy with me and with others, designed to inflict damage upon the Australian Labour Party when an election was pending, and that he did this by accepting instructions from me, and even phraseology which I am alleged to have submitted to him.

Against myself, as Prime Minister of the country, he makes a bewildering variety of charges. First, he says that I 'saved up' the Petrov matter for election purposes until April 1954, though, as he alleges, I knew all about it as far back as 1953. His witness on this matter is a book published in the name of one Bialoguski, Bialoguski being, on his own view, a man of no credit, except when he speaks against me. Second, he says that I suppressed public knowledge of the payment of five thousand pounds to Petrov until after polling-day. Third, he says that I encouraged or directed Mr Windeyer to exaggerate and deceive in his opening address and, if I understood his speech—I do not undertake to guarantee that I did—that I drafted some of Mr Windeyer's opening speech. Fourth, he says that I grossly betrayed my trust by giving wide publicity to allegations without first finding evidence in support of them. Fifth, he says, with a singular and

190

imaginative effort, that I conspired against Madame Ollier, 'spirited her out of the country'—his very words—and had her held incommunicado—a beautiful phrase—so that the investigation of episodes concerning her could be unfairly conducted. There may be other charges against me, the chief of which is that I am Prime Minister, but I have not been able either to isolate or define them.

But he had not devoted the whole of his speech to attack. He also defended certain people, who had been referred to in the reports. He defended one Dr Burton, who had been head of the External Affairs department when Evatt was Minister, and against whom the judges had made no adverse finding at all!

He defended one Sharkey, a leading Australian Communist, against the well-proved charge that he received from Moscow $25,000 as some recompense for the costs incurred in his campaign, conducted in the closest collaboration with the Leader of the Opposition, against the Communist Party Dissolution Act. As I do not think that a single member of the Opposition doubted that Sharkey had received this money, this item of defence did not advance Evatt's cause one jot.

He then proceeded to defend one Clayton, who was prominent under his code-name in the Moscow papers, and who had been found by the judges, on the clearest possible evidence, to be the chief member of the Communist spy ring in Australia!

And, most remarkably of all, he had prayed in aid, as his chief and indeed only witness, the remote but unheard and un-cross-examined M. Molotov.

At this stage of my speech I paused to say:

What I have already said will, without any verbal decorations, satisfy all sane and sensible people that *the right honourable gentleman, suffering from persecution delusions, is introducing us into a world of sheer fantasy*.

I then went on to speak of the character and attainments of the judges. I added a few words about the other accused, Mr Victor Windeyer, Q.C., who had been leading counsel assisting the royal commission:

191

. . . who was, quite properly, so convinced that he must be free of any influence that, from first to last, with the exceptions that I will refer to, he said he did not wish to be instructed—I use the word in its technical sense—by the Commonwealth Law Department as counsel are normally instructed by solicitors. Who is Mr Windeyer? He is a lawyer, a former distinguished lecturer in law, and a great soldier; a major-general, a military Commander of the British Empire, the holder of a Distinguished Service Order and bar, and three times mentioned in dispatches; a veteran of Tobruk, of Alamein, of the capture of Finschhafen; for some years from 1950 the citizen forces member of the Military Board. Any New South Wales lawyer must know that the name of Windeyer, like the name of Owen, represents all that is best in New South Wales legal tradition.

The head of ASIO, Brigadier Spry, I have already described, though I shall later on point out the vital fact, utterly discreditable to his attacker, that a blind, bigoted, extravagant, and unfounded attack upon the security service of the nation was probably the most effective way to give aid and comfort to our enemies, actual or potential.

As for myself, I concluded my description of the persons in the drama by saying a few words about myself as perhaps the principal accused.

I am not here to defend myself, but I must permit myself to say that I have, for over a quarter of a century, served the Australian people in the very heat of political controversy, that for almost fifteen years those who are closest to me have unanimously maintained me as their leader, and that I am, therefore, not entirely unknown, either in character or act, to the Australian people. Yet, according to the right honourable gentleman, I, last year or the year before, made myself a party to a swindle and was able to secure the collaboration of those distinguished men whom I have named in order to make that swindle effective.

I pointed out that the judges found favourably to the Petrovs as honest witnesses after Petrov had been in the witness-box on thirty-seven days for approximately seventy-four hours in all,

192

and after Mrs Petrov had been in the witness-box for approximately thirty hours.

I now turn briefly to the case of Madame Ollier, about whom evidence had been given. The judges had disposed of this quite definitely. They found that the French Ambassador had sent the lady to Noumea, to get her away from access to secret communications and ciphers, and away from any dangerous associations she might have formed. She was interrogated in Noumea, arrested there and sent to France for further interrogation.

The evidence about Madame Ollier was, briefly, that one of the Moscow letters had given directions that she should be approached as a possible source of cipher and secret information, that one of the Soviet men had arranged meetings with her at Canberra and Cooma and that he had presented her with a watch costing thirty-five pounds. The judges found that the results of these manœuvres were 'almost negligible'. In France, Madame Ollier admitted these contacts and the receipt of the watch, but as she had been imprisoned for two months, the matter was dropped. Her only significance in this story is that in her case the Soviet methods of espionage were clearly traced from Moscow to Canberra to Cooma.

I concluded my speech by making two statements, one about Evatt's outrageous attack upon the security service and the other about the international consequences of the Petrov defection, which I think I should set out in full.

The business of counter-espionage is a business which requires great character, great courage, great skill and considerable freedom of action. Honest Australians will be more easy in their minds to learn from this royal commission report that our security organization has been so effective that in the last six years practically no information has been secured by Communist agencies. All this is so elementary and so clear that one is at a loss to understand why the Leader of the Opposition, the alternative Prime Minister of this country, should be at such pains to destroy the reputation and the efficacy of the security service. On behalf of that service, I reject and condemn the allegations that have been made that it has acted in a political way. The men who constitute it are patriotic, skilful, and industrious men. *It will be a poor thing indeed if men in such a service are given to understand that if their investigations are not agreeable to the Leader of the Opposition, they may expect to encounter dismissal and infamy if a change of government occurs.* . . .

I do not hesitate to say that this is one of the right honourable gentleman's principal purposes in this matter, He has not concealed his violent hatred of that service or of the people that make it up. It will be, I hope and repeat, abundantly clear that, should he become the head of the Government of this country, the present senior personnel of that service will be dismissed, and the possibility of getting adequate recruits utterly and perhaps permanently destroyed. This is a dreadful manœuvre.

My other passage provides a concise statement of the results which had followed the defection of the Petrovs.

The information provided by the Petrovs, only some of which came within the scope of the royal commission, has proved invaluable to other democratic countries. *Petrov himself, as we know from the United Kingdom authorities, is the most senior defector from any of the Soviet intelligence services since 1937. As such, he has been able to supply more information than any previous single defector regarding the espionage activities of the M.V.D.* Both of the Petrovs have, in fact, since April 1954, been continuously supplying information, some affecting the security of Australia and, possibly more importantly, some providing general intelligence of assistance to the Western democracies, which intelligence has not been, and of course cannot be, published.

I want to inform the House that communications with the United Kingdom security authorities show specifically that the information obtained from Petrov is in many cases confirmed by information held abroad, and, in other cases, has enabled a material addition to be made to their information. *In point of fact, scores and scores of Soviet intelligence operatives working in democratic countries have been identified as a result of the disclosures of the Petrovs.* In addition to all this, they have, of course, supplied invaluable information regarding Soviet intelligence methods and techniques of espionage.

My parting shot, before I sat down, was:

If there is a charge to be made, it is this. The Leader of the Opposition has, from first to last in this matter, for his own purposes, in his own interests and with the enthusiastic support of every Communist in Australia, sought to discredit the judiciary, to subvert the authority of the security organization, to cry down decent and patriotic Australians and to build up the Communist fifth column. I am, therefore, compelled to say that, in the name of all these good and honourable men, in the name of public decency, in the name of the safety of Australia, *the man on trial in this debate is the right honourable gentleman himself*.

Conclusion

The results of the Petrov defections and the royal commission's proceedings and findings may now be summed up.

Inside Australia, Communist methods of espionage had been probed and exposed, all persons with access to secret information had been put on warning of those methods, and the efficiency and integrity of ASIO had been established. These matters alone would have justified the appointment of the royal commission, since many of the facts concerning individuals would never have come to light, and Dr Evatt himself would have remained unaware of the associations or activities of some of his staff.

Further than this, from the point of view of Australia, it meant several things of great importance.

Public officials and Members of Parliament, particularly those handling or having access to confidential information, were alerted to Soviet methods; the cultivation of selected officials; the skilful use of the social meeting and particularly that modern menace to discreet diplomacy, the cocktail party; the spying-out of personal weaknesses; the shrewd use of parliamentary journalists enjoying frequent access to ministers and other politicians. Such methods were of course most important in relation to the Department of External Affairs, where the most valuable secrets might be sought for. After the disclosures before the royal commission, there could be no excuse for carelessness, and every reason for caution.

And above all, Australians, an increasing number of whom were beginning to discount political attacks on Communism and to treat them as theoretical or dogmatic, had presented to them by a non-political and authoritative tribunal the harsh realities of Soviet spying under diplomatic cover and of the activities of their Australian Communist collaborators.

The information produced for the security services of other countries, notably Great Britain, the U.S.A. and Canada, was of outstanding significance. Much of this information was, as I have shown, provided by the Petrovs after their defection, but, I repeat, did not come within the scope of the royal commission since it related to the activities of people outside Australia.

But this valuable information was the consequence of the defections, and cannot be divorced from the Petrov story.

The internal effects of all these disclosures on Australian politics could have been negligible—because both parties had said that they were opposed to Communism, and perhaps some of the strongest opponents were to be found on the Opposition benches—had it not been for the strange performance of the Leader of the Opposition both before the judges and in Parliament. He had, wittingly or unwittingly, cast himself for the role of Communist defender and apologist. This made a grave split in his party inevitable. The consequences of that split were to be a vital element in Australian politics for many years.

In 1953 the Opposition contained a group of members of strong character and deep convictions who rejected Communism on political and moral grounds, and were known as the Anti-Communist Labour Party. They were to walk the political gangplank in due course, and they knew it. But they did not lose their courage nor conceal their beliefs. In 1957 they formed a separate party, the Democratic Labour Party, which, though it now has only two members, and those in the Senate, has had a profound effect on succeeding elections.

The effects of Evatt's strange advocacy were therefore most

damaging to his own party. Be it noted that this damage was not the natural consequence of the Petrov defections or of anything that was known before the 1954 election, but of what happened subsequently.

Evatt had ruined himself as a real political force. His crowning calamity was his strange invocation of Molotov. The laughter in the House when he made his disclosure was sardonic and sustained, and really disposed of Evatt as a potential Prime Minister. For he had revealed, in a single passage, either that he was so hopelessly lacking in balance that any evidence would satisfy him, or that he was so simple that great affairs ought not to be entrusted to his judgment. True, he was still leader of his party at the general election of late 1955, for the Labour Party, radical though it believes itself to be, has a tradition of loyalty to its leaders. But he was no longer a political force. I have refreshed my memory by reading the full text of his policy speech of 9 November 1955, delivered only a few weeks after the debate on the final Petrov report. It reminds me that, in spite of his charges and heat in the debates, he was prudent enough to make no reference to the matter at all.

The public rejection of his charges against me, charges which, had they been believed by the electors, would have ensured my defeat, was eloquent enough. They gave me a larger majority, and thereafter continued to maintain me as their Prime Minister until my voluntary retirement over ten years later.

3

Miscellaneous

19

Looking Forward

Britain

And now, at the age of seventy-five, I claim the old man's privilege of peering into the future and saying a few controversial things about what I think I can see. I start with Britain. Australia still has, and will continue to have, a lively interest in the political and economic future of Great Britain. Will she go into Europe and, if so, how and on what terms? Will she go in for economic reasons, or for political reasons, or for both? The interesting thing about these questions, so easy to put and so hard to answer, is that most advocates of entry appear to make a distinction between the short-range and the long-range considerations which have influenced their minds. That there will be short-range economic disabilities appears to be conceded. Indeed, the White Paper presented to the House of Commons early this year, frankly conceding that exactness of estimate is just not possible, did set out upper and lower limits of the prospective *loss*. A country with fairly chronic balance-of-payments problems would not contemplate such a loss with equanimity, nor would its electors be expected to take comfort from the prospect, unless the postponed, long-range benefits could be confidently expected.

I am, as I said earlier in this book, a firm believer in long-range policies, which, if soundly based, are the essence of statesmanship. But they are frequently unpopular in the short run. Great efforts will be required in the public-relations field if Britain is not to go into the European venture as a heavily divided country.

All three parties in the British Parliament seem to be committed, as parties, to Britain's accession to the Treaty of Rome on terms which have yet to be defined, but which will need to be agreeable to the existing parties. They believe that belonging to an internal free-trade area which would give an enormous home market for British production would have economic advantages outweighing the losses in certain directions that would initially accrue. This is an economic problem and I do not wish to discuss it beyond saying that I hope that they are right. For, once in the Common Market, they cannot get out except by the consent of all parties. I rather gather that though the parties in the House are pro-European, the people outside Parliament are not so sure. This is explained by respected political leaders with whom I have discussed the matter as being not so much a hostile attitude as a doubting one; one which will change as the nature of the Common Market becomes more clearly understood. I can claim no authority when it comes to interpreting the British mind. But I think that there are deep-seated instincts and a sort of patriotic insularity which combine to make the Englishman distrust the idea of subordinating his interests and his political rights to any institution established in Europe, empowered to give him orders but not responsible to him. He may be well versed in the popular art of speaking contemptuously about members of Parliament; but he does not really mean it; for he knows at the back of his mind that just as the electors put members in, so they can throw them out. Britain is the home of responsible government, of the supremacy of Parliament, and of the rule of the law, the law involved being British.

I have friends on all sides of politics in Britain, and they speak to me quite freely about this matter. Some of them have a gleam in the eye when they visualize, on the economic front, a British–European home market about the same size as that of the United States. They resist the notion of Britain outside Europe, with a limited industrial future, becoming less and less significant in world trade and influence. Others are not so confident about the economic consequences of the treaty, but have an equally fiery gleam in the eye when they contemplate the political consequences. As I shall point out later, they are not, for weighty reasons, European Federalists, but they see great need of and ample room for a political association of the Western European nations, including Britain, deeply influenced and perhaps led by Britain, and developing common policies in the fields of foreign affairs and defence.

They recall that Britain, which for many years contributed,

from outside, to a somewhat fragile balance of power on the Continent, has on great occasions paid a great price without having had an effective voice, at the crucial times, in the policies and events which produced or permitted great wars to break out.

They feel deeply that Britain can no longer stand aloof; that she must be in Europe; an effective presence and voice in a European community of nations. They do not disregard the economic factors. On the contrary, they believe that those very factors will be favourably influenced by the political ones.

Now, these are great issues, and will be resolved by the statesmanship of a great country. All I desire to do is to record, quite objectively, some of the consequences of Britain's accession to the Treaty of Rome as I see them. Those consequences may well prove to be acceptable and even desirable. But they will certainly involve great changes in the British world as we have known it; and I think that we should understand them now and not suddenly discover them later on.

Now, confronting this problem, Britain seems to me to have a choice of attitudes.

She might, of course, determine to have no special arrangements with Europe at all, except for those defensive arrangements which exist under NATO. I concede that, although this is a theoretical possibility, the pressure of events and the growing complexity of the international trade and finance would make it unreal.

She might deal with the matter by making ordinary trade or other commercial treaties with some or all of the European powers. Such treaties would produce mutual obligations which would be, in international practice, binding; but they would be limited in their time of operation. I have yet to hear of any trade treaty which was permanent, in the sense that the Treaty of Rome is expressed to be permanent. Another thing about international treaties is that they do not normally throw up institutions which are given an overriding authority over any of the domestic affairs of the contracting parties. It is true that some well-known modern treaties do give rise to institutions: e.g. NATO, SEATO, ANZUS, each of which has a council and a central organization. But in such cases, while international obligations can and do arise, there is no derogation from the normal *domestic* authority of the individual nations concerned. The importance of this consideration was emphasized by the paper issued by the then Lord Chancellor to assist the Parliament at Westminster in its deliberations when he said:

The novel features of the European Treaties lie first in the powers conferred on the Community institutions to issue subordinate instruments which themselves may impose obligations on the Member States or may take effect directly as law within them; and secondly in the powers of those institutions to administer and enforce (subject to the control of the European Court) much of the law deriving from the Treaties and the instruments made under them.

The Lord Chancellor referred to various conventions relating to carriage by air or sea or the regulation of sea fisheries, but his paper appeared to concede that it was a very long and novel step from such treaties to one which creates institutions which may exercise authority directly in relation to the domestic affairs of a State, including economic and financial policy and social provisions.

So I must say that ordinary trade treaties between Britain and European countries would be very far removed from what is now under consideration. There can be no doubt that if Britain became a member of the European Economic community by acceding to the Treaty of Rome, she would be accepting community law, i.e. the whole body of legal rights and obligations deriving from the treaty or its instruments, and to that extent would reduce the authority of her own Parliament, and the scope of her own law.

I shall return to this matter later. But I would first like to put the problem into a Commonwealth setting.

It is true that one must not yearn for the old days that are gone. It must be recognized that the old British Empire was an accident of adventurous seafaring history and in no sense the product of a deliberate conception. It was, as it happens, just one more example of the inductive methods of the British mind; the navigators went and found places, and were followed by the traders, and colonies came into being, and then the idea of an Empire arose as something which embraced them all.

In the present century, the Empire idea, which had achieved a great emotional content, faded as the former colonies one by one achieved a full nationhood of their own. It faded but it did not entirely disappear; most of it took a new form. It became a British Commonwealth which had a structural bond in the fact that it was united by a common allegiance to the Crown, though each member country was recognized as completely autonomous. Further changes then occurred. Republics were admitted to membership; the name was changed to 'the Commonwealth'. Some members retained their allegiance to the throne, but the fashion is increasingly for newer members to become republics. I have exhibited my fears about the future of the Commonwealth in *Afternoon Light*; and I shall not repeat them. But in this chapter I must say that as I look forward to the future, I do not see the disintegration of the new Commonwealth being halted. It is certainly no longer a structure but a loose association of nations who would like to be friendly but have few common principles and, so far as I can judge, no cause on which they are prepared to speak to the world in clear and united tones. Heads of Government in the Commonwealth will, no doubt, continue to meet occasionally for an exchange of views and the ventilation of differences; if its differences are so acute as they were and are in the case of Rhodesia, they might even repeat the error of referring those differences to the United Nations, with the kind of result with which we are distressingly familiar. Looking to the future, I see this new Commonwealth of ours becoming steadily less comprehensible, tending more and more, under the driving influence of many of the newer nations, to duplicate the strange and divisive activities of the United Nations without adding a coherent body of ideas to its deliberations.

But with all these unhappy thoughts in my mind, the result of much practical experience, I have always hoped that at least Great Britain, Australia, New Zealand and Canada would, as all proud subjects of the Queen and bound together in terms of traditions, history and institutions, remain as a solid core of combined and influential opinion in a very disordered world.

Now I have written something earlier in this book about Australia's relationship with New Zealand, a relationship which I am sure will continue to be a source of strength to both of us. Canada is still an old member of the Commonwealth; but I read that the present Prime Minister is publicly contemplating the possibility that, at some future date, Canada may choose to become a republic. The very proposal would no doubt give rise to bitter differences in Canada. But the mere fact of great controversy would tend to weaken the bonds of common allegiance which now hold some of us together. But what of Britain herself, the heart and centre of the Commonwealth? If she accedes to the Treaty of Rome, at least two consequences must arise. One is that she will be joined with the European partners on a basis of internal free trade and a common tariff wall as against the world. This will, of course, spell the end of the Commonwealth preferences which have existed since the celebrated Ottawa Agreement. Those preferences may seem of little importance to Britain today, though I should point out that in my final year of office Australia was Britain's second largest export market, of a sterling value of £300,000,000; and that of the goods which produced that amount, about ninety per cent received preferential treatment in the Australian tariff. Australia herself obtained benefits from the preferential system. More than sixty-five per cent of the Australian exports to Britain received some form of preference and those exports totalled in that year £190,000,000 sterling. But accession to the Treaty of Rome will, when that accession becomes fully operative (I assume there will be some transitional period), inevitably and by force of the treaty itself bring preferences to an end.

I have already said that the judgment on the relative values from the British point of view is a matter for the British Government and Parliament, and that I am not intending to set myself up as an advocate of one view or another. In the case of Australia, the very proposal that Britain should enter the Common Market has accelerated our successful search for other markets and Australia is for those reasons becoming increasingly capable of absorbing shocks; though grave shocks there would be to several Australian

206

primary industries should British entry be unconditional. But these considerations mean that, of necessity, we look less and less to Great Britain as on the economic axis of our thinking.

The other consequence affects the structure of the Commonwealth itself; for if, as I believe and have said, Great Britain foregoes some of her own sovereignty to become a European member of a European organism, she clearly will not be any longer an autonomous country like Australia. She will, of course, still be the principal home of the Crown to which we owe a common allegiance. But the Commonwealth will need to be redefined. I will be told with much good sense that it has gone through many phases of redefinition and that what is called our genius for compromise will absorb this change. But a change, and a very material change, it will unquestionably be.

I do not wish to make too much of a point about this, for I confess that, as one who has lived with and known something of the legalisms of federations, my tendency is to resist anything which seems to be an unnecessary constitutional change. I am undoubtedly more reluctant than are those of more recent generations to remove the ancient landmark.

But I ask permission to offer my view, if only for the historical record.

As time goes on and the politically uniting elements of the Treaty of Rome, in spite of the lessons of modern European history, become more established, it is conceivable, on the basis of other associations of nations we have seen, that it may develop into a European federation. I know that this is warmly denied by my friends in Britain and I firmly believe that they do not desire it. But in every confederation or association of nations with institutions which can give domestic orders to all of its members, history has justified Lord Bryce's famous observation that two forces begin to operate: the centripetal and the centrifugal. There will either be an accumulation of central power and the emergence of a federation on the normal pattern, or there will be pressures to disintegrate and return to the *status quo ante*.

Of course it is clear that should Britain, contrary to current intentions, become a state in a European federation, its sovereignty in the full sense would disappear; for, in a federation, no state is sovereign but merely exercises some sovereignty in a limited field, the sovereignty of the federation as a whole becoming the dominant factor.

But, putting federation and its inevitable legal implications on one side, I now look more closely at the Treaty of Rome itself.

The principles laid down in the treaty, to become in due course binding upon all members, are very significant.

'The establishment of a common customs tariff' and 'a common commercial policy towards third countries' will of course represent a profound change for Britain's independent management of such matters. Special arrangements with Commonwealth countries or with the United States will be ruled out.

In these matters, Britain's present 'autonomy' will become limited.

Free trade, and the abolition of quantitative restrictions between the member states, will of course expose the European market to the duty-free competition of British products; a prospect which the advocates of British accession find most encouraging and of crucial importance. And, having regard to the great British achievements in science and technology, they may well be right. They see in this a powerful inducement to British industry to increase its exertions and improve its efficiency. I hope that this will turn out to be so; but it is clear that the competitive position *in Britain* of European manufacturers, already in many aspects notably efficient, will, with duty-free entry, present the British manufacturer with a great challenge.

A third provision is for 'the abolition, as between member states, of the obstacles to the free movement of persons, services, and capital'.

British control over its own immigration policies, now giving rise to acute and sometimes bitter controversy in England, will therefore be sharply limited, and her present problems may well be intensified. For French and Italian immigration policies would, by the free movement of persons, affect those of Britain.

I have also taken a look at the structural effect of the Treaty of Rome. The executive body would appear to be the Commission. It is at present composed of nine members chosen as the treaty runs for 'their general competence and of indisputable independence'. This is somewhat rhetorical language, but it should be realized that the Commission really is a completely bureaucratic body. It is full-time, it is an appointed body and it is in no sense a 'responsible Government', in the sense in which British countries use that term. Indeed the treaty provides that the members of the Commission shall perform their duties in the general interest of the community with complete independence and 'in the performance of their duties they shall not seek or accept instructions from any Government or other body'. The Commission reaches most of its conclusions by a majority and the orders it issues are binding on the member states. Its duties are to ensure the application of the provisions of the treaty, some of the principal elements of which I have already described. It will be realized that British accession to the Treaty of Rome must, in relation to many affairs which are now British domestic affairs, take these out of the control of the Parliament of Westminster and the ministers responsible to it.

The then Foreign Secretary, Mr George Brown, made an authoritative statement at the Hague which confirms one's impression that there may be more to come. He said:

We recognize that the community is a dynamic organization which has already evolved and will continue to evolve. If it is to be true to the spirit of the treaties which established it, the community's institutions will develop and its activities will extend to wider fields beyond the activities covered by the existing provisions of the treaties. We believe that Europe can emerge as a community expressing its own point of view and exercising influence in world affairs, not only in the commercial and economic but also in the political and defence fields. We shall play our full part in this process.

This view was confirmed by the Lord Chancellor in these words:

If this country became a member of the European communities, it would be accepting community law. By 'community law' is meant the whole body of legal rights and obligations deriving from the treaties or their instruments, whether conferred or imposed on the member states, on individuals or undertakings, or on the community institutions. A substantial body of legislation would be required to enable us to accept the law.

The expression 'to enable us to accept the law' should not be misunderstood. Once a member state becomes bound by the treaty, which is expressed to be concluded for an unlimited period and therefore has permanency, the consent of all the contracting parties being needed for a change, the British Parliament would not appear to have any choice about the matter. It could not amend 'the law' except by consent, and the British legislation incorporating the law in the body of legislation in Britain would not be exercising its own judgment or the judgment of the electors, but would be carrying out its duty to the European community.

The normal function of the judiciary in Britain would also have limitations imposed upon it; because the Treaty of Rome provides for the establishment of a Court of Justice which is to be set up to 'ensure observance of the treaty'. Any member state which considers that another member state has failed to fulfil any of its obligations under the treaty may refer the matter to the Court of Justice. If the Court of Justice finds that the member state has failed to fulfil any of those obligations, such state is compelled to take the measures required for the implementation of the judgment of the court. There is also power to confer on the court full jurisdiction in respect of penalties provided for in regulations. When one considers the wide scope of the treaty and the obligations it imposes on member states, to only a few of which I have referred, it will be seen that the power of this non-British court will be very extensive. For the matters which will be considered before it include the interpretation of the treaty, the validity and interpretations of acts of the institutions of the community, and so on. Indeed, where such a question is raised in a case before a domestic court or tribunal which is normally empowered to give a final decision, such court or tribunal is to refer the matter to the new Court of Justice.

The Court of Justice will be competent to hear cases concerning the fulfilment by member states of the obligations arising under the treaty provision for a European investment bank.

I need not go on, for I am not undertaking the huge task of making a complete analysis of the Treaty of Rome. My only purpose has been to show that there are many important matters affecting the domestic economy and social policies of the British Parliament which would ultimately be removed from its jurisdiction. My only constitutional concern has been to show that the normal concept of sovereignty which is applied to the British Parliament would be qualified in a large number of very important ways.

I concede that I have not made any points which have not been carefully studied by both the Government and the Opposition at Westminster and that they may well regard my observations (if they ever read them) as quite otiose. They may, and no doubt do, conceive accession to the Treaty of Rome as a taking-part in the creation of what is, within limits and certainly not in specific form, a supra-national institution. Many careful thinkers have, over a period of years, looked to the time when acute nationalism will be submerged in supra-national institutions, the very nature of which must be that the old notions of sovereignty must give way or be modified. This is, I think, a splendid ideal which would be revolutionary in its effect. A world full of conflicting national sovereignties would some day come to welcome it as an instrument of peace.

If, in the long run, Britain avoids becoming a constituent state in a European federation but has nevertheless been prepared, for the economic and political reasons which may seem good to her, to accept some loss of her autonomy which stops short of Federation, then some of my observations will turn out to be irrelevant. I fully understand the difficulties in the way of establishing a European Federation with or without Great Britain; for I recall that the great wars of this century have all begun in

Europe and that hostilities which have become deep-seated over centuries are not easily put on one side in order to achieve political union. I point out, however, that it will be agreed that if Australia joined the United States of America as a constituent state (which I don't even concede to be a remote possibility) it would be quite clear that it would cease to be a member of the Commonwealth. It could not become an American state and remain an independent sovereign autonomous member of the Commonwealth. The same thing would, of course, be true if Great Britain became (contrary to our present expectations) a state in a European federation. What we call the Commonwealth would then, of course, become a body without a head and would not survive.

Britain's Particular Relationship to Australia and New Zealand

It has become the vogue for some writers in Australia to refer to me, apparently under the impression that they are using a derogatory expression, as an 'anglophile'. I certainly am, and would be sadly disappointed if I thought that a majority of my fellow citizens were not of the same mind. I love Britain because I love Australia, and like to think that I have done her some service. I cannot go anywhere in Australia without being reminded of our British inheritance; our system of responsible government and Parliamentary institutions, our adherence to the rule of law and, indeed, our systems of law themselves; our traditions of integrity in high places and of incorruptibility in our Civil Service. We derived all these things from Westminster. Our language comes to us from Britain and so does the bulk of our literature. To have no love for a relatively small community in the North Sea which created and handed on these vital matters would be, to my mind, a miserable act of ingratitude. The fact that in Australia we have received all these things, and have made all our own notable contributions to their development, not only fills me with pride but strengthens my affection.

Another term which I think is intended to be used in a derogatory sense is that I am one of 'the Queen's men'. Indeed, there was recently published a book, whose contents are singularly inaccurate, in which I am described as 'Menzies, the last of the Queen's men'. Well, I am sure that I am not the last, by a long chalk. In Australia we are all, by our own law, 'British subjects and Australian citizens'. We are British subjects because we owe our allegiance to the Queen, an allegiance which so far from weakening our independence gives it pride and strength.

But am I in a minority? Is Australia drifting away from Britain? Well, I am prepared to concede two things. The first is that there exists some movement towards a republic. It has rather more support than I would wish to see, but I don't think that it has the stuff of endurance in it. Indeed, the recent magnificently human and successful Royal Visit to Australia has dealt it a heavy body blow. It has, I believe, some support among a few 'intellectuals', and it *may* enjoy some favour among the many thousands of European immigrants who have become Australian citizens (and, by naturalization, British subjects) since the war. I realize, of course, that European immigrants, coming to Australia and settling here, cannot be expected to share, in one generation or two, the inherited instincts of those of British stock. But when we think of Australia's great post-war immigration flow, splendidly initiated by Arthur Calwell in the post-war Labour Government, and carried on in growing volume by my own administration, we must also realize that throughout the whole period more immigrants came to us from Britain than from all of the European sources, and that the republican idea has, so far as I can learn, not made much progress in Britain. I do not propose to repeat my arguments against republicanism in my country, for I fully set out my views in an earlier book. I merely say that until the so-called republicans make clear to the rest of us what kind of republic and what system of government they aim at, we can, I think, ignore them.

But, at the same time, there seems to be a perceptible lessening of the old instinctive feelings about our relationship with Great Britain. There are, no doubt, some identifiable reasons for this. Britain though still a considerable naval power, is no longer the mistress of the seas; and her old sea-power, something which helped to keep the world's peace, including the peace of Australia, has been much diminished. The policy of the Wilson Government to reduce British military commitments east of Suez has, doubtless, intensified our feeling that Britain can no longer be a large factor in our forward defence. But I doubt whether this is a determining factor. We Australians are acutely conscious of the fact that Britain has her economic problems and is inevitably concerned with her balance-of-payments problems; that her international economic problems are not reasonably to be attributed to any default on her part but, on the contrary, to her enormous sacrifices made in two great wars for the protection of the free world. It is, indeed, one of the ironies of modern history that Britain, first into the field on both occasions, has paid far more for victory than quite a few of the countries to whose liberation from the enemy she made such remarkable contributions. As I believe that most Australians realize these crucial facts, I am not inclined to think that we are over-critical about some of the consequences in our part of the world. We regret those consequences; we regret that there should not be a powerful presence on the part of Great Britain in South-East Asia and the South-West Pacific. We would, of course, be happy to see some such presence maintained, and now, in the light of the recent British election, have a revival of hope. But to a reasonable man there is nothing in these events which would induce him to convert his friendship for Britain into either cynicism or hostility.

I think that the real reasons for this drift to which I have referred are mostly subconscious. More and more Australia is feeling her own surge of power. The Commonwealth, as a structure, no longer looms so large in our minds. We are passing through an era of the most astonishing development, particularly of our mineral resources. Our population is growing with great rapidity. We feel that we are masters in our own house, can make our own arrangements with our neighbours and our friends, can expand our trade and make our own contributions to international conferences and agreements. We are, therefore, inevitably concentrating upon our own affairs and finding it a full-time job. Under these circumstances it is easy either to forget our old associations or to give them too little weight in our thinking. But this is a state of mind that cannot last. In the long evenings when the day's work is done and the television programmes unusually boring, we will think about some of these matters more and more.

Now, as an 'anglophile', let me propound a few questions. Are we concerned with Britain's prosperity as well as our own? Clearly we must be, for though Britain is no longer the greatest power in the world, she is still a great asset to the world; in science, in diplomatic experience, in administrative skills, in wisdom. If Britain were weakened to a point where she became a sick and ineffective country the loss would be, in a direct sense, hers; but it would be ours also because from the Australian point of view, not only in trade and commerce but in the more impalpable things of the mind and the spirit, a strong Britain is essential.

This hope that I express would be somewhat dimmed if I thought that there was any truth in the view I occasionally hear expressed in England that we Australians are going American; not by some deliberate constitutional change, which the United States would no more wish than we would, but by yielding to a sort of lateral thrust which is affecting our habits of mind and, to an extent, our very speech. That our speech is nowadays influenced by America is, no doubt, quite true. The influence of the films and of television is very great, particularly among the young. Another example is to be found in the sporting Press, whose jargon yearly comes closer to that of the American sporting Press, though it has not yet reached the same strange heights or depths. But these are superficial things, regrettable as a purist may find them. Another and more important factor is that we have a large influx (to an extent temporary) of American businessmen, engineers, production experts and the like. They are, as a rule, not only valuable contributors to our progress but well received by the people they encounter. The Australian–American Association in Australia is large, active and flourishing. These are all good things, and they will no doubt leave their mark upon traditional Australian habits of thought and work. But they do not in any sense mean that we are moving away from Britain. There is, as I have frequently said in Australia, no conflict between our own independent pride and aspirations, our fidelity to Britain (from which, after all, the ancestors of most of us came), and our warm friendship with the United States and our appreciation of the contribution which that country has shown itself willing to make to our own advancement and security.

In the strengthening of British–Australian relations High Commissioners have a great part to play. In my time men like Lord Carrington, Sir William Oliver, and Sir Charles Johnston built up the British 'image' in Australia. In London former colleagues like Sir Eric Harrison, whose strong convictions admitted of no ambiguities, and now Sir Alexander Downer, who shares my deep affection for both countries and is singularly capable of expressing his own, have kept the flag flying.

But much more is needed. I am increasingly conscious of the fact that elements which were once taken for granted must now be identified and promoted. I hope to see, before I die, a flourishing British–Australian Association both in Britain and Australia. For I remind my fellow-countrymen that more good things in life are lost by indifference than ever were lost by active hostility.

Nationalism

When the United Nations Organization was being established, there was a widespread belief that we were making a notable experiment in a direction which favoured an internationalism which would reduce the occasions of conflict in the world. After the war it was thought that nations would, seeing the advantages of international action, become less nationalistic; less self-contained; more conscious of the existence and interest of other countries. I confess that I have seen no symptoms that this result has been achieved. On the contrary, I would think that the tendency all around the world and particularly in the newer countries is to intensify nationalism. We are frequently told that strange and revolutionary events in many of the new countries are merely evidence of a struggle for nationalism. Yet there are some paradoxes. These new nations get their national existence acknowledged by membership of the United Nations, but when they attend the General Assembly they fall readily into groups or blocs designed to impose their ideas upon other nations. They are much more concerned, vocally at any rate, to criticize and condemn other nations than to look at themselves and ask how they can make themselves fit into international affairs in a constructive way.

Just as the Commonwealth has begun to fall to pieces because many of the new members, feeling and expressing no obligation to the Commonwealth, devote their energies to telling other members how they ought to run their own affairs, so in the United Nations an exactly similar process goes on. If that process continues, the United Nations will disintegrate for reasons exactly similar to those which we have observed in action in the Commonwealth itself.

Australia, the United States and South-East Asia

Australians are so close to the countries of South-East Asia and its adjoining islands, so much exposed to attack should the Communists get control of the area, and yet with so much to gain by friendly intercourse and the forwarding of our common interests should the Communists be held back, that any forward look in the Pacific must be, for me, a northerly one.

I see, moving down from the North—Peking to Hanoi, to the war-torn jungles of Laos and South Vietnam and Cambodia—Chinese Communism with its undiluted Marx–Engels doctrines and practices. No smooth talk about 'peaceful co-existence'—but Mao's famous and brutal phrase, 'Political power grows out of the barrel of a gun.'

I know that there are those who say that Communism in Asia does not possess a monolithic character or common purpose, and that the 'Domino Theory' is wrong. They say that a take-over in South Vietnam should have no terrors for countries like Australia. But one of the consequences of the inevitable pragmatisms of politics is that statesmen cannot afford the luxury of accepting theories as facts.

I subscribe to the Domino Theory in exactly the same way as

that temporarily obscured but very great U.S.A. Secretary of State Dean Rusk subscribed to it. For the aggressiveness of Chinese Communism has been demonstrated in action. Its active presence in South Vietnam is clear and damaging. Its penetration of Laos is notorious. It has begun to operate its usual apparatus in Thailand and Cambodia, with a National Liberation Front already active. On the precedent of South Vietnam, the blessed word *liberation* means liberation from non-Communist government, and subordination to Communist control from Hanoi.

I have no doubt that if the Vietnam war ends with some compromise which denies South Vietnam a real and protected independence, Laos, Cambodia, Thailand, Malaysia, Singapore and Indonesia will be vulnerable. If it turns out that SEATO has failed to protect South Vietnam, these other countries will have at best a precarious tenure of non-Communist self-government.

Clearly, vital significance will attach to the policies of the United States, where the defeatist and substantially isolationist views of well-publicized Democratic dissenters and critics are enjoying some success. They are even demanding that President Nixon should announce a 'timetable' of phased withdrawal of American troops! Such an announcement could help only the enemy; but this does not appear to disturb those whose chief desire appears to be to have peace at any price, and to weaken the American will to fight.

As I look forward, my first feeling is one of grave anxiety. In common with the majority of my fellow Australians, I am disturbed by these recent symptoms. The United States is now the greatest power in the world. In earlier years it was clearly isolationist, and could afford to announce the Monroe Doctrine and its detachment from the problems of the old world in Europe or the new world in the East, because Britain was the greatest naval power; while the long-range aircraft, the inter-continental ballistic missile, and the nuclear and thermonuclear weapons had not been devised. The First World War snatched her out of her isolationism, but her abstention from membership of the League of Nations turned her thoughts once more to home. Her crucial participation in the Second World War, and her magnificent and generous policy thereafter, changed the picture. Power always connotes responsibility in a civilized country. We had all seen the dreadful Hitlerian tragedy of power without responsibility, and have no desire to see it again. It was the great American sense of responsibility which took her into the Marshall plan, into the Berlin airlift, into NATO, into Korea, into SEATO and Vietnam, into ANZUS.

It was inevitable that questioning voices should be raised in the United States, for the burdens lie heavy on the American people. 'Why should we be the world's gendarme?' But, as I took the liberty of pointing out in a recent lecture at the University of Texas, there is a vital middle course between being a defender everywhere abroad, and a defender nowhere except at home. I have always believed and said no more than this, that great powers have great responsibilities, and that the greatest has the greatest. We in Australia are by no means a great power; but we are sufficiently rich and strong to have responsibilities to our neighbours and discharge them, as we do in relation to Papua and New Guinea, the Colombo Plan, SEATO and its consequences, and in various other ways.

The truth is that a great power cannot make itself available at call anywhere, as if it were a fire-brigade. It must select tasks commensurate with its resources and the willingness of its people. As a world power, it will know the sources of world danger to the freedom of which it is an exemplar and defender. America's policy and actions in relation to Western Europe are a splendid example; but they are reasonably predicated upon Western European powers, including Britain, taking their fair share of the burden. It is not called upon to intervene in every local conflict, or, for that matter, in every limited war. But it intervened in Vietnam because, more clearly than any of the European powers, it saw the defence of South Vietnam as a defence against the aggression of Communist China, an aggression which is backed by a vast population and a developing technology, including nuclear capacity, and which, if unrestrained, could threaten the peace and security of the whole world.

219

Looking to the future, I cannot see the United States going isolationist; withdrawing its overseas support, and leaving the rest of the world to took after itself. From a moral point of view, such a policy would be repellent to respectable and respected American opinion. From a hard-bitten, practical point of view, it would, in the long run, gravely damage the United States.

I expect President Nixon's announced policy, not of abandonment of all overseas commitments but of selectivity in the choice of commitments, to prevail. From Australia's point of view, his clear affirmation of existing treaties such as ANZUS is of vital importance.

But I remind myself that ANZUS with South-East Asia outside of Communist control is one thing; but that ANZUS with a Communist South-East Asia would be another. The same treaty, of course; but the practical problems quite different.

My final observation is that, given a satisfactory conclusion to the Vietnam war, Australia will be more and more occupied with the great tasks of establishing our relations with these countries on a basis of friendship and co-operation; with an increasing supply of technical assistance and financial and economic aid being provided by Australia.

For we should see these nations, protected against aggression, not only as a *cordon sanitaire* between us and the potential enemy, but as a source of economic strength, making an important contribution to the world, and providing a good neighbourhood for them and for ourselves.

Australia and Papua–New Guinea

There is a current political controversy in Australia about how soon, and on what terms, the Australian Territory of Papua and our Trust Territory of New Guinea, which are jointly administered, should be given completely political independence.

For the bulk of the time during which I was Prime Minister, the responsible Minister for these territories was Paul Hasluck, now Governor-General of Australia. His policy, supported by us, was to develop, in that area of many separate tribes and languages, natural industries, education and health services, transport facilities, and, progressively, institutions of local government. Later on, he moved to participation by the indigenous peoples in the central legislative and executive field. He constantly and successfully worked for bigger and better Australian financial subventions.

Hasty viewers of, or commentators on, the Papua–New Guinea scene can have little conception of the complexity of the tasks which confronted Hasluck, and of the significance of what he achieved. It is not within my self-appointed task to go into details; but I wish to go on record as saying that the historically recognized achievements of the famous Murray's colonial achievements under the government of Britain, great as they were, were no more significant, and as I think less significant, than what was done by Paul Hasluck in the long years during which I held him to this great task; a task at once thankless and rewarding. Whatever comes or goes in the future, he has a great place in Papua–New Guinea history.

Their people are much more fit for self-government than when Hasluck began. The ultimate granting of political independence was always our objective. Whether the time is ripe should be a matter for their own decision, and not a matter for Canberra alone. We should not prematurely wash our hands of responsibility for the government of the territories, and run the risk of another Congo. On the other hand, we should not delay action too long, so that when self-government comes it arrives in an atmosphere of resentment and hostility. In other words, 'much too soon' would provoke disaster; 'a little too soon' would be preferable to 'a little too late'.

That these territories will achieve independence, I have no doubt. That they will, after political independence, need large economic and financial aid from Australia is inevitable. That they will get it is certain. They will not become a State in the Australian Federation; the difficulties so created would, in my opinion, be politically insuperable.

But I believe that they will remain our friends, growing in prosperity and living standards in what, as I have said, I hope will be a peaceful and co-operative South-East Asian neighbourhood.

20

A Literary Encounter

An old friend used to say to me, 'If you recall one good story about a man, write it down. His biographer will thank you. For one good story will sometimes tell you more about a man than a long analysis.'

It is because I believe this to be true that I am now, while my memory is clear, recording something of a famous literary figure, now dead, whom I had the good fortune to meet.

My narrative concerns two notable Scotsmen who lived in England. One of them was William Shepherd Morrison, who ended his life as Lord Dunrossil, Governor-General of Australia, and the other the famous dramatist J. M. Barrie.

I knew Morrison very well. All his friends called him 'Shakes', but his name was William Shepherd Morrison. A lot of people thought his name was William Shakespeare Morrison, but that was only because he was fond of declaiming Shakespeare when he was a young man. He was born in the Hebrides. He had a great rangy height, a Highland, swarthy face, and a lovely shock of hair which was quite black when I first knew it. He had a lovely accent, a beautiful burr on the tongue, great eloquence and superb wit. He was prominent in Parliament. He was really one of the most attractive men whom I saw many years ago in the whole of England and I wrongly thought that he might very well some day become Prime Minister.

Thirty-four years ago I went down to put in a weekend with him in the Cotswold country, in a little place called Withington on the Coln, where he had a stone house which was part of an old monastic institution. And he said to me on, I think, the Saturday, 'I would like you to come over with me to Stanway Hall in the West Country, to meet J. M. Barrie.' Well, of course, this was like Paradise or the prospect of Paradise for me, and so off we went. Stanway Hall has a lovely Inigo Jones gateway, and was the home of the famous Cynthia Asquith. J. M. Barrie was her house guest.

On the way across, 'Shakes' said to me, 'Well, I want to warn you that J.M., though he is an old friend of mine, is a difficult man. If he likes you, he may say a few words to you. If he doesn't like you, he will be as silent as the tomb.' This was a rather threatening prospect; but my ambition to meet Barrie and to have even a one-sided conversation with him was of course very great.

And so we arrived. It was a grey sort of day. We arrived just as the members of the household were about to have tea. It was all set up in the dining-room at a big table. After being presented to our hostess, I found myself placed next to the great J. M. Barrie himself. This was a good start; but after the start, everything went wrong. I did my best to be conversational and intelligent and, within my natural limitations, I did my best. But the old man didn't even grunt at me. He just remained completely silent; and, remembering what Shakes had said to me, I thought, Well, this is the end of it. This great expedition will be one of the great failures of my life.

A little later, when the tea had been dispatched, the old man got up, went to a side-table and began to shuffle himself into a thick overcoat. Cynthia Asquith said to him, 'J.M., what on earth are you doing?' He said, 'I am going out into the garden with Mingies'—that being the Scots pronunciation of my name. From my point of view, it was as if the sun had burst through the clouds. I hopped up very quickly and we went out into the grounds.

There was a little cricket field there. Barrie was a great lover of cricket. All the Australian cricketers who went to England for a long time knew him. He leaned against the veranda post of a little pavilion, and spoke affectionately about Don Bradman and other famous Australian cricketers. He was even kind enough to repeat to me a famous remark that he had made to them. 'I was a slow bowler myself. I was so slow that if I didn't like the ball after I delivered it, I could run after it and take it back.'

Anyhow, he was delightful. We went down to the big barn where a number of his plays had had their first performance when

223

he was trying them out. And we walked around discussing this and that and, of course, I got on to the subject of speech-making. Not being a dramatist or novelist myself, I had to get on to the home ground, so to speak. It was a good opportunity to do so because, in my opinion, J. M. Barrie's rectorial address at St Andrews University, the famous address on 'Courage', is one of the very great speeches in the English language.

I took the opportunity of asking him how he went about preparing and making that speech. Had he written it or did he use impromptu language and have it recorded, or what? And he said no, that he had written it. 'I wrote it and I delivered it, and a fortnight afterwards I couldna have told you what I said.' Well that interested me, because that was exactly how Lloyd George told me he used to make his speeches; write them, recite them by heart, and then hope for the best.

Barrie very courteously asked me how I went about making speeches and I answered him; and then he looked at me with a twinkle in the eye and he said to me, 'Menzies,' he said, 'have you ever written a play?' And I said, 'No. No. No. No. It's a very odd thing for a politician to have to confess, but I could never think of a plot. I think I could write the dialogue but I never could think of a plot.' And he said, 'Oh, you ought to look into this. You know, when I write a novel, say ninety thousand words, that is a lot of writing. I write a play, twenty thousand words, and they give me three times as much money for it!' And thus it was that I discovered that even the great in the field of literature have their commercial moments. Anthony Trollope was not the only one.

We went inside and there was a long table on which they played shove-halfpenny. I understand it is a game of great skill. Anyhow, J. M. Barrie demonstrated it to me. He was full of enthusiasm by this time and as communicative as he had been silent at the tea-table, and so he demonstrated all the fine points about it.

He then directed my attention to the ceiling of the big room, and there I saw something I had never seen before. There were

224

postage-stamps stuck on the ceiling (and the ceiling was a high one), and I said, 'What is all this about?' 'Well,' he said, 'you see, you take a stamp—a used stamp, mind you—that has still got a little gum on it; and you take a penny and you lick the stamp and you put the gummy side up and then you spin the penny up. It takes a lot of skill, mind you—you spin it up in a horizontal plane and when it reaches the ceiling it presses the stamp and you get your money back.' I have not attempted to reproduce the Scots accent or the whimsy of gesture; but it was superb.

I was delighted beyond words, and on the way back to Shakes's house I was going into raptures about this incident when Shakes said to me, 'Yes, I entirely agree with you. But what do you think happened with us? Alison' (that was his wife, now his widow, a charming person), 'Alison and I had J.M. to dinner one night at Withington, and after dinner the old boy got to work with the stamps and the coins and we had probably fifty or sixty stamps firmly adhering to our ceiling in the dining-room. A most historic document. And I said to Alison, "In the morning we will put a little perspex, or something of that kind, over the stamps along the ceiling, and we will preserve it; because this will be an object of curiosity for people for years to come and something that our children will be delighted to have, rich with memories of the great J. M. Barrie." And do you know, old man,' he said, shaking his head, 'the next morning when we came down all eager to get the material down the street in the village and go back and fix it, we found that a zealous housemaid had swept the ceiling clean. And,' he said, 'that I would regard as one of the minor but identifiable tragedies of my life.'

4

The Law, Grave and Gay

21

Sir Owen Dixon

I am giving myself the pleasure of giving some account of a judge now retired; by common consent the greatest lawyer in Australian legal history, Sir Owen Dixon, formerly Chief Justice of Australia.

I admit that I am most heartily biased in his favour. But my prejudice is not blind, nor is it the product of hearsay; it is what you might call a first-hand prejudice.

I had graduated from the Melbourne University at the top of my year, with first-class final honours, after a series of academic distinctions in my earlier years. Before I could be called to the Bar, I had to serve twelve months' articles of clerkship with a solicitor. This term I served with a respectable solicitor of some small practice in conveyancing, but with no common-law practice at all. This was a poor preparation for the work of a barrister, but at least it gave me leisure to keep up my legal reading.

It is the practice of a newly called barrister to 'read' in the chambers of some leading junior. He reads the briefs that come in; he is encouraged to discuss them with his chief. He is, of course, free to accept briefs of his own and, if he is lucky, as I was, gets a few. But his great advantage is that he sees a busy junior at work, and at close quarters. The law comes alive for him. He begins to know how little he knows and what a world of difference there is between academic learning and the same learning when applied to the tangled facts of life.

I had the great good fortune to be accepted by Owen Dixon as the first pupil he had taken. He had an enormous practice, and was already regarded as the Bar's leading lawyer, though he had not yet chosen to 'take silk'.

I soon lost any self-conceit which may have been induced by my success as a student. When Dixon would invite my views on some matter that had come on to his table, and I nervously offered them, he would nod gravely and then go on to develop an argument that, invariably, though in a kindly way, showed me that I had no more than touched the surface of the matter, that it had aspects of which I had not dreamed. I did not take long to learn that I had almost everything to learn. An occasional simple brief of my own for some case in a Court of Petty Sessions was useful, no doubt, in restoring some of my confidence.

I should explain for the benefit of the general reader that in the legal world the word *junior* is a technical term, meaning a barrister of any age who has not been appointed one of Her Majesty's Counsel—a Q.C. When he is appointed, he is said to 'take silk'. A junior wears a 'stuff' gown in court, a Q.C. a silk one. Age has nothing to do with it. A Q.C. of forty may find himself leading a junior of sixty.

What advantage is there in taking silk, apart from the supposed honour and glory? Well, the answer is that, at my Bar, a Q.C. cannot normally appear without a junior, who will be expected to do a great deal of devilling—and not infrequently does—and who will be paid a fee approximately two-thirds of that of his leader. There are advantages in these arrangements for the client as well as counsel. A very busy junior becomes over-burdened with work. He is under pressure for long hours of the day and night, and (as I was to find out myself in due course) ultimately takes silk out of sheer self-defence. He will then be largely free from such work as the drafting of pleadings and interrogatories before trial, and will therefore be able to concentrate his full attention on the points of law which arise in the case, on the all-important matter of forensic tactics, and on the ultimate advocacy. This is all in the interests of that efficiency which the client is entitled to expect.

A busy junior may take a pupil or pupils; a Q.C. may not. The reason for this will at once be apparent. If a Q.C. had a pupil (who is after all a junior barrister with the right to practise) visibly sitting in his chambers, there would be a tendency for that pupil to get the junior brief, to the disadvantage of other perhaps more competent juniors. This is properly regarded as most undesirable, and embarrassing for the instructing solicitor, and so the rule of 'no pupils' for a Q.C. stands approved.

I now leave this explanatory digression, which may be helpful to those who look at the practice of the law from the outside, and are inclined to make rude remarks about its domestic rules, and come back to Owen Dixon.

He had obtained degrees in Arts and Law at the University of Melbourne, at a time when Latin and Greek were compulsory for Arts, and Latin compulsory for Law. He loved the classical languages. When I was his pupil, and he occasionally went away for a week-end on horse-back, he always had in his pocket some Greek or Latin classic. His university degrees were moderate enough for a man of Dixon's uncommon talents. But as I got to know him, I got to realize that as a student he must have been much more interested in far-ranging studies—learning for learning's sake—than in the mere passing of examinations based upon set courses and prescribed books.

There was a certain amount of heredity in all this. His father J. W. Dixon, whom I remember as a splendidly bearded but entirely deaf man, practising as a solicitor, was himself a brilliant lawyer. But he was a victim of a spectacular train smash in the Melbourne suburbs, and never had adequate hearing thereafter. But there was scholarship and law in the household of the young Owen Dixon, and he inherited and developed it.

I mention this because, among highly political educational reformers, there is now a quite fatuous argument that the children of homes where books are read and ideas are exchanged are 'unduly privileged' as against the children of illiterate homes, and that in the awarding of scholarships and bursaries they ought to be penalized, or, in what I believe to be racing parlance, be made to carry extra weight in order to 'bring them back to the field'.

In a world in which every civilized country needs the greatest possible supply of top talent, this argument is nonsense. But I mention it in passing. At my age, I am entitled to be a little discursive. The effect upon Dixon of the classics, and of his deep unprescribed reading in legal history, was profound. Whenever

231

he exposed his mind to me, I found that I was entering a new world of thought.

He was briefed in many cases involving the Australian Commonwealth Constitution. This was a branch of the law to which I had given a great deal of attention as a student under Harrison Moore, and I hoped that I knew something about it. But the first time a case for opinion in this field came into Dixon's chambers I began a new course of study.

I have now forgotten what the matter was about. But the solicitor had done his homework, and in his brief to Dixon he furnished many pages of notes on and references to reported cases on related matters. Dixon simply took from the front of the brief a short statement of the facts and the questions to be answered, detached the other pages and put them on one side, asked me to read the short statement, and then said to me, 'Menzies, it's a great mistake to allow yourself to be side-tracked by what may turn out to be judicial errors. Our job is to interpret the Constitution, not to interpret other people's interpretations. Let us now read the Constitution and interpret it as a comprehensive statute. Let us pay particular attention to the basic structure of the Constitution and to every section which may bear upon our problem, and see if we can reach a conclusion. When we have reached one, we shall then turn to the decided cases. If they support our conclusion, we may take it that we are right. If they don't, we must examine them to see whether they can be distinguished from our case successfully. If they are indistinguishable, we shall have to decide that our client be advised to attack them as wrongly decided, or advise him that our opinion is AB, that the decisions make it clear that the High Court will decide against that opinion, and that he should act accordingly.'

Dixon had great wit, though much of it had a subtle quality which does not lend itself to easy report. But I must recount a lovely remark he made on one occasion in the Victorian Practice Court, where the late Mr Justice Schutt was hearing an argument on an originating summons, on a point of equity.

I was waiting for the next case to come on. Also waiting was the late H. I. Cohen, whose virtues did not include that of reticence.

Dixon, a great lawyer and a great latinist, was presenting an argument to Schutt, who was not only a highly regarded equity judge but also a Latin scholar. During a pause in the argument Cohen suddenly stood up and intervened; ostensibly to explain what the real point in the case was, which by inference both Dixon and Schutt had missed. 'In what capacity do you appear, Mr Cohen?' said Schutt. 'Oh,' replied Cohen rather loftily, 'simply as *amicus curiae*, Your Honour.' 'Oh no,' said Dixon, 'my learned friend is appearing as *amicus certus in re incerta*.' You have only to translate *certus* as 'cocksure,' and the full flavour of this retort will be tasted.

Dixon's personality was, in a sense, elusive. He was a tall, lean man; unmarried, and so incessantly devoted to work that we cast him for the role of perpetual bachelor. When he suddenly announced his engagement to Alice Brooksbank, the daughter of an Anglican clergyman, the Bar was dumbfounded; we had not thought that he found any time for a private life, to say nothing of the more tender emotions. But it turned out that as usual his judgment was impeccable. With me, from the time when I became his pupil until today, when he has retired from his labours, he has always been warm-hearted, tolerant of my deficiencies, and revealing in his thought. But he is not this to all people. When I was his pupil, I used to be quite startled when somebody like the late barrister Wilbur Ham, a master of polished profanity, would look in for a talk. Instantly Dixon became the complete cynic, his nervous cough always heralding a devastating blast at somebody or something. He would freely and unpityingly analyse people and expose their mental deficiencies in what seemed to me to be a heartless manner.

But I came to know that this was a nervous mannerism. When, in later years, I sometimes appeared in court as his junior, he would, at our end of the Bar table, keep up a running fire of *sotto voce* comment on our opponent's conduct of the case, so that I almost hated the days when I myself was his opponent. But I

16

came to know that this was a defect of his quality. He had mastered the first principle in the art of advocacy; that you must understand your opponent's case at least as well as you understand your own. It will therefore sometimes happen that, concentrated as you are upon the proceedings in court, you will be critical of the way your opponent is handling his case.

In spite of this odd characteristic, he was vastly popular at the Bar. The reason is not far to seek. For barristers with a knotty problem, he was a first port of call and an accepted authority. 'Dixon, I've got a tricky problem of law. Could you give me a hint?' And they always got it, ungrudgingly. I record a small illustration. A barrister named 'Billy' Williams, a sort of court jester who will figure elsewhere in this book, had been given a case for opinion, Lord knows why, by some optimistic solicitor. I was reading with Dixon at the time. The door burst open, Williams walked in, planted himself in a characteristic pose in front of the fireplace, and put his problem to Dixon. Dixon laughed and said, 'Well, Billy, I would have thought the answer was so-and-so, and for these reasons.' Williams thanked him profusely, and left. Dixon turned to me, winked, and said, 'He'll be back!' In ten minutes he was. 'Owen, there's just one little aspect of what you told me on which I'm not quite clear.' Dixon explained. Billy left. In another ten minutes he arrived again, this time bringing a few sheets of paper and a pencil, walked straight to Dixon's table, and said, 'Be a good fellow, Owen, and write that down for me.' Dixon complied, Billy sent out an accurate opinion, the solicitor was pleased, and Billy got his fee!

When I say as I do now that Dixon was the greatest legal advocate of my time in Australia, I emphasize the word *legal*. As an advocate on matters of fact which involved the cross-examining of witnesses and sometimes the addressing of juries he was, in my opinion, not outstanding. He found it difficult, in cross-examining anybody except an expert witness of high mental attainments, to get on to the same wave-length as the witness. This difficulty was accentuated when he came to address a jury.

His intellectual subtleties eluded them; frequently they wrongly but excusably thought that he was talking down to them.

But with all these criticisms, if they are criticisms, he did enrich me with one observation of shrewd and penetrating wisdom. 'You must never forget, Menzies, that to bowl out a witness on some matter of logical deduction is no great matter. But the longer you practise the more you will come to realize that honest witnesses in a workaday world are usually illogical. When you encounter a witness of impeccable logic, watch him carefully! He may turn out to be an honest man with an unusually well-ordered mind; but he may well turn out to be a retrospective liar!'

But as a *legal* advocate, i.e. as counsel appearing in a court on matters of law, Dixon was supreme. One reason for this was that his singular mastery of the law was well known to and greatly respected by the judges before whom he appeared. His arguments therefore invariably carried great weight; they were not to be lightly brushed aside.

His argument could, in many cases, finally be rejected; for counsel argues the case entrusted to him by the solicitor briefing him and has no professional right to choose only the winnable cases. But his argument always commanded respect. Of course, he had a close knowledge of the forensic qualities and methods of his leading opponents, and of the judicial strengths and weaknesses of the judges before whom he appeared.

I can illustrate these observations by referring to one case in which I was engaged as a junior, which went to the High Court on appeal from the Full Supreme Court of Victoria. Dixon had been brought in to lead for our opponents in the appeal. The late Sir John Latham was my leader, and before the Supreme Court we had won on a variety of legal grounds, some weaker than others. Latham was a highly competent lawyer; in later years he was to be a distinguished Chief Justice of the High Court. But his defect as an advocate was that his manner and method seemed cold and pedantic. He had been a lecturer in logic at the university in his earlier days; he had lectured in the law of contract in my student days; and the habits of the lecturer persisted. In his view and practice, the argument had to be presented to the judge or judges in an inevitable and ordered sequence, with a sort of unspoken suggestion that the listener was being instructed, even on the most elementary principles. He never seemed to me to adjust his tactics or his emphasis as the argument proceeded.

Dixon opened for the appellant. His methods were exactly opposite to those of my leader. His tactical sense was impeccable, and, as I have explained, he had, even at the Bar, a sort of judicial authority. He could, to put it quite bluntly, do or say things which in another man would be regarded as impudent, and get away with them.

So it was on this occasion. He opened his argument by demolishing the weakest of the grounds upon which we had relied in the Supreme Court. He then destroyed the second weakest, and had already created a 'winning' atmosphere. To our astonishment, he began to sit down. 'But,' said the Chief Justice, 'aren't you going to deal with the other points in the case, Mr Dixon?' Dixon gave a great laugh, which almost chilled my blood, and said, 'Well, Your Honours, those points, which are somewhat obscure to me, should really be explained by my learned opponent, so that we'll all be able to consider them!' And down he sat, and up stood Latham. Latham fell into this brilliantly baited trap. He took the points in their logical order, and began to explain them with pedantic care, explaining some propositions of law which were really elementary, just as if the judges needed instruction. The inevitable happened, as Dixon had designed that it should. The judges' questions became more and more hostile and penetrating. They were searching for answers to our winning points, and as they were distinguished lawyers, Latham found himself in a tough fight, not with his opponent at the Bar table, who sat silent, but with the court itself. And we lost the appeal.

When I say that I believe Dixon to have been the greatest constitutional lawyer in Australia's history, I should explain what tests I apply before producing this superlative.

Did he bring to the task of interpreting the Australian Commonwealth Constitution, a written and detailed document, the amendment of which involves a complex process, and which has therefore been but seldom amended, a first-class understanding of the principles of the Common Law? He did. So did many others.

Did he approach that task strictly as a lawyer with legal concepts and not, as some have undoubtedly done in the United States, as a lawyer with political and sociological concepts which give colour to decision? He did; and he made no bones about it.

When he was appointed Chief Justice of the High Court of Australia in 1952, he stated his view, which may well have startled some lawyers who had come to believe that constitutional interpretation was an agreeable mixture of social philosophy and statutory interpretation.

He said:

Federalism means a demarcation of powers, and this casts upon the court a responsibility of deciding whether legislation is within the boundaries of allotted powers. Unfortunately that responsibility is very widely misunderstood, misunderstood, largely, by the popular use and misuse of terms which are not applicable, and it is not sufficiently recognized that the court's sole function is to interpret a constitutional description of power or restraint upon power and say whether a given measure falls on one side of a line consequently drawn or on the other, and that it has nothing whatever to do with the merits or demerits of the measure. Such a function has led us all, I think, to believe that close adherence to legal reasoning is the only way to maintain confidence of all parties in federal conflicts. It may be that the court is thought to be excessively legalistic. I should be sorry to think that it is anything else. There is no other safe guide to judicial decision in great conflicts than a strict and complete legalism.

This, of course, meant, not that he favoured interpreting the Constitution's particular provisions in a strict and isolated way, but that, as I illustrated earlier, he approached the task by examining the Constitution as a whole, giving due weight to its federal structure, and recognizing the impact of that structure upon the *continuing* existence and functioning of both Commonwealth and States. In short, he applied legal concepts, and not political ones.

I shall illustrate.

On the bench, in several leading cases, he clarified the basis of the decision in the famous Engineers' Case, about which I have written at length in *Central Power in the Australian Commonwealth*. He pointed out that the decision that the Commonwealth's industrial power extended to cover industrial employees of a State Government or instrumentality did not mean that a Commonwealth legislative power could be exercised by the Commonwealth Parliament in any way it chose so as to control the activities or for that matter the continued existence of the State Governments. To him the federal structure was an over-riding consideration.

The prima facie rule is now that a power to legislate with regard to a given subject matter enables the Parliament to make laws which, upon that subject, affect the operations of the States and their agencies. That, as I have pointed out more than once, is the effect of the Engineers' Case stripped of embellishment and reduced to the form of a legal proposition. It is subject, however, to certain reservations.

These reservations were worked out in later cases. I will illustrate. The Commonwealth's power over taxation was in these words: 'Taxation; but so as not to discriminate between States or parts of States.' This power so expressed and interpreted without limit, except that set up by the prohibition of one form of discrimination, would appear to authorize a taxation law which discriminated against *all* State Governments equally.

But, since the power to tax, as has been well said, is the power to destroy, such a law would be inconsistent with the continued existence of the States in the federal system, and would therefore be invalid. Dixon himself expressed the principle in a later case.

The Commonwealth Parliament, seeking to strengthen the Commonwealth Bank, a Government bank, as against the privately owned trading banks, had passed a Banking Act under its power over banking, precluding a bank from doing banking business for a State or any authority of a State except with the consent of the Commonwealth Treasurer. An 'authority' of a State included a local government body set up under State Law. The Corporation of the City of Melbourne challenged the validity of this Banking Act as involving a discrimination against the States, and the High Court found the challenged law invalid.

Dixon expressed the matter succinctly in these words:

The distinction has been constantly drawn between a law of general application and a provision singling out Governments and placing special burdens upon the exercise of powers or the fulfilment of functions constitutionally belonging to them. It is but a consequence of the conception upon which the Constitution is framed. The foundation of the Constitution is the conception of a central Government and a number of State Governments separately organized. The Constitution predicates their continued existence as independent entities. Among them it distributes the powers of governing the country.

My obvious disqualification for the task of writing about Owen Dixon is that I am dangerously one-eyed. I remember that, many years ago, I had offered some opinion to my wife (not on a legal matter, I hasten to say, for my wife knew nothing about the law, and therefore had healthy non-professional views of lawyers). She exhibiting some doubt, I said, 'Well, Dixon thinks so, and that's good enough for me.' Her retort was marvellous. 'Bob, I think you ought to realize that Dixon is not God!' All I could think of by way of reply was, 'You're quite right, my dear; but only just.'

But I am writing about him, because time marches on; new generations of lawyers are arising who know not Caesar. With our modern temptation to think that all knowledge began with us, Dixon's memory could, for a time, fade. So here I am, striking a blow for survival. I am sure that, just as a constitutional lawyer in far-off Australia recalls as giants in the history of the United States Supreme Court John Marshall and Oliver Wendell Holmes,

Junior, and Felix Frankfurter, so will future generations of Australian lawyers recall Owen Dixon, who has left an ineradicable mark upon the constitutional history of Australia.

He established the interpretation of our constitution as a pure matter of law and of legal concepts. He had never been engaged in politics, and always seemed to me to have little interest in them; certainly no partisanship; no sociological objectives to achieve. At the same time he regarded the Constitution as a frame of government, designed to deal not just with the world of 1901, but with future problems and circumstances, always on a federal basis; not to be narrowly interpreted in a rigid manner and without imagination, but at the same time to be scrutinized as a legal document in the light of received legal concepts. He rejected the notion that the Constitution, being in its origin and effect a political document, should be interpreted in the light of current political views by judges of a political frame of mind.

Above all, he understood the nature and significance of federalism as the dominant factor in the Constitution.

In the High Court as it was when I first appeared before it, and for some years thereafter, the Socratic method had reached its peak. There would probably be four or five judges joining in the argument, each pursuing his own line and expecting to be answered by counsel. Under these circumstances an advocate needed to have the faculty of never losing sight of his own line, and returning to it as opportunity offered. It is small wonder that some leading counsel were reluctant to appear in the High Court, preferring the role of the cross-examiner to that of the cross-examined. In those days the High Court appeared, from the point of view of the bar table, to be not so much a team as a group of highly individual and almost competing judicial lawyers.

It must be said that Latham, as Chief Justice, produced a higher degree of concert. But it was left to Owen Dixon to complete the task. For Dixon's acknowledged legal talents had their effect upon his colleagues, who numbered among them some

240

lawyers of great eminence and mutual understanding. If counsel still knew that he would have to face the music, he still knew that it would be a powerful music, played by masters under a master conductor. It is small wonder that the judgments of the High Court became known and respected not only in Washington but among the Law Lords of the Judicial Committee of the Privy Council.

I have said that Dixon's reputation as a judicial lawyer extended far beyond the boundaries of Australia. A legal friend has just brought to my attention two remarks made by distinguished English judges which illustrate this quite vividly. Lord Morton of Henryton, of the Judicial Committee of the Privy Council, when opening a legal convention in Australia, referred to Sir Owen Dixon as 'one of the great judges of all time'. The present Lord Chief Justice of England, Lord Parker, said in one of his judgments in the Queen's Bench Division:

For my part I need only refer—and I do so without hesitation—to the judgment of Dixon J., the now present Chief Justice, a man whose judgment commands the greatest respect not only in Australia and in this country but I venture to think throughout the world.

That Dixon was a fine scholar in the classical tradition, which is now perhaps a little outmoded, I have already indicated. But he was a great legal scholar, using the word *scholar* in its most elevated sense. He always saw through the text-books and the statutes to the historic background, and thus determined the significance of every change. Legal history in its infinite variety has sometimes been regarded as a fit subject for the classroom; an academic exercise, but of no great practical value. But when Dixon's judicial work comes to be examined it will be found that he, perhaps more than any other man, wove the stuff of legal history into the fabric of modern statute and modern decision.

He set tremendously high standards for the High Court. He saw more clearly than most that though litigation must produce its practical results from the points of the litigant, the function of the High Court was broader than that. He saw that the court had a profound duty to the jurisprudence of the country, to its legal scholarship; and that it should make its contribution in both fields.

Dixon, on the bench, though always courteous to counsel, had one habit of speech when making an observation in the course of argument which some found confusing. It is worth recording, for it exhibits an interesting aspect of Dixon's mind.

Some barristers, including one or two who were quite eminent in my time at the Bar, had what I may term the 'alphabetical' method of presenting an argument. Instead of selecting the crucial points on which the argument could be won or lost, and dealing with them as clearly and persuasively as possible, they would proceed inexorably from A to B to C, and so on, as if every step had to be separately established. Dixon justifiably found this method of advocacy tiresome and irritating. So, when he submitted a proposition to counsel, his method was frequently elliptical. If, as he saw it, proposition B made C and D quite inevitable, he would go straight to D with the remark he was putting from the bench. Those who were in full command of their cases would understand this and act upon it. Those whose advocacy was more pedestrian, and who were not familiar with Dixon's methods, would flounder. Dixon's desire always was to get to the point or points of substance and suggest or elicit helpful argument about them, thus shortening the proceedings in the interests of all concerned. This, it must be conceded, had some of the charm of novelty.

In my young days, great cases in the High Court tended to proceed differently. It should be understood that in our High Court—unlike the Supreme Court of the United States, where the full arguments are submitted in writing, and only a brief oral argument permitted, normally for half an hour or an hour—the whole argument is submitted orally, and there are no time-limits.

Great cases therefore tended to be legal marathons. One story was told at the Bar of a case in which the late Sir Edward

Mitchell, K.C., was engaged. He had commenced his argument on a Tuesday morning, had mapped out his course, and was following it slowly and ponderously. One of the judges, on Tuesday afternoon, invited Mitchell's attention to a point, and asked what he had to say about it. Mitchell's reply was a classic: 'I propose to deal with that matter on Thursday afternoon.'

In this necessarily brief chapter I have written of Owen Dixon the lawyer and judge. But he performed great services in non-legal fields on at least three occasions which took him away from his judicial duties. At the outset of the Second World War he became the active Chairman of the Australian Central Wool Committee. Wool was the principal export from Australia and its sale and transport were likely to be grievously affected by the vast interruptions of war. What to do about the wool clip and its storage and its ultimate disposal involved many complexities in what is in reality the most complex of industries. He moved in these matters with the skill of a master thinker. At the same time he was chairman of various shipping and transport boards whose work was closely associated with the wool problem. That the wool industry came through the Second World War in good shape was in no small degree due to his work.

From 1942 to 1944 he served as Australian Minister at Washington and took part in the crucial discussions which occurred in Washington during that vexed period. That he succeeded in making a mark with American statesmen is beyond question; I have listened to much evidence of that fact. He must have been an unusual sort of diplomat, because he was equipped to enter into and to take part in the intellectual life of the country as very few people have been.

Years later in 1950 he was appointed by the United Nations to make an attempt to bring about a settlement of the vexed question of Kashmir, and the contending claims of India and Pakistan. That he failed to achieve success in that mission was not to his discredit, but was largely due to the intransigent attitude of some of the leaders with whom he negotiated.

But I do not attempt to deal adequately with those incidents in his life, for my purpose has been, and is, however indifferently achieved, to make some account of him as he operated in the legal field. I have no doubt that it was by reason of his acknowledged eminence in that field that his career was crowned by the rare award of the Order of Merit by Her Majesty the Queen.

22

Some Legal Memoirs, Mostly Light-hearted

It is one of the oddities of legal memory that those sound and serious lawyers who became businesslike and efficient judges, who were involved in no scenes and provoked no humour, survive chiefly in the Law Reports; while, from a human point of view, the 'characters' survive.

Looking back over my youth at the Bar, I realize that most of my happiest reminiscences derive from my relatively few years of practice in the County Court. Perhaps there was rather more informality than one encountered in the Supreme Court of Victoria or the High Court of Australia, though I must confess that there was some fun to be had (respectfully, of course) in those elevated tribunes. For all I know, the County Court has become the preserve of businesslike lawyers, pressed for time. But there were characters in my day. Their entertainment value was in some cases superior to their legal attainments, but as I grow older I remember them with a sort of nostalgic affection. There have been many books of legal reminiscences. Most of them have concerned the well known or the famous. So perhaps I may be forgiven for making a change by writing about the less well known and the less famous.

It is of some of the characters of my County Court days that I now write.

George Dethridge, a barrister of competence, first became a County Court judge, and was later appointed Chief Judge of the Commonwealth Court of Conciliation and Arbitration. In this latter capacity he soon learned to avoid humour, and in particular irony, which retailed very badly at union meetings at the week-end, and was in any case reported by the newspapers with literal witlessness. But, in his few years on the County Court, he made the most of his opportunities. A man of middle height and of medium build, he carried his head rather thrown back, wore glasses on a watered ribbon, had a sort of barking and emphatic manner of speech which was easily mistaken for pomposity, and concealed beneath it a quick mind and a somewhat Rabelaisian humour.

One day, into my chambers came a well-known solicitor to retain my services on behalf of the proprietor of an illegal suburban sweep who was being sued by the Commonwealth for income-tax.

I pointed out that nobody could know less about the techniques of gambling than I did; and that in any event the illegality of a profit did not exempt it from the clutches of the tax-gatherer. The solicitor retorted that the reason he wanted my services was that I had been appearing a lot in cases on constitutional law, and that he wanted me to challenge (in the County Court!) the validity of the Commonwealth income-tax laws. Naturally, I said he should bring in his client, so that I could give him a fair warning about his chances of success. The client turned out to be a somewhat asthmatic but sporting character, who positively beamed at me when I said that the odds against success were at least 1,000 to 1. 'Good odds!' he said. 'I'll go on, so long as you can give me a run for my money!' I assured him that I could argue for an hour or two, if that was what he meant, and we parted and remained good friends.

The case came on before Dethridge. Counsel for the Commonwealth opened his case. Following the Victorian County Court practice, I then had to state, orally, the defences.

When I said, solemnly, that the defences were (1) that the Commonwealth Income-Tax Assessment Act was invalid, as being not authorized by the Commonwealth Constitution, and (2) that the Commonwealth Income-Tax Act (prescribing the rates of tax) was invalid for the like reason, Dethridge barked hilariously. With a quick glance to see that no reporters were present, he said, 'Mr Menzies, as a taxpayer I agree with you most heartily. But perhaps as a judge I should hear a little more!'

I then got to work. The whole issue had in fact been put to rest in the High Court after a series of decisions in which, naturally, there had been some conflict of judicial opinion and some marked variations of expression.

In most of these cases Mr Justice Isaacs, who was later to become Chief Justice of Australia, had been an active and vocal participant. Isaacs was a considerable scholar and a prodigious worker, deficient in humour and addicted to the writing of voluminous dissenting judgments; this addiction arose partly from vanity—he liked as many goods as possible in the shop window—and partly from a quite real difference of approach to the problems of Constitutional interpretation.

Naturally, giving my enthusiastic but illegal client his run for his money, I resorted a good deal to Mr Justice Isaacs. When I had quoted a passage which helped me a little, Dethridge could stand it no longer.

'Really, Mr Menzies' (with a quick glance to confirm the absence of the Press) 'what's the use of quoting this to me. No doubt Isaacs was dissenting, as usual!'

'No, sir,' I replied, 'on this occasion the learned judge was delivering a judgment which concurred in the result with the majority.'

DETHRIDGE: 'With great respect, I find that almost impossible to believe!'

MENZIES: 'I hand up to Your Honour the volume of the Law Reports, open at this passage.'

DETHRIDGE (*after a visibly astonished perusal*): 'Well, well, well! So Isaacs concurred! What an event! Went the whole hog for once, in spite of his religion!'

Naturally, we lost. But my client wheezed his way out of court, defeated but delighted.

My other story of Dethridge is, I fear, even more indelicate. But modern novelists have altered our expectations of delicacy, and I will therefore recount it.

I was briefed to appear (I've forgotten on what side) in a case in the County Court at Kerang, in a farming area—wheat and sheep—in the north-west of the State of Victoria. The action was one for damages for breach of warranty on a sale of sheep. It was common ground that the vendor of a number of ewes—locally called 'yowes'—had said that the rams and the ewes had been 'joined' at such and such a time. The vital question, to be solved by expert evidence, was whether this expression meant merely that the rams and the ewes had been given their opportunity, and that no particular result had been guaranteed, or whether it meant that the ewes were in lamb.

It was a fascinating case. Dethridge was on the Bench, watered ribbon, whimsy and all. Most of the members of the jury were farmers. The witnesses were farmers, who gave 'expert' evidence of a conflicting kind. My opponent at the Bar table and I made no doubt powerful speeches (at least I like to think that they were), and the judge summed up. Nobody enjoyed the case more than Dethridge. I can see him now, looking at the jury for form's sake and up to Heaven for inspiration, swinging his glasses on their ribbon, saying, 'Gentlemen, this is eminently a case for you. It turns on the meaning of a simple English word, *joined*. Like all simple English words, it is capable of quite a few interpretations. Thus, I might, in all innocence, say that I had joined my wife at a railway station. *Wouldn't mean what any of you sheep men think it means!*'

I'm sorry I can't remember the jury's verdict. But I fear that I must have been on the losing side; for I never had a brief to appear in Kerang again.

One other story of Judge Dethridge is worth recording since it exhibits his satirical capacity, I think, extremely well.

There was a building case being heard before him. All the usual paraphernalia of a building case was on view. A very tedious young gentleman was the counsel for one of the parties. The case involved, among other things, the quality of the woodwork in the house and involved allegations that veranda posts and other timber elements were infested by white ants and that consequently the work was not of a quality that should be paid for.

At the end of the case the young counsel proceeded to make his final address to Dethridge who, of course, by this time had a pretty good idea of what he regarded as the facts and was not over patient at having a long address. Counsel was quite unconscious of this, and went on and on and on, until the judge could stand it no longer. At this stage the young man produced a brown paper parcel which was one of the exhibits and proceeded to open it up to show some white-ant-infested timber. He was indiscreet enough to say to the judge, 'I hope, Your Honour, that you will not mind me putting this out on the Bar table where we have timber as well, and I know you would not want to have white ants in this court-room.' Quick as a flash, Dethridge said, 'White ants, white ants! I don't mind a scrap about the white ants; what I can't stand, sir, is the borer, the borer.'

William Ah Ket did not ever sit on the Bench, though he would have been a very competent judge. He was a phenomenon at the Victorian Bar, a full-blooded Chinese born in the northeast of Victoria. He was a sound lawyer and a good advocate. His bland oriental features gave nothing away; his keen sense of fun was concealed behind an almost immovable mask. A certain prejudice among clients against having a Chinese barrister to an extent limited his practice, though instructing solicitors thought very well of him. He was considerably senior to me but we were great friends.

I will tell two tales to illustrate him.

He had a brief to appear in a distant country town. To be in court on Tuesday morning, he caught a Monday train from Melbourne. At that time commercial travellers from Melbourne caught Monday trains; and there were quite a few of them in the train which Ah Ket caught. The train was almost crowded but Ket found an empty compartment, tossed his bag into the rack, and settled down for the journey. At the last moment a 'commercial', finding no room elsewhere, reluctantly joined Ah Ket, and sat opposite to him. For a time there was silence (Ket later described the scene to me with solemn pleasure), but within half an hour the natural passion of the traveller broke out as follows:

COMMERCIAL: 'Have you been in this country long, John? Do you savee English?'

AH KET: 'Ah yes, twenty year, thirty year. Likee country very muchee.'

And so it proceeded, Ket keeping up this curious lingo, and the traveller matching it.

Finally, after some hours of this splendid farce, Ket arrived at his station, which was also the destination of his travelling-companion. The solicitor instructing Ket was at the station. There was a solitary horse and cab, which all three entered. The solicitor at once began to discuss his case with Ket. The conversation was very learned. The commercial grew paler and paler as the proof of his own folly piled up against him! I used to tell Willy Ket that the story should have ended with the traveller falling out of the cab and breaking his leg. But Ket's reply was characteristic: 'Oh, no, he could see that I was a Chow, and wanted to be sociable; so I was!'

On another occasion he was briefed to appear in a suburban Court of Petty Sessions constituted by several honorary Justices of the Peace and presided over by one. The Chairman was a retired school-teacher, of great vanity, ignorance of the law, and intolerance. Usually the parties were represented by local solicitors well known to the J.P.s, and so listened to with reasonable respect.

But let a party be represented by a barrister sent out from the city and the Chairman was in his element. He would put this fellow in his place! On the occasion to which I refer, Ah Ket was briefed to appear in a civil matter in which the facts were not in serious dispute, but one or two questions of law were involved.

Solemnly Ah Ket stood up to open his case. He explained the undisputed facts and then (knowing the reputation of the Chairman) said, 'I now address myself to the legal problem, knowing that Your Worship will consider it judicially. The case may be put in this way.' And on he went to elaborate a legal proposition until finally the Chairman burst out, 'I don't agree with one word of what you're saying, Mr Ket. It is clearly wrong!'

Ket, not a whit abashed, his bland oriental features unfurrowed replied, 'May I take it that your opinion is concurred in by your colleagues, Your Worship?' A hurried and whispered consultation, and then a triumphant assertion: 'Yes, it is!' (and, under his breath, 'That disposes of you!').

KET: 'I am glad to hear Your Worship's statement. As I have been stating the case for the defendant, I take it that I may now have judgment in my favour.'

A wonderful case of 'the biter bit'.

Another character was '*Billy*' *Williams*, to whom I made some reference earlier.

He was a large, round-faced, amiable man, with little knowledge of the law but a fine gift of low comedy. When he was at the bar, he could occasionally laugh a case in or out of court. I will record one example.

He was appearing for a plaintiff before a judge and jury. The action was one for damages for fraudulent misrepresentation on a sale of property. Williams was opening his case to the jury. He was speaking from the end of the Bar table farthest from the jury. Between him and the jury were opposing counsel and, sitting opposite, the defendant's solicitor and the defendant himself. Billy was in fine rumbustious form. He recounted the various ways in which the defendant had 'robbed' the plaintiff. He reached a point at which he said, 'Here's a letter that this scamp wrote. I'll read it to you, gentlemen!' There was a dramatic pause while Billy fumbled for his reading-glasses. Professing not to find them, he suddenly peered forward and said to the wretched defendant, 'Have you stolen my glasses too?'

Gravely irregular, I concede, but it made the atmosphere!

But it is, of course, easier to laugh a case out than in. So a plaintiff's advocate must be careful, as many have discovered to their sorrow. For a defendant, there is more scope. I will recount,

17*

as briefly as I can, one of Billy's successes in this field. The year was 1917. In Australia, conscription was proposed, and hotly debated. A body called the Returned Soldiers' No-Conscription League was formed. The Melbourne *Age* reported a public meeting at which a decorated returned soldier said that this League was only about a hundred strong 'and that these individuals had been sent back to Australia as undesirables'.

One Canavan, a member of the League, sued the *Age* for damages for libel. It would appear to be a fairly formidable case, since the words were, as indeed the jury found, defamatory.

Williams gave a superb theatrical performance. I can, as if it were yesterday, remember him addressing the jury.

'The plaintiff isn't mentioned, gentlemen. You can imagine him meeting his friends that day, and one of them saying to him over a pot of beer, "Why don't you have a go at them, Jim?" So Jim, who has great doubts, but would like some money, goes to the solicitors.' Here Williams gave a highly hilarious word-picture, garnished with gestures, of the solicitors, who were well known, advising that as Canavan was not named the prospects were poor. '"But we'll consult counsel!" And my learned friend, with wonderful ingenuity, is trying to persuade you that this man, whom nobody ever mentioned or heard of, has been wronged and should have some money!' And so he went on, until everybody was laughing, and the jury found 'no reference to the plaintiff'. The judge did his best. In fact, he ordered a new trial, subsequently disallowed by the High Court on appeal on grounds which I have never thought satisfactory. But Billy had triumphed; he had created an atmosphere of farce, and Canavan paid the costs.

In due or undue course Williams became a County Court judge. He had a slightly bawdy mind which would have endeared him to a modern theatrical producer. When he did make an offbeat remark from the Bench he did so with a beatific unsmiling countenance. I remember well the best example, for I was in his court at the time. The case being heard was an action for damages for injuries suffered in a street accident. Counsel for the plaintiff, to establish what the plaintiff's loss of salary had been, had called the general manager of the business in which the plaintiff was employed.

The manager proved to be a small, excessively dignified, not to say pompous man. He had evidently decided that he must use good language, with no colloquialisms.

What happened can be put into question-and-answer form.

COUNSEL: 'At the time of the accident, was the plaintiff working for your company?'

WITNESS: 'At the time of the happening of the events which led to this litigation, the plaintiff was in the employment of the company of which I have the honour to be general manager.'

COUNSEL: 'What was he paid?'

WITNESS: 'He was in receipt of an emolument of six hundred pounds per ānum.'

THE JUDGE: 'This is fascinating and unusual. I have heard of people paying through the *nose* but this method is new to me!'

But I think that my most hilarious recollection of Billy Williams concerns a great case over which he presided. It was a criminal proceeding. It arose out of the activities of a gang of criminals who lived in the industrial suburb of Fitzroy and who were quite famous as a collection of what might properly be called gangsters. They fell out with each other over the favours of a young woman who was vaguely (?) attached to their circle, and this gave rise to certain affrays which were compendiously described in the newspapers as the 'Fitzroy vendetta'.

Finally one of them came up before Williams in General Sessions on a shooting charge. At the end of the first day Billy was walking down Queen Street, Melbourne, looking rather gloomy and introspective, which was not usual for him. A solicitor, who knew him well, and who was walking in the opposite direction, stopped him and said, 'Billy, you're looking pretty troubled. What is it, old man? Is there anything that I could help you about?' 'Oh, no,' said Williams. 'The fact is that I'm in charge of this "Fitzroy vendetta" case and I'm very worried about it.' 'But,' said the solicitor, 'why should you worry about it? You don't live in Fitzroy. Don't you still live in St Kilda Road?' 'Oh, yes! That's right, old man.' 'Well, you don't have to pronounce this fellow guilty or not guilty; the jury will attend to that matter. All you have to do is to sum up, quite fairly, and leave the rest to the jury. Why should you be worried?' 'Well,' said old Billy, his characteristic twinkle emerging from behind the façade of gloom, 'you know what it's like, old man; ever since I knew I was to be the judge in this case I've made inquiries all over Melbourne; from everybody I met I made inquiries. And, do you know, in spite of all this, old man, I can't find out one thing about this Fitzroy vendetta: I can't find out what side the Baillieus are on.'

Now that story is incomprehensible, and indeed offensive, unless one remembers that the great family of the Baillieus in Melbourne was not only a family of the greatest distinction, W. L. Baillieu having been the virtual founder of the great industries of Broken Hill and Port Pirie, but it was also a large family. The Baillieus were, in fact, remarkable people. But it had become almost a cant phrase among the envious to imagine that the Baillieus had a finger in every pie and that they must make money out of almost everything that went on in Melbourne.

That explains Billy's story. I wouldn't repeat it now if I had not, on more than one occasion, repeated it to members of the Baillieu family, to their immense delight.

George Arnot Maxwell, who died in 1935, was the greatest criminal advocate I ever heard. He had terrific earnestness, a fine Scots burr on his tongue, a beak of a nose, a flashing eye (until he went blind, of which more hereafter), a genius for self-persuasion (I do not think that, once he got going, he ever believed he was appearing for a guilty man) and a capacity for persuading a jury that its members must be as astute to find excuses and doubts on behalf of the accused as they would be in their own cause 'on the dread day of judgment itself'.

When I was a junior, getting a good deal of work in the County Court, Maxwell was in his heyday. He and my father were old friends, and he was always kind to me. We had adjoining lockers in the robing-room of the Law Courts at Melbourne, and so frequently exchanged a little gossip as we arrayed ourselves for battle in wig and gown. In this way I obtained sidelights on his mind and methods. In addition, though I had no taste for criminal work, and did but little of it, I had a great taste for Maxwell, and many times looked into the Criminal Court to see and hear him.

A good sample of our robing-room gossip recurs to me.

'Good morning, Maxie, what angel of light are you appearing for this morning?'.

'Well, Bob, I fearr he's no angel. A wretched young man called Honeybubble. A clear case, caught in the act. Oh dearr! Oh dearr! All I'll be doin' is to put up a bit of a plea for maircy!'

So off we went, I to my modest fee in the County Court, Maxwell to his 'bit of a plea'. To my astonishment, at 1 p.m. when the courts adjourned for lunch and I returned to the robing-room, there was Maxwell!

'How did that young scoundrel Honeybubble go, Maxie? Your plea for mercy seems to have taken an uncommonly long time!'

'Oh dearr! Bob, you must not speak like that. The puir lad has been wrongly charged. He's pleaded not guilty. Oh dearr! Oh dearr! It will be a gross miscarriage of justice if he's convicted.'

Well, there it is. I've forgotten but I have no doubt that young Honeybubble got off.

Maxwell was not a very great cross-examiner. His power was in the address to the jury, which was quite hypnotic. He could take hold of some apparent irrelevancy and elevate it into a crucial fact. Once, Charles Lowe (later Sir Charles Lowe of the Victorian Supreme Court) and I were at Ballarat, the old mining city, to appear against each other in a civil action in the Supreme

Court, which was on circuit. As usual, the 'liberty of the subject' cases, the criminal cases, were taken first. And so it came about that Lowe and I sat in court and heard Maxwell defending a young man who was charged, on what appeared to be impressive evidence, with a sexual offence against a young woman whom he was driving home from a country dance. The defence was consent. Maxwell was, we thought, labouring heavily. The jury seemed listless. Lowe and I were impatient. The prosecutrix had been cross-examined in detail. Yes, the journey had begun pleasantly. Yes, at one stage she had, with memories of the dance, been singing some of the current music-hall numbers. She named a dozen of them. Maxwell proceeded solemnly to address. And then, suddenly, the almost fantastic drama arrives.

'Gentlemen, you may picture the scene. The dead of night. This fine lusty young man driving this handsome young woman home, through the Bullarook Forest; the lights shining through the darkness and the wheels cr-runching on the lonely gr-ravel road. The dancing was over, but the blood was still pulsing in their veins. Ah! What a setting for romance! And then, in the silence of the night, with nothing but the trees for witness, this young woman begins to sing, and what does she sing to this lusty young man? She sings the current music-hall ditties, and then she reaches the climax, and into the night air there come the words of invitation:

'Abie! Abie! Abie my boy,
What are we waiting for now?'

Lowe and I had almost to be carried out, but the jury promptly acquitted!

When Maxwell was addressing a jury, he turned everything to his advantage. On one occasion a somewhat testy judge (there were some in my day) interrupted Maxwell's address with a somewhat untimely query. Maxwell turned, with flashing indignation, and protested. The judge, with something of a sneer, said, '*I'm* not taking sides. I'm indifferent to the result!'

Instantly, Maxwell turned to the jury. It was his great chance.

'Gentlemen, His Honour is indifferent. But *I'm not* indifferent, gentlemen!' (It sounded like thunder with a Scots accent.) *'Nor is the poor wretch in the dock indifferent*, gentlemen. His Honour will take his dinner at his club tonight, whatever happens. *But where will the prisoner be dining?* The answer is for you, gentlemen. *You cannot, under solemn oath, be indifferent; for as you do justice here, in this place, on airth, so you will receive it on the last day.'*

It seems, written down, to be mere professional fustian. But I shall never forget the pause: the jury wide-eyed, Maxwell's head shaking with emotion, the judge silent and withdrawn.

While his powers were still high, Maxwell became blind. His eagle eye was dimmed. Such a crushing blow would have unmanned and defeated most advocates. Maxwell met it with great courage and remarkable shrewdness. He knew that he had never been a delver into the books of the law; that his blindness should not finish him; that he might even use it, on occasion, to the advantage of his client. Some people thought this mere humbug; I thought it a triumph of the spirit. And so it came about that one day I slipped away from my own court and into the gloomy old Criminal Court, to see how the great blind advocate was going. He was addressing the jury. He was dealing scathingly with the principal witness for the prosecution. Familiar as he was with every detail of the courtroom in which he had practised so long, he stood, deliberately, as I realized, facing a point four or five feet away from the foreman's end of the jury box; speaking, as it were, into space.

'Gentlemen, it has pleased Providence to take from me the power of sight. I cannot see you. I could not see the witness. *But I could hear him, gentlemen, and he sounded like a damned rrrogue!'*

Here is another story about a man who was probably the best known police-court solicitor of my junior days. He was *N. H. Sonenberg.*

He was a short, whimsical, humorous character, intensely

shrewd; he did an enormous business in the Courts of Petty Sessions in dealing with petty crimes and also, not infrequently, appeared himself in the Court of General Sessions or even in the Criminal Court, before juries.

Solicitors of this type ('amalgams') are not always highly regarded by the Bar. But I can at once say that Sonenberg was universally trusted; his honesty was unimpeachable; he was liked by all the judges and by all the practising counsel.

One afternoon, just before he was leaving his office, a man came in to see him and told him that he was being prosecuted at the city court the following morning on some relatively petty criminal charge. Sonenberg asked him to tell his story. He told it. 'Sonny' then, in a characteristic way, said, 'All right, son, if that's the story you tell, there's no reason why you should be convicted. But, of course, it's all a matter of whether the court believes you. Do you want me to appear for you?' 'Oh yes, Mr Sonenberg; tomorrow morning.' Sonenberg said, 'Very well. That will cost you ten guineas and I will see you at the court in the morning, before the case begins. I have a few other cases there myself.'

The client made as if to leave. Sonny stopped him and said, 'Son, what about the ten guineas?' With a sort of a leer the client replied, 'Oh, Mr Sonenberg! But you can trust me, you can trust me, surely, until tomorrow?' Sonny replied with a broad grin, 'Son, look here.' And he turned around to a little shelf of law books which represented his technical equipment, pulled down a very old edition of Lewin on Trusts, banged it on the corner of the table so that half an inch of dust flew off and then said, 'Son, that's the leading text-book on Trusts; as you can see, we haven't used it in this office for twenty-five years.'

In British countries, we are now so accustomed to the modern rank of Queen's Counsel for members of the Inner Bar that we may forget that there have been other ranks, including the most honourable one of Sergeant. This reflection reminds me of another rank, and of another man, *Colonel McInerney*, who was a well-known solicitor in Melbourne. He was a big, tall man, with a booming voice and a touch of the Irish in him. He did a good deal of work in the police courts, and conducted some of his own office's cases in the County Court; this being permissible in the State of Victoria. His advocacy made up in robustness what it lacked in subtlety.

On one occasion he had appeared for a wife who was claiming maintenance from her husband, in the Court of Petty Sessions at Prahran, a suburb of Melbourne. The defendant had successfully taken a point of venue, that the case should have been heard in another suburb, Fitzroy. McInerney took the case to the County Court, where it came before Judge 'Billy' Williams. McInerney, in the height of his form, kept roaring out that the case 'should have been heard at Prahran'. Billy submitted to the barrage for a time, and then intervened, with a twinkle in the eye, 'Gently, gently, Mr McInerney. If you go on like this, it will be heard at Prahran quite easily!'

But the choicest incident occurred when the great McInerney went up into chambers to get some simple order from the dryly whimsical Judge Box. The order was granted without much question. The same afternoon, up came a clerk from Mr McInerney's office to get the order signed. It had been drafted so as to begin: *Upon hearing Colonel McInerney for the applicant* . . . Judge Box struck out the *Colonel* and substituted *Mr*.

Up came McInerney in a fury. With great Hibernian fury he told the judge that he had become a colonel in the service of the Queen in the Boer War, and that he would not tolerate the omission of his rank. Box looked up at him, speculated a little, took his pen and made an alteration in the order. 'Well,' he said in his slow and characteristic way, 'I have done my best for you. I have given you the highest rank that the law recognizes. I have made you *Sergeant* McInerney!'

Every experienced lawyer is familiar with the phenomenon of the *litigant who appears in person*. The layman is disposed to think with pity of the unfortunate fellow who, by reason of poverty, finds justice denied to him by the machinations of the clever barrister retained by the rich opponent.

This picture is by no means always true. Indeed, some of the most persistent and vexatious litigants I have known habitually appeared in person for no other reason than that, after a few weeks' unscientific reading in the Public Library, they esteemed themselves quite competent to understand and argue the law. Such people infuriate judges, commonly behave with a sort of crazy arrogance, and are almost invariably wrong.

But the genuine litigant in person, who suffers from honest poverty and not from a form of litigious mania, is in my experience treated fairly and helpfully, as my one completely hearsay story will show. It was told by the late *Mr Justice Schutt*, of the Victorian Supreme Court.

Schutt was a rare character. He had been a powerful footballer, became a good equity lawyer, was a most quiet and persuasive legal advocate, and won unwonted praises in the High Court of Australia. He was a good latinist, a noted wit in the Melbourne Savage Club, of which he was for years the presiding genius, and carried on to the bench the aura of one who had been perhaps the best-liked man at the Bar.

To those qualities he added the possession of a good deal of money, a willingness (not always found in such circumstances) to spend it, a love of travel, and a fondness for genial company. Thus it was that in the long vacation, which in Victoria lasts from a few days before Christmas until the end of January, Schutt would promptly set out on a sea journey: sometimes to Ceylon, where he was for years most appropriately addressed by the head waiter at the Galle Face, proudly wearing his tortoiseshell comb, as 'Benign my lord'; and on one noted occasion as far as to New York.

On this occasion, Schutt carried a letter of introduction to an American judge in that city. He sent it in, and rang up the judge. After some preliminary difficulties of accent (a common language is a great bond of union) the judge invited him to come to court next day, where the Marshal would meet him. He arrived, was escorted on to the bench itself, was warmly welcomed by the judge, and sat down. A long, hearty, and animated conversation ensued. At the end of about half an hour, during which Schutt had begun to feel that the business of the court was being interrupted (though admittedly counsel at the Bar table had continued to speak with great fluency!), he said that he thought he should leave.

A dialogue then occurred which was so splendid that I will recount it in direct form. It embodies the whole of the rest of my story.

THE JUDGE: 'Now don't you worry about that, Judge! I'm enjoying your little visit with me! Don't you worry about that lawyer talking away down there. Lean forward, Judge.' *Schutt leans forward.* 'You see that little guy down there, with the book? He's been writing it all down. When it gets to the end of the day I'll cast my eye over it and see what's in it. So don't worry, Judge. By the way, Judge, how long have you been a judge down there in your country?'

SCHUTT: 'Oh, about ten years.'

JUDGE: 'Well, now, that's a long time. Say, Judge, do you ever have any litigants appearing in person in your court?'

SCHUTT: 'Quite a few.'

JUDGE: Say, don't you think they're a terrible problem? I do, you know, Judge; I had been sitting up here about a year when I had my first. My Gard, he was a terrible fool. He knew just nothing. At the other end of the table was a smart downtown lawyer, putting witnesses on to the stand, one after the other. It was all one way. This fool of a litigant in person knew nothing, and asked nothing, all day.

When I got into bed that night, I couldn't sleep well. Suddenly I sat up in bed. A tremendous thought had struck me. I remembered, Judge, that when I came on to the bench, I took an oath to do justice! Gee, Judge, that was a solemn thought. I couldn't sleep again. Next morning, when I came on to the bench, I may have looked a little jaded, but, sir, my mind was active.

This smart downtown lawyer put a new witness on the stand, and got his evidence in chief. Then I took a hand. The first few questions I put, I felt a little rusty. You know how it feels, Judge. Then after a while, it began to come back to me. After a while more, I found I hadn't forgotten how to cross-examine. After a while longer, I became real good. And in the end, Judge, by Gard, *we won*!'

Not all of the fun was reserved for the lower courts. The gravity of the High Court itself was occasionally disturbed. No court that contained *Sir Frank Gavan Duffy* could be prosaic for long. For Gavan Duffy, who ultimately became Chief Justice, enjoyed the Socratic methods of the High Court, freely questioned and answered counsel, and enjoyed the argument hugely, as became a born and experienced dialectician. If his judgments were usually brief and sometimes perfunctory, his activities in the argument had usually helped the judgment of others.

When I was first appearing in the High Court he was exceedingly kind to me. He did not spare me from his cross-examination, but he clearly approved of my obstinate refusal to surrender at the first shot. His methods were fascinating. He would draw me out by a series of questions, which became more and more difficult for me to answer. I will explain my meaning by one example. His first question to me, after consideration, I answered, 'Yes.' He then, in a sense, took me out to sea. As I was about to sink for the third time, I gave a sickly grin, and said, 'Your Honour, I seem to feel that when I said yes some time ago, I should have said no. Could I now say no and let us start all over again?'

Gavan Duffy hugely enjoyed this kind of thing. Though his dialectics were not always appreciated by some of his colleagues, I have no doubt that they did me a world of much-needed good.

But when he chose to sting, he could sting like an adder. Wit is not necessarily genial, and his was frequently barbed. I will give three examples, two of which relate to cases in which I was appearing, and the other of which is hearsay, but I have no doubt true.

The first relates to a somewhat painful memory I have of being briefed to argue what I believed to be a hopeless case of some complexity, in the High Court, before the full Bench. Gavan Duffy was near one end of the row of judges (he had not yet become Chief Justice) and the late Sir Hayden Starke (who had married Duffy's daughter) was near the other end. I want to say at once, without presumption, that I honour Starke's memory, just as I respected his massive legal ability and formidable personality whenever I appeared before him. But he would not temper the wind to the shorn lamb. On this occasion he tore my poor argument to pieces, while I did my best to hold its tatters together. Duffy came to the rescue by tossing a series of helpful arguments to me. Naturally, I seized on each of them in turn, and tried to put them, in my own words, to the Bench.

At last, Starke could not take it any more, and said to me, 'Mr Menzies, your argument is nonsense.' Before I could say a word, Duffy, my protector, leaned forward and said to me, 'What was that my brother Starke said?' Playing for time, I replied that I thought that Mr Justice Starke had not looked with favour on my argument.

'Wasn't this an argument which I had suggested to you?' said Duffy, fairly bristling. All I could say was that I thought it was, but that I had no doubt conveyed it rather clumsily. But Duffy had girded his loins to the battle, and said, 'That is not so. You conveyed it admirably.'

Whereupon Starke said, in a grumbling sort of way, 'I didn't realize that this was an argument suggested by my brother Duffy. If I had, I wouldn't have spoken as I did. But treating it as Counsel's argument, I thought it was nonsense, as indeed it is!' From Duffy came the final dart. 'I gather that my brother Starke is apologizing. If so, the apology is worthy of him, *both in matter and manner*!'

I have hesitated about recording this incident, but I really believe that it illustrates some aspects of both judges; and in any case it occurred in open court.

My second example I can give with a good deal of pleasure.

Following on the famous Engineers' Case, I had been engaged in several cases in which the constitutional doctrine of a more expansive interpretation of Commonwealth powers had been applied. Then came a similar case originating in Queensland, and I was briefed to appear as junior to the politically celebrated T. J. Ryan, K.C., Attorney-General in the Queensland Labour Government. Ryan had a great Press reputation as an advocate, but he was no constitutional lawyer, and had me briefed because I was familiar with the legal issues.

Ryan called at my chambers in Melbourne on the day before the case was to come on, for a conference. It was obvious that he had done no work on his brief. He put two questions to me. What were the issues in the case? and what was our argument?

I answered both questions as clearly as I could, and then sat expectantly to listen to my leader. But all he did was to close the conference, and say that he would see me in the morning. So there we were next day appearing before the full High Court, with the celebrated but dreary Sir Edward Mitchell, K.C., appearing against us, and opening the argument. Mitchell had plenty of material in the judgments of the earlier High Court, judgments which had been questioned in the Engineers' Case and were now readily challengeable, as I had carefully explained to Ryan in my chambers.

When Ryan rose to reply, however, although he began by stating in rough form the broad conclusion that we aimed to establish, he was singularly barren of reasons. The judges, who regarded Ryan's claims to legal eminence as unfounded, fell to the task of cross-examining him with some relish. Duffy in particular, kept putting to him some of the earlier judgments, and asking him to explain why they should not be followed. Ryan began to flounder badly. The bluff manner in which he had begun became crumpled. He turned to me and made a whispered cry for help. I stood up and whispered in his ear that he must point out the ways in which later decisions of the court, of which I had given him a list, and the reports of which were on the bar table, had either weakened or destroyed the authority of these early decisions.

The court waited fairly patiently while this strange colloquy went on, a colloquy which of course would have been completely unnecessary if Ryan had done any work on the matter. When I sat down, to my horror I heard my leader reply to Duffy by saying, in a scoffing manner, 'Oh, those judgments! They were only the judgments of the first High Court!'

This was too much for Duffy. In a voice acutely expressive of contempt, he said, 'I understand you perfectly. Your argument is that it is better to be a live dog than a dead lion.'

In a few minutes the 'live dog' was heard to ask that I should be allowed to follow. This I did with relief. After an hour I noticed that Ryan had left the court, and he didn't put in an appearance again.

I need only add that, on the strength of the recent decisions, the High Court decided in our favour; and the well-advertised Ryan was able to chalk up another great victory!

My third example is this. One of the senior High Court judges was Sir George Rich. Personally, I liked him very much. He was not a talkative judge. Social contacts with him outside court were invariably pleasant. He spiced his conversation with Latin tags, was delighted when they were occasionally understood, and had strong and frequently defamatory opinions of some other lawyers which were much enjoyed by his table companions, and particularly by me. But truth requires me to say that he was inclined to be indolent. He certainly wrote a few individual judgments which were a joy to read; but on the whole he preferred to attach his name to a joint judgment, the labour of writing which he left to his judicial partner. For some years we were familiar with joint judgments of Isaacs and Rich J.J.; in other years with judgments by Gavan Duffy and Rich J.J. These were shorter, because although, as I have said, Duffy was a renowned dialectician during the course of argument, he believed in short judgments.

The day was to come when Rich was ill-advised enough, in a

conversation off the Bench, to rebuke Duffy. 'Duffy,' he said, 'the trouble with you is that you talk too much from the Bench.' He got a quick and acid reply: 'Small wonder, since I have to talk for two!'

5

Cricket and Cricketers

23

The Prime Minister's Eleven

Early in October 1951, a West Indian cricket team began to arrive, a few players at a time, in Sydney. I saw in the Press that no match had been arranged for a week or two. This seemed a rather casual beginning for an international tour, so I rang up the then Chairman of the Board of Cricket Control in Sydney and told him that I would like to put on a one-day festival match for them at Canberra, against a team selected by me. I added that this was my personal proposition, not a Government matter; that I would personally guarantee the expenses, including the transport of the players; and that if any profit resulted it would go to the Canberra Legacy Club. (Legacy is a magnificent Australian association of ex-servicemen devoted to helping the widows and children of fallen comrades.) The Chairman was cautious. 'What kind of team would you pick? I don't want any secret weapons disclosed to the enemy!' My reply was that I proposed to have a few players who had retired from Test cricket, several who were still playing, a couple of members of Parliament, and three local players; no new first-class bowlers, no secret weapons.

He agreed, I thought a little reluctantly. But his fears were not as great as mine; for if the match was washed out by rain, or the public attendance small, I would be up for a sizeable sum of money!

The West Indies players readily agreed, and the date was fixed.

My captain was Jack Fingleton. I had Bill O'Reilly, Martin Donnelly, Lindsay Hassett, Neil Harvey, Sam Loxton and Ian Johnson. The M.P.s were the late Athol Townley and Bill Falkinder, both good Tasmanian cricketers. The three local players were T. Freebody, K. Gibb and I. McLellan. I invited the irrepressible Ernie McCormick to come to Canberra and act as one of the umpires.

On the evening before the match I entertained my team,

together with some of the Canberra officials, to dinner at the Prime Minister's Lodge. I doubt whether this course would have been favoured by considerations of training, but I did it as a means of enabling my local players to get to know some of the 'greats' (and I continued it in subsequent matches). The dinner went very well and was followed by much cricket talk in my study and on a side portico. My wife, as usual, kept in the background and saw that the provisioning was adequate. She was assisted by my daughter, Heather, who was then unmarried. But the dinner and the subsequent talk were purely a men's affair.

We had as house guests Hassett, Johnson, Harvey and Loxton. As I had work to do in my office next morning, I went to bed at about 11 p.m.; most of the guests remained to a later hour and some, as I discovered, to a very late hour. I learned next day that Lindsay Hassett, who is both whimsical and durable, decided at 2 a.m. to take a stroll in the Lodge grounds, all by himself. Coming back into the house, he saw on the hall table a very large brass bowl containing a mass of flowers. It was so large and heavy that it might have been regarded as immovable. But Lindsay picked it up, walked up the stairway and found his way along a corridor to my daughter's bedroom, she being sound asleep. He tiptoed into the room, and placed the vast bowl carefully alongside her bed. She woke, blinked her eyes at this strange spectacle and Lindsay promptly said with a bow, 'Just a little floral tribute, my dear,' and walked out.

I was to recall this event a few matches later when Lindsay was once more a house guest, and had, in my study, to the imminent danger of the bric-à-brac about the room, a heated argument with Sam Loxton as to the proper execution of the hook. As they were both demonstrating with the fire-irons I was glad to discover later that no damage had been done, though thereafter I took suitable precautions in the disposition of breakable objects on the shelves in the room.

Next morning, Lindsay came down to breakfast a trifle late and looking, if I may say so, jaded by his training exercises of the previous night. He had with him a little bottle of eye-lotion, and had a dropper in his hand. He had clearly been putting a few drops in his own eyes and thought that he might do the same service to the other house guests. This he proceeded to do. When he came to me, who had been early to bed the previous night, he tipped my head back and said, putting some drops into my eyes, 'This will do you the world of good after your excesses.'

One of the arrangements I made with both the captains was that nobody should go out for a duck and that any ball that looked in transit as if it might be a difficult one at the beginning of a batsman's innings was to be called 'No ball' by the umpires. So long as no duck was involved, the usual rules of cricket were to apply.

The match began in clear weather and Jack Fingleton was one of the opening batsmen for my team, which had won the toss. The bowler was Trim, who delivered a fast good-length ball just outside the off stump. Jack played a forward defensive shot and the ball flew low in the air towards first slip. Ernie McCormick was the umpire, but forgot his instructions. Instead of instantly calling 'No ball' he stood just looking at it, and it was well caught by Weekes. So my captain, one of the great Test openers in Australian cricket history, was out for a duck. I shall always remember his small and loyal son calling out, making cries of protesting anguish and rage at such a misfortune.

Apart from this unhappy incident, we saw good cricket until the tea adjournment when the heavens opened and the rain fell and the match was over. Between eleven o'clock and tea the better part of four hundred runs had been scored, so the carnival spirit was established; except that Ernie McCormick had to put up with a good deal of abuse from me and from others.

That night I gave a dinner to both teams and various other men connected with them, or with the match. As I had a couple of hours between the abandonment of the match and dinner time, I wrote a few pieces of doggerel. Fingleton, who is, of course, a talented professional journalist, wrote a lively account of the match for *The Cricketer* in London and used these verses.

271

The only one that I care to remember at present is a piece of singularly free verse which I wrote about this unhappy initial incident:

What, Fingleton?
Not even a singleton?
Oh, what a fruitless journey,
Thanks to a singularly slow piece of thinking by Ernie.

It was a great financial relief to me when this match ended with a profit, all expenditure paid, of £180, which went to the Legacy Club.

As further matches came to be played, attendances increased and so did the profit. The Canberra Legacy Club looks back on these events with some satisfaction, because I find that the total profit on the seven matches was just under £5,500.

I was extremely busy with affairs of state and could not have offered to take on this enterprise unless I had had in all matters concerning the arrangements for the game, the preparation of the pitch and other administrative details the invaluable assistance of Ian Emmerton, Secretary to the Joint House Committee at Parliament House; Charles Morrison, the President of the local Cricket Association; and Jim Backen of my own department. Throughout what was to become a series of matches, they did, in addition to their normal official duties, generous and splendid work, and I am happy to record their names.

During my long period of office, these matches became a regular feature and were, I have good reason to believe, very popular with the players; so popular, that within the month preceding any particular match I frequently encountered leading Australian cricketers who said to me with a yearning look in the eye, 'Have you picked your team yet?' In all, as I have said, seven matches were played, the first one, as mentioned above, against the West Indies. The next one was in December 1954, against the M.C.C. touring team, Lindsay Hassett being my captain. The third one was in February, 1959, against the M.C.C., with Ian Johnson my captain. The fourth one was against the West Indies in Feb-

ruary 1961, with Ray Lindwall captain. The fifth one, to which
I shall make some special reference, was in February 1963
against the M.C.C.; Sir Donald Bradman was my captain. The
sixth was in February 1964 against South Africa under Neil
Harvey; and the seventh was in December 1965 against the
M.C.C., for which Richie Benaud was my captain.

I retired from office a month later and am sad to record that
there has been no Prime Minister's XI match since.

One of the objects of these festival games was to give the
cricket-lovers of Canberra an opportunity of seeing the great
players in action. It is, therefore, quite interesting to recall that,
in my teams over this period, they saw a great number of past
or current or future Australian Test players, including Fingleton,
O'Reilly, Hassett, Harvey, Loxton, Johnson, Miller, Benaud,
Lindwall, Morris, Craig, Booth, O'Neill, McDonald, Lawry,
Connolly, Bradman, Cowper, Grout, Mackay, Davidson, McKen-
zie, Stackpole, Burke and Sheahan. On each occasion my request
to the two captains was that good and serious cricket should be
played for the bulk of the day, a little hilarity being permitted in
the third session. This rule was fairly reasonably adhered to,
though not always. When it was not adhered to, the crowd
offered its opinions in terms of which I warmly approved. But
on the whole we saw some good cricket and had great fun.

I seem to keep coming back to Lindsay Hassett. I admit that
I have a very soft spot for him and, indeed, his presence always
guaranteed the cheerful spirit of the game. But he excelled himself in the 1959 match against the M.C.C. This was a game of
terrific scoring: 620 runs were made in the day, so it can be
judged that there was some loose bowling and some unexpected
bowlers. Colin Cowdrey made a century. When he reached the
century, he decided, very sensibly, that he would call it a day
and get out. Lindsay Hassett was fielding at fairly short forward
leg. So Colin hit a lollipop shot in the air over Lindsay's head,
but it was just too far for Lindsay to reach it when he ran after
it. It was observed that Lindsay promptly walked to the square-
leg umpire, borrowed his white hat, returning then to his place

in the field. Colin repeated the shot, but this time hit the ball to a distance where Lindsay might reach it. Lindsay ran after the ball, looking over his shoulder at it. He could have caught it with ease in an orthodox way, but that was too dull for Lindsay. He held the umpire's hat under it! Colin was given out, Lindsay tore the lining out of the hat and threw the residue to the umpire.

A reputable diplomat sitting next to me in the pavilion said, 'But, sir, that's not out. You can't get a man out that way.' I made the not very original but classical rejoinder, 'You'll see he is out because he is marching out now and he will be recorded as "caught Hassett" in the morning newspaper.'

Grave and reverend seniors may rebel at this farcical record; but I love to remember it because it was a splendid reminder that cricket is a game and that the strict rigour of the game can sometimes be suitably relaxed.

Another hilarious episode concerns Lindsay Hassett, though it concerns Arthur Morris even more. They were both playing in my team in this particular match. Arthur Morris had brought along a practically brand-new bat. When it came to Lindsay's turn to go out and bat he, quite light-heartedly, picked up the first bat he could see, which happened to be the one belonging to Arthur. To those who are illiterate about cricketers, I must recall that Arthur Morris was a left-hander, one of the greatest that we have ever had, and that Lindsay was a right-hander, also among the very great. But this was Lindsay's day of pleasure. After all it was a carnival match, and one should not treat it as if it were a Test match.

So, as I say, Lindsay grabbed up Arthur Morris's bat and walked in to play. When he had finished what I remember as a somewhat sketchy sort of innings, he was dismissed and walked back towards the pavilion. As he neared the pavilion, the schoolchildren of Canberra, as usual at these matches, surrounded him asking for an autograph. Lindsay hurriedly picked out one bright-faced schoolboy and, with a magnificent gesture, gave him the bat. Now this made the schoolboy's cricketing life for him, but had no particular appeal for Arthur Morris who, when Lindsay entered the dressing-room, said, 'Don't you know that that was my bat that you gave away, and that it's almost a new one?' Lindsay, with that superb grin that he has made all his own, put his hand on Arthur's shoulder and said, 'What does it matter? You can easily get another one, but the kid couldn't.' Arthur speedily recovered; he is a warm-hearted man himself.

When the match against the M.C.C. had been fixed for 6 February 1963, I had many suggestions made to me that it would be well received in Canberra if I could persuade Sir Donald Bradman to play. I pointed out that it was a long time since he had played and that it would be quite unfair to him to ask him to come out of his retirement. However, I yielded to persuasion and I spoke to Don, whom I can claim to be an old friend of mine, and, to my delight, when he found what was the destination of the profits, he agreed. It was a most dramatic moment when, before a record crowd, the well-known figure was seen walking to the wickets.

He began in style by playing an off-drive to the boundary in his most characteristic manner. Statham came on at the other end and, calling on his very considerable powers, he bowled a ball to Bradman which Bradman just came down on, the ball spinning back towards the stumps. The old Bradman would, of course, have kept it out of his stumps by one of those quick reactions of his. But his reactions were slower and so the bails just fell. Poor Brian Statham was most dejected. The umpire should have no-balled him, for the common good. Still, there must be some limit to illegality, even in a Prime Minister's Match.

So Don Bradman was out for four, but he produced for us a record attendance and the highest profit we ever got for Legacy on any single game.

Some time before this, Emmerton and Morrison and I had been at work on the departments concerned, and had secured the construction of a very fine pavilion which is called the Donald Bradman Pavilion and which was, in fact, opened by him on the day of this match.

24

Apartheid and Sport

When I first started to write this chapter, hundreds of 'protesters' in England were doing their best to impede the playing of Rugby matches in England by the South Africans. They appeared to believe that by engaging in their noisy tactics either they would persuade the South African Parliament to alter its apartheid policy or they would at least go home satisfied that they had played a valiant part in isolating South Africa from the rest of the world.

The next thing, of course, is to invade the cricket field, hoping to deprive some of the greatest living cricketers of international competition, and Englishmen of the pleasure of their company. How could the South African cricketers purge themselves of offence? By giving a Press interview in which, jointly and severally, they denounced their own Government? Not even such a magnificent and irrelevant gesture would satisfy their narrow-minded opponents. For the complaint appears to be that they have been chosen by a 'racialist' Government on principles which exclude non-whites from a representative South African team. In short, the militants object to the structure and policy of South African government, and are, therefore, presumably prepared to denounce everything that comes out of South Africa.

Yet, strangely enough, this belief does not lead them (as yet!) to stage tedious demonstrations in Threadneedle Street, outside the Bank of England, against the receipt of South African gold into the gold reserves of Britain; or in Bond Street, outside the windows of famous jewellers, to protest against the sale of South African diamonds to an unsuspecting public, many of whom (including no doubt some of the protesters) have inadvertently given South African diamonds to their fiancées or their wives.

If the rule of pure logic is fully observed, the protesters ought also, in defiance of the law, which they treat with contempt, to be obstructing the traffic outside the offices of the Board of Trade in London, demanding a complete cutting-off of trade with South Africa.

In short, if the objective of the protesters is the complete isolation of South Africa from the rest of the world, starting with Great Britain, why don't they say so? Folly could go no farther. The softening of the asperities of apartheid, or the progressive review of the policy itself, may be looked for if, on as many levels as possible, there is contact with other nations and peoples, a free interchange of ideas with them, the *inclusion* of South Africa in a modern and active free world in which the march towards democratic freedom and electoral equality proceeds.

A proud and (may I say it?) obstinate people may be persuaded, but they will not be coerced. The cause of the Bantu or the Cape Coloured, and their future prospects as citizens, are not advanced, but actually hindered, by these illogical and unlawful extravaganzas.

I may well, of course, be wrong. Perhaps the attack, for some reason unknown to me, concentrates itself on *sporting* activities; in 1969, on a handful of trained and expert footballers who might, for all that is known, be opponents or critics of South Africa's racial policies in their hearts, or might, quite conceivably, have that enthusiastic passion for football which drives out political passion.

As I write, we are promised by the protesters (who include some professing Christians) that a South African cricket tour of England will be interfered with, and perhaps destroyed. Some of the most brilliant exponents, like Graeme Pollock, are to be deprived of the chance of playing cricket in the ancient and lovely home of cricket. And the spectators, the cricket-lovers, will (whether they approve of it or not) be preserved from the corrupting influence which would radiate out from the pitch, and the Government at Pretoria will be taught its lesson!

The absurdity of these antics becomes evident if one considers other international sports and entertainments, and the protesters' attitude to countries other than South Africa.

Take the Soviet Union, a country where, under tight authoritarian control, there are no democratic rights for anybody, and, as in the case of Czechoslovakia, a suppression of any liberal movement in the satellite countries. Yet Russian tennis-players are welcomed at Wimbledon; Russian crews are permitted without protest to sully the waters of the Thames; 'amateur' Russian athletes run freely at the White City; and, crowning offence, the graceful and skilful dancers of the Bolshoi Ballet are greeted with enthusiasm by English audiences!

These things happen, and properly, because the English people, with massive common sense, distinguish between sport and politics. They have learned to co-exist as peacefully as possible with the Soviet Union, to do business with it, and not to interfere in the internal politics of a nation *whose internal politics they detest*.

If these football and cricket protesters extended their activities to the people who come to England from the Soviet Union, and made those activities effective, political relations would be seriously strained and the delicate processes of diplomacy would become seriously deranged.

Whenever a mob is allowed to influence our foreign policy and relations, our position *vis-à-vis* other nations is weakened.

At the end of 1968, I visited Pretoria and was a guest of Dr Vorster, the Prime Minister, whom I had never met before. In the course of various long conversations with him and others I learned something about the D'Oliveira Case.

I had been under the impression that when D'Oliveira was omitted from the originally selected M.C.C. team for South Africa, and David Sheppard and his followers at once raised the political issue by accusing the selectors of yielding to political considerations, Dr Vorster had seen in the subsequent selection of D'Oliveira an attempt to impose political pressure from the England end, and had reacted to it in a predictable political way.

But I found out that there was another aspect of the case. D'Oliveira is a Cape Coloured (i.e., a man of half-blood) born in South Africa, a great cricketer and the idol of the 'coloured' population. Any cricket-field decision adverse to D'Oliveira, it

278

was thought by some of those I spoke to, would almost certainly provoke demonstrations or even riots which would be damaging to the game and its spirit and atmosphere.

Now, what sort of man is the South African Prime Minister? Is he, as his distant critics assert, a racialist fiend incarnate?

The answer is that he is not. He is, of course, a conservative, but he is not a reactionary. But both he and his predecessor, Dr Verwoerd, have been treated in the most wrong-headed manner by outsiders. Dr Verwoerd was a highly educated man of great integrity, and with a courtesy and tolerance in negotiation which put his attackers to shame. But I found him almost immovable on the national policy. Yet, only a few months before he was murdered, his Government took a decision that Bantu and Coloured could be included in the South African team for the Mexico Olympic Games. Their thanks for this significant decision was to be kicked in the teeth by the Olympic authorities, who yielded to blackmail and withdrew the invitation.*

Dr Verwoerd began negotiations with one of the more northerly African nations, Malawi, for the establishment of diplomatic relations. They were successfully concluded early in 1967 by Dr Vorster, and are operating with satisfaction to both sides.

When I asked Vorster how territorial 'separate development', the creation of a self-governing Transkei, was going, and how effective the votes of Bantu in the other South African states could be in Transkei elections, I learned for the first time (I should have known before!) that these electors could vote effectively where they lived.

In short, I feel that there are processes at work at the top in South Africa which will be encouraged by international contact and retarded by international boycott.

As a cricket-lover of long standing, as one who believes, in spite of the queer exuberance of some cricket spectators in India, that international cricket is a powerful diplomatic contributor to

* The Olympic authorities have now gone further and have banned South Africa from future participation in the Games.

international understanding and a widening tolerance, I am shocked by these latter-day demonstrations, which I regard as ill informed and counter-productive.

Strangely enough, South African golfers (so far) are not molested by these lawless mobs. I recently pointed this out to a friend of mine, who retorted by saying, 'Ah, yes, but Gary Player is an individual; and since the same man cannot be both black and white at the same time, it cannot be said that he is the product of a racialist policy!' 'But,' I replied, 'suppose two white golfers came to play in foursomes, wouldn't they be a team, and therefore be in the same case as the Springbok footballers?' Undoubtedly. In a mad world all things are possible.

But let me return to the case of Soviet Russia, and inquire why the protesters in their queer activities discriminate in favour of the Communists. I had always thought that the basis of opposition to apartheid was that it denied to some millions of South Africans democratic political and social rights equal to those of white men and women. What of Russia, which denies democratic rights to all?

But no; *apartheid* is a rude word. It is a policy which taints South African sportsmen and therefore presumably taints everything that comes out of South Africa. When I point out to people that *apartheid* simply means 'separate development', and that it surely must be conceded that every nation must have the right to its own form of government or social structure, the popular reply is that 'separate development' is simply a modern term of excuse. That is easily answered by looking at a little history. For the policy goes back to the great J. C. Smuts, who, in his many visits to Britain and his many immortal services in two world wars, was never treated with contumely by any of the people of Britain whom he was helping to preserve.

It was as far back as 1917, when Smuts was actually in the Empire War Cabinet in London, that he made a great speech about the problems of mixed races in a country like South Africa, which South Africa's critics nowadays find so easy to solve.

I will set out two passages from that speech. They are not

short; but they exhibit, as no words of mine could, the basis of his thinking, and that of his successors.

I wish we had made more progress and also discovered some political axiom and knowledge how to deal politically with our immense native problem. But although in this regard nothing can be taken as axiomatic, we have gained a great deal of experience in our history, and there is now shaping in South Africa a policy which is becoming expressed in our institutions which may have very far-reaching effects in the future civilization of the African Continent. We have realized that political ideas which apply to our white civilization largely do not apply to the administration of native affairs. To apply the same institutions on an equal basis to white and black alike does not lead to the best results, and so a practice has grown up in South Africa of creating parallel institutions – giving the natives their own separate institutions on parallel lines with institutions for whites. It may be that on those parallel lines we may yet be able to solve a problem which may otherwise be insoluble. . . .

Instead of mixing up black and white in the old haphazard way, which instead of lifting up the black degraded the white, we are now trying to lay down a policy of keeping them apart as much as possible in our institutions. In land ownership, settlement and forms of government we are trying to keep them apart, and in that way laying down in outline a general policy which it may take a hundred years to work out, but which in the end may be the solution of our native problem. Thus in South Africa you will have in the long run large areas cultivated by blacks and governed by blacks, where they will look after themselves in all their forms of living and development, while in the rest of the country you will have your white communities, which will govern themselves separately according to the accepted European principles. The natives will, of course, be free to go and to work in the white areas, but as far as possible the administration of white and black areas will be separated, and such that each will be satisfied and developed according to its own proper lines. This is the attempt which we are making now in South Africa to solve the juxtaposition of white and black in the same country, and although the principles underlying our legislation could not be considered in any way axiomatic, I am sure that we are groping towards the right lines, which in the end tend to be the solution of the most difficult problem confronting us.

Many people found their attack upon apartheid upon well-publicized incidents of alleged excesses in administration, injustices to individuals, and of scenes of violence such as those which occurred at Sharpeville, after which the Opposition at Canberra demanded that Australia cut off trade with South Africa! The answer to that was easy. I pointed out that a large proportion of our imports from South Africa consisted of items produced almost entirely by black or coloured labour, and that it would be a strangely ironical thing if, under the pretence of helping these people, we put them out of work.

At the same time, I felt that many of the protests were a sort of racism in reverse; and that they were voiced only when white people were involved. There were vast massacres, involving many hundreds of thousands of Indians, after the partition of the sub-continent into India and Pakistan, and much misery suffered by the refugees. Yet I cannot remember any protests from platform or pulpit. Coloured people were killing coloured people for religious or political reasons; but no white people were involved.

I have been at pains to explain what I believe to be the basis of apartheid in South Africa. That is not to say that I believe (peace be to the memory of the great Smuts) that it will be justified by history. As I said once to Verwoerd, 'The more the policy succeeds in the short run, the more certain it is that it will fail in the long run.' For the more successful the education and health services provided for the Bantu (and they are better than those provided in other African nations), the more surely the day will come when the Bantu will no longer be content to be treated as second-class citizens. There may well be a horrible explosion, and with the backing or encouragement of some intransigent northern African states, much blood may be shed.

The answer to this will not be made overnight. The solution will be achieved gradually. It would not be made easier or more likely if the unthinking boycotters succeeded in isolating South Africa and driving her people to live with resentful minds, feeding on their own prejudices. In short, to adapt my earlier phrase, the more the protesters succeed, the more certain will be the failure of their avowed objectives.

Such demonstrations, which lead inevitably to violence and unlawful activities, are, as Quintin Hogg said in December, evidence of the 'slide into anarchy', of which there are too many symptoms today.

The law is that you can play a football match against a white South African team if you wish; that is your absolute right.

When Liberal and Labour members of Parliament say that they mean to stay away from such matches in principle I respect them, but when they say that they will try to interfere with other people's rights to make up their own minds on these subjects and that some of them will run on to the pitch I accuse them of encouraging the slide into anarchy, of being enemies to the law, because they intend to break the law, and of being enemies of freedom, because they intend to interfere with the freedom of others.

Great Britain and South Africa have a current agreement about the naval use of Simonstown, so important for the protection of the growingly important Cape route to the Indian Ocean and the countries bordering upon it, including, of course, my own country, Australia. I can only suppose that the protesters are indifferent to what I believe to be the great defence significance for millions of us of South Africa's posture and facilities.

South Africa was a foundation member of the British Commonwealth. She was driven out of that Commonwealth some years ago against my will, as I have described elsewhere. I deplore the activities of so-called lovers of international sport who now wish to treat her citizens with contumely, and in a fatuous way shout completely futile insults at a far-distant government.

June 1970

Since I wrote this chapter, the blow has fallen. The English cricket authorities stood firm against the threats of a noisy minority; the British Government, to its great discredit, succumbed, and made an official 'request' to the cricket authorities (which was a virtual order) to cancel the tour of the South Africans; this the cricketers, not unnaturally, felt unable to reject.

The immediate effect upon international cricket is to terminate, for many years, South Africa–England matches, to the great disadvantage of cricket in both countries, particularly English cricket. For to play against a team which is currently the best in the world would have done a great deal for the standards of English cricket.

But, after all, 'cricket is only a game', say those who pride themselves on seeing all things in due proportion. To which I rejoin that cricket is not only a lovely but a lawful game, and cricket-lovers have (or had) a legal right to watch it in peace. Until this surrender by the British Government, threats of riotous assembly were not lawful. Malicious injury to property was not lawful. The threat to inflict it was not lawful. No Act of Parliament had been passed to legalize any of these crimes. True, it is always piously asserted by those who foment such demonstrations that they wish peace and would deplore violence. But are they so incredibly naïve as to think that they can attract to their banners rough and violent elements, anarchists who hate government and are happiest when they can provoke battles with the hated police, and then wash their hands of the consequences?

The Government, by purely executive action, has now yielded the ground to the law breakers, and has given them great encouragement to go on, and to go further. The decision is an incitement to lawlessness. The long-established and noble Rule of Law, one of the greatest products of the character and tradition of British history, has suffered a deadly blow. Blackmail has become respectable. Should it be said that this comment is extravagant, that I make a mountain out of a mole-hill, the retort is easy.

So far, since the establishment of the supremacy of Parliament and the widening of the franchise, revolution has been out of fashion; violence and riot and physical threats in support of political or other objectives have been rejected by decent public opinion. But a precedent has now been officially established. Any well-organized minority group which wishes to impose its will upon the peaceable majority in relation to any matter now knows what to do. If the anarchists, the professional agitators, and their dupes can give themselves an air of respectability by securing the blessing of some clergymen, so much the better; for then essentially unchristian activities will be made to appear to have Christian sanction.

Finally, to recur to a point I made earlier, what will be the effect in South Africa of this successful step towards the isolation of South Africa?

Will the principles of apartheid, subscribed to by both major parties in South Africa, be meekly abandoned? Will the lot of the black and coloured people of South Africa be improved? Of course not! An insult has been offered to South Africa; its effect is much more likely to harden South African attitudes, and to postpone that steady 'softening of the asperities of apartheid' which, as I have said, would inevitably result from growing contacts with the rest of the world.

But I can see that I have opened the way to the retort — 'But they insulted us by refusing to receive an English touring party which included d'Oliveira'. If that is the doctrine, an insult for an insult, an eye for an eye, what becomes of the New Testament, my Lord Bishop?

25

Some Great Left-handers

I want to say something about a matter which has always attracted me. I am not an anatomist or physiologist; either of whom could no doubt explain it. How is it that, in the highest classes of batsmanship, the left-hander so frequently appears to me to be the more elegant—the poet of cricket—while the right-hander almost always gives me the prose?

I had, in my team in the first Prime Minister's XI match, for the delight of cricket-lovers in the national capital, two of the most elegant left-hand stroke-makers then playing—Neil Harvey and Martin Donnelly—each of them batting with a fluency and carefree ease which had been exhibited long before them by the immortal Frank Woolley and was to be exhibited again by Graeme Pollock of South Africa, and Gary Sobers of the West Indies.

When one sets out to write about splendour of style, one soon becomes involved in hopeless difficulties of definition. As well try to define beauty, or charm, without reducing both to banality.

I can perhaps best describe what I am trying to say about Harvey, or Woolley, by contrasting them with other great masters, of equal greatness in technique and execution, who were right-handed batsmen and had a genius of their own. Consider Charles Macartney. He respected no bowler. Standing there erect (he was not tall) at the wickets, he looked aggressive, and he was. He treated the ball as an enemy, to be hit and hit hard, as if he hated it. Frank Woolley, on the other hand, seemed to deal with the ball as if it were a friend, to be dismissed from the presence in a kindly way, with so little obvious physical effort that the ball was at the boundary almost before you had seen the stroke. That Macartney was one of the greatest batsmen Australia has ever had no cricket-lover will deny, but he had not that willowy, effortless, rhythmic elegance of the great left-hander.

From this point of view, Lawry, though, I would suppose, one

of the soundest opening batsmen now playing, is not a characteristic left-hander. He preserves a watchful defence and is sparing
of scoring shots, though he has them all. He regards time as
having been made for slaves. His job is to wear the bowlers down
and to deal severely with the loose ball. He is a great and successful artisan; but he is not a great artist.

I have seen the master batsmen of the last fifty years and have
had great joy from the watching. There was, for example, a
certain splendour about Walter Hammond. He was a thoroughly
masculine bat. With his great shoulders and superb footwork, he
seemed always to be in the correct position to hit the ball with the
maximum of force. His square driving I shall never forget. But
one knew, as one watched him, that here was the 'power game'
in excelsis. Watching Woolley, one of course knew that there
was power; but one did not think of it in the presence of so much
ease and beauty.

The great Don Bradman, as I have said on other occasions,
defies all rules or definitions. As he is a human being, he must
somewhere have had a weak spot; though bowlers found it
difficult to discover. The immense *authority* of his batting, the
complete justice with which he dealt with each ball on its merits
and dispatched it on what seemed to be its predestined errand have
made him the undisputed master batsman of my time. Century
followed century with almost monotonous inevitability. We
could find no fault in him. Yet perfection itself has a sort of
sculptural quality. One begins to yearn for a little artistic
aberration which would make mere mortals feel less awed, but
possibly a little happier.

And thus it is that I must occasionally turn away from a flaw-
less Bradman and recall having seen Woolley and Harvey playing
shorter innings, but playing them with a carefree *panache*
exhibiting the gaiety of cricket.

But I must pause to emphasize that what I have said, and will
say, about the poetry of the great left-handers and the prose of
the right-handers must of course admit of exceptions. In *Afternoon Light* I wrote of McCabe's batting at Trent Bridge in 1938,

287

and described him as 'a supreme artist', practising art for its own sake.

Having made a profound bow in his direction, I return to my broad proposition about the great left-handers, and to my impressions about the special anatomy of their batting. I will take six of the great, some of them unknown to my younger readers.

Vernon Ransford played for Australia at a good period, in 1909 and 1911. Though he made a notable century at Lord's in a Test match in 1909, playing for M. A. Noble's great team, which won the Ashes, and, in the tour averages in that year, was third only to Bardsley and Armstrong, with 1,783 runs at an average of over 43, I remember him not simply for great scores, but for his superb style, both at the wickets and in the field. He had smoothness in every movement in both capacities. I have only to shut my eyes today to see him fielding in the outfield on the large Melbourne Cricket Ground. He ran like a deer. When he got near the ball, always at a beautifully judged point of interception, his left hand, far outstretched, would seize the ball and instantly throw it from where the hand was, with no pause or winding-up, but with uncanny accuracy, to the stumps. I have seen many famous outfields, but I cannot remember another who fielded and threw in quite this manner.

And then I come again to *Frank Woolley*, the 'pride of Kent', the joy of England, and, for that matter, of every observer who ever saw him. Whenever, in my mind's eye, I see Woolley straight-driving the ball with effortless ease, I think of Peter May doing the same kind of thing. I always thought Peter a right-handed Woolley. I have never thought of any other right-handed batsman in the same way. Perhaps Peter has a left-hander's anatomy reversed. His batting was touched by poetry.

Of course, my enthusiasm may involve me in being misunderstood. There is great art in poetry, though it is sometimes disguised in some modern verse. But there is also great art in great prose, which cannot be written except by a master. But most of the prose we read is prosaic, and it is in that sense that I have used the word. Ponsford's great bat spoke a powerful prose on many famous occasions. Had Bradman not arrived, Ponsford could properly be regarded as the master batsman of the period. I still think that he was the most devastating batsman against slow spinners that I have ever seen. But 'Ponny' would have resented any allegation that there was poetry in his bat.

Arthur Morris and *Neil Harvey* were of the same vintage; and what a splendid vintage it was. A vintage for a connoisseur. Each had his own style and attributes. Harvey was all ease and elegance; never an ugly movement or stroke. His nimble foot-work provided for defence and attack alike. His eyes were quick to anticipate, whether at the wicket or in the field. Indeed, had he been much less prolific with the bat, it would have been still worth a long journey to see him field in the covers. It is normally a busy area to patrol in any game. It requires faculty of antici-pation, quick judgment of the speed and direction of the ball, great certainty of hand, and speed and accuracy of return. Harvey had them all, as many an ambitious batsman found to his cost. I have seen many great cover fieldsmen in my time, from J. B. Hobbs to Paul Sheahan, but I have never seen a better one than Neil Harvey.

I remember one summer's day when young Neil, till then almost unknown, played for Victoria against a touring side on the Melbourne cricket ground. Strangely enough, I was at home, in the suburbs. My elder son was at the ground. That afternoon, he rang me up and said, with great excitement in his voice, 'Dad, you must come in. There's a lad called Neil Harvey batting and I've never seen anything so exciting before.'

I couldn't go in, but I later discovered the accuracy of my son's words. *Exciting*: that is the true description of Harvey's batting throughout his famous career. He made five Test centuries against England, and, I'll warrant, enchanted the onlookers every time.

Arthur Morris, though perceptibly different in method, was equally a master batsman. He made eight Test centuries against England, two of them in one match at Adelaide. He took the brunt of the new-ball attack as an opener (Harvey usually batted as No. 3). He lost no opportunity of scoring, for, in contrast to so many modern 'negative' batsmen, he was, like Harvey, both a defender and an attacker. His footwork had a character of its own. Instead of appearing to lean away a little as he made a cover drive, as Harvey did (though Harvey's footwork was immaculate), he had a little habit of making a slight shuffle along the batting crease as he got into position to play an off stroke.

This exposed him to the risk of an occasional l.b.w. decision. But his eagle eye seldom failed. His movement left him in position to play his off shots with singular effectiveness and great power, and place them with penetration. This latter art eludes most batsmen, but Arthur Morris was its master.

The first time I ever saw the South African *Graeme Pollock* play an innings, I turned to my neighbour and said, 'By Jove, this chap reminds me of Frank Woolley.' The reply was that that was a very bold thing to say. It was, perhaps, a little premature. I have seen quite a few cases of young and competent batsmen being hailed as 'a second Bradman', to the disadvantage of their own subsequent careers. But Pollock has proved, time after time, that he justifies the comparison with Woolley, both in style and in effortless effectiveness. As we move into the seventies, I believe that he is the brightest star in the batting firmament. For the lovers of cricket as cricket—and there are many of them in England—it will be a tragedy if the 'demonstrators' are allowed to have their way.

My final name is, of course, *Gary Sobers*, one of the very greatest cricketers in the whole history of cricket. He is three cricketers in one. He is an effortless and devastating bat, the only mystery about whom is that he puts himself in too low in the batting order; for after all, he is a born No. 3. He is a fast opening bowler with control over both length and direction, and with a deceptive capacity to make an unexpected change of pace. Later on, when the shine has gone off the ball, he emerges as a slow-medium spinner. In each of these capacities he has helped mightily to win many matches for the West Indies (and, I regret to say, writing as a Victorian, for South Australia). It is fascinating to see him going out to the wicket to bat. His slim and loose-limbed body leans forward eagerly; he looks anxious to be 'at them'. Not for him the long business of digging in, or wearing the bowlers down. He is there to attack, and attack he does. In every stroke he makes there is smoothness, and a combination of both beauty and power. It may well be that, like some other great cricketers who play the English season as well as their own, he is nowadays giving himself no let-up, and bestowing his cricketing gifts with too lavish a hand. But after all, cricket is merely my onlooking pleasure; it is his business.

When writing this chapter, I had the rich benefit of conversations with Hans Ebeling, who was a successful bowler for Australia in his time, is on the Committee of the Melbourne Cricket Club, and in my experience is a veritable fountain of reminiscence and judgment. I also consulted my good friend Ian Johnson, who is now the dynamic and successful secretary of the club. As a former captain of Australia and a fine off-spinner who had fought the good fight with many noted batsmen, his opinion is to be both sought and respected. His list of great left-handed batsmen includes Bert Sutcliffe of New Zealand. That I have not written anything about him is not caused by any disagreement with Ian Johnson's judgment, but by the melancholy fact, for me, that I hardly ever saw him at the wicket.

You do not need to tell me, dear reader, that in these scrappy remarks I have been illogical and inexpert. Of course I am both. If any batsman found himself governed by the immutable principles of deductive logic, he would soon disappear from the most delightfully illogical game on earth. And if inexpertness proved to be a disqualification what would become of so many writers of the sporting Press?

But, just as I can seldom recall averages (those I have quoted in this chapter I have dredged out of the columns of *Wisden*), or even what side won any particular Test series, I can always recall men, and events, and oddities of style and those gleaming flashes of pure beauty which suddenly illuminate the memory.

Index

293